THE
GARDENING
ENCYCLOPEDIA

ORBIS · LONDON

First published in this edition 1984
by Orbis Publishing Limited, London
Reprinted 1985

© 1982 Orbis Publishing Limited
All rights reserved.

ISBN: 0-85613-732-4

Printed in Italy by Imago

Previous page: Clematis montana *Nelly Moser* (photo Ray Proctor).

Acknowledgements
Bernard Alfieri, Heather Angel, Ardea, A-Z Collection, Barnaby's Picture Library, Ron Boardman, Michael Boys, Pat Brindley, S. T. Buczaki, Robert J. Corbin, John K. B. Cowley, Ernest Crowson, Michael Davies/NHPA, Samuel Dobie & Son, Fisons, Monica Fuller, Brian Furner, Michael Gibson, Halls Homes & Greenhouses, Iris Hardwick Library, Hozelock, ICI, Archivio IGDA, Leslie Johns, Clay Jones, Michael Leale, Marshall Cavendish, May & Baker, Elsa E. Megson, Tania Midgeley, Ken Muir, Murphy Chemicals, National Vegetable Research Station, Nutting & Thoday, Kenneth I. Oldroyd, Oxford Scientific Films, Pan Brittanica Industries, Picturepoint, Ray Proctor, Shell International Petroleum, Donald Smith, Harry Smith Horticultural Photographic Collection, Suttons Seeds, Thompson & Morgan, Brian Tysterman, W. J. Unwin, Weed Research Organisation, D. Wildridge, Wolf Tools.

Contents

THE FLOWER GARDEN

Planning your garden

This long, narrow plot, typical of so many back gardens, calls for an imaginative layout, so we have steered away from the tunnel-like effect of narrow side borders and a central rectangle of grass or paving and created instead a series of curving lines and irregular shapes. In this way the eye is attracted by informal groupings of flowering plants and shrubs (which avoid the considerable upkeep required by more formal herbaceous borders), while the rose-covered trellis acts as a natural break in the length.

We have filled the garden with easy-to-care-for evergreens, flowering shrubs and trees, seasonal bulbs and roses for the paired pergolas. Annuals planted at appropriate times of the year and flowering plants in tubs on the patio provide additional patches of instant colour, as and where they are needed.

The paved patio runs the whole width of the garden, providing a convenient eating-out and relaxation area near the house on sunny days and somewhere to scrape the mud off your boots on the wet ones. There is room for a lean-to greenhouse to be erected against the north wall if you feel tempted to invest in one, and facing the end wall of the garden, screened by the rose-covered trellis, is a sizable shed for all those tools, toys and miscellaneous garden furniture.

Ground plan, showing the main features of the Flower Garden plot, which measures 22 metres (72 feet) long by 7·5 metres (25 feet) wide

silver birch
bulb area
azaleas
honesty
horse chestnut
campanula
camellia
seed bed
hostas
firethorn
shed
quince
trellis with roses
pergola with roses
pergola with roses
lavender (dwarf)
stepping stones on grass
winter heathers
grey cineraria
camellia
spindle bush
buddleia
thyme
lesser periwinkle
African lilies
madonna lilies
laburnum
cornflowers
hypericum
hellebore
catmint
Virginian stock
pinks
iris
houseleek
alyssum (saxatile)
nasturtiums
cotoneaster
mahonia
annuals
African marigolds
gladiolus
chrysanthemums
dahlias
hollyhocks
French marigolds
Christmas rose
box
broom
terrace
tub
trellis on wall

honeysuckle
clematis
sedum (spectabile)
hydrangea
ceanothus
rhododendrons
syringa
garrya

winter jasmine
hydrangea
climbing candytuft
convolvulus
cornpoppies
Russian vine
barberry

Spartium (Spanish broom) is a shrub that thrives near the sea on light, sandy soil. It can be grown elsewhere, but you will not get such good blooms

Turfing or seeding?

For the lawn, with its attractive curved edges, we opted for turf – which need not be such an expensive outlay as you might imagine (unless you hanker after the bowling-green effect of a really luxury lawn). The great advantage of turf is that it gives you a quicker result than if you had settled for sowing from seed.

Food for compost

If you have not already got a compost heap, start saving vegetable waste as soon as you can. The compost is vital to the well-being of your garden – as important as a fridge is to a cook. If possible, keep *two* waste bins in the kitchen – one solely for vegetable matter which can be added to your compost. Avoid saving very smelly things like fish bones, though – and meat bones take far too long to break down.

Know your weeds

There are several weeds that produce colourful displays and fill a border quite prettily, but their spreading roots may be doing untold damage beneath the surface. It is important to be able to tell the difference between growing weeds and good plant stock. In a later section of this book we shall help you to distinguish the 'good' weeds from the 'bad' ones – and how to control them.

Inheriting the earth

If you are already the owner of a well-cared-for garden, you are spared the trials, and may lose the pleasures, of creating a totally new one. But you still have plenty of room to exercise your talents by redesigning the planting areas,

choosing new shrubs – even reshaping the lawn, and advice in later sections will tell you exactly how to do all this.

A little caution is called for, however, if you have recently acquired a garden of unknown quantity. Do not rush ahead with a complete replanting job as there are many perennials that die down and remain dormant underneath the earth for months at a time, and you may not know that they are there. One of the most enjoyable experiences here is being happily surprised as a small shoot in late spring grows unaccountably tall and blossoms, for instance, into a hollyhock come mid

Some plants grow happily anywhere, such as cotoneaster (shown here) and berberis. Both these shrubs are tolerant of all soils, including chalk or limestone

---

ACID OR ALKALINE?

Before planting it is necessary to know if your soil is acid (peaty) or alkaline (limey). Some plants, such as heathers and rhododendrons, like acidity; a few, such as clematis and viburnum, like alkalinity; but most prefer a slightly acid-neutral soil.

Soil acidity or alkalinity is expressed in terms of its pH value. This can be measured by using a proprietary soil-testing kit.

Something like pure water is neither acid nor alkaline and has a neutral pH of 7. The higher the pH reading, the higher the alkalinity; the lower the reading, the more acid. pH 6.5 (slightly acid) is the level at which most plants flourish best.

If too acid, lime should be added; if too alkaline, an acid substance such as peat should be dug in.

Calluna (ling, often called heather). These shrubs grow best in peaty (acid) soil. Similar conditions can be created by importing the right type of acid soil

summer. If you keep a note in your garden file of the plants that appear out of seemingly bare earth as you identify them, it will be of enormous help to you in any redesigning plans you may have.

During this watchful period you must not neglect basic maintenance such as pruning and so on, as this is of vital importance.

Know your neighbours

Different districts have their own peculiar quirks, and so indeed do individual gardens in the same street. Useful local knowledge can be gathered from conversations over the garden wall. You'll soon find out what grows well in your area by this method and by looking at other nearby gardens.

You'll also be told of great disasters of the past, and so learn by the mistakes of others, and of great successes which you may well emulate.

Don't be afraid to stop and speak to someone working his patch – gardeners are great talkers, and as often as not you'll end up by having cuttings of admired plants bestowed on you.

Starting from scratch?

If you have just moved into a new house with an as yet unplanned space for a garden, this means that you have the opportunity to create your own design from nothing. In the following pages we shall be telling you how you can transform such a site into a thriving colourful garden.

Before getting down to work, however, it is essential to prepare a rough plan of what you hope to achieve.

Starting your garden from scratch

When faced with a derelict patch instead of a garden, you must first of all clear the site by removing all the litter and rubbish that is lying about. Some of the bricks, stones and timbers may be useful later on, so pile them into a corner.

If the amount of rubbish is not too great, you can put it into strong polythene bags but don't overfill them, or they become too heavy to move around. For large loads of rubbish you will have to hire a skip for which you will need a licence from the local council.

The next clearance job is to remove all unwanted plants from the garden site, including such things as brambles, weeds, tree stumps and even old, weedy turf.

If you come across any plants worth keeping at this stage, leave them where they are or carefully dig them up, with plenty of soil around the roots, and plant them in a prepared trench that has been well dug over until they can be put into final positions.

Drawing up the ground plan

Having done all this, you can then see more easily how to set about the next task, which is to draw up a rough plan of the available area.

You will need a long measuring tape (borrowed or hired if necessary), a ball of coarse twine, some stakes, a sheet of strong paper clipped to a board and a pencil. Begin by taking the measurements of existing structures such as the walls.

Don't forget to mark on your ground plan where the points of the compass fall, so sun-loving and shade-preferring plants can be given the positions they need. Any existing features should also be marked in, such as the three trees in our garden – laburnum, silver birch and horse chestnut.

Now transfer the details from this first rough drawing to a sheet of graph paper, using a simple scale. Be sure to allow for the whole garden to be shown on a single sheet. On this ground plan you should have accurate measurements of structures and existing plants.

Outlining special features

First of all decide what special features you want in your garden and list them on a separate sheet of paper. In this design for instance, the paved patio, the shaping of the borders and lawn areas, the shed with its rose-covered trellis and matching pergolas are all important, some for practical reasons, others for helping to break up this long, narrow garden. The sample garden feature plan at right shows how these are indicated on the graph paper, with the essential measurements needed to transfer your plan into reality outdoors.

Whatever you plan at this stage, don't get carried away and make your garden too complicated and overfull. It is always more effective if the design is kept relatively simple and interest maintained throughout the year by your plants.

Once you have finalized your plan in general outline, get the building-type work done before you start making preparations for planting. If you construct the paved patio near the house first, you will have a solid base from which to carry out other work as well as a resting place for sunny days.

Preparing the patio area

From your graph of the garden you will be able to calculate the quantities of materials you require. We chose York stone, for its old-world character and lasting quality, but there are many suitable alternatives, such as pre-cast slabs in various colours and textures.

Before laying the paving, it is essential to peg out and level the site, taking care not to bridge the damp proof course and under-floor ventilation bricks of the house wall.

As the lawn comes right up to the terrace, it makes for easy mowing if you set the paving a little lower than the intended final level of the lawn surface. (If the paving is higher than the lawn, mowing becomes very difficult and you will have to use shears to cut the grass along the edge.) The grass here will help to hide any unevenness in the front edge of the paved patio.

Siting the shed

The next important feature is the shed, centred within the garden's width but towards the far end so as to give a visual break to the length of the site. It is hidden from the house by a screen of trellis-climbing plants and other perennials in a shaped bed below.

Our shed measures some 3×2m (10 ft $\times$ 6 ft 6 in) and the door and window face west, with access via the stepping-stone path. If you decide on an easy-to-erect prefabricated one, the only essential is that it should be on a level base, preferably of brick, concrete or wooden sleepers. If

Creating a new garden is hard work but the finished product is well worth it, as these photographs show

possible, allow an air space below to prevent the floor timbers from rotting. You will need to fix guttering and a water barrel or soakaway to collect rain water and prevent puddles forming around the base.

Digging a new garden

Unfortunately, all the heavy work – digging the site and levelling by raking – comes at the beginning. This is also the time to buy in, and spread where necessary, any extra topsoil you need to mix in with the existing soil. Dig it over to at least the depth of the spade blade or fork tines (prongs). This rule applies to the whole garden.

Digging can be very hard work, and it is advisable not to do too much at one time; take it at your own pace, and dig correctly to minimize aches and pains. It doesn't matter how dry the soil is, but don't try to dig when it is very wet.

If the soil seems to be compacted (very hard and heavy) or very light, such as sandy or chalky, it would be a good idea to dig in some compost, manure, peat or similar soil-conditioning material.

Decide in which direction you are going to dig; in this garden, for instance, it is best to start from the far end and work backwards, trench by trench, to the paved patio. In this way you will avoid treading on the dug soil.

Digging in comfort

Always stand face on to the line of soil to be dug, and never try to dig too large a lump of soil at any one time. The least tiring way to dig is to stand close to the upright spade or fork, and if you are right-handed place your right foot on the cross-piece over the blade or tines, with your left hand on the handle and right one about halfway down. Press the head of the tool into the ground to its full

depth by putting your weight onto the foot on the cross-piece. Then place your right elbow on your right knee and use this knee as a fulcrum (leverage point) to lift the soil free from the ground and turn it over and forwards. Another way is to use the edge of the undug soil on which you are standing as the lifting and pivoting point. If the soil is very compacted you may have to cut the edge of each spadeful by pressing the implement in at right angles before digging the soil.

If manual digging seems too arduous a task, you can hire a powered cultivator (from your local hire service shop) which turns the soil over quickly, rather like a miniature plough.

If time allows, it pays to leave the soil for a week or so to settle naturally. Then, when the weather is fine and the ground not too wet, you should go over the whole site with a rake and roughly level it. If you want slightly raised soil anywhere, as round the silver birch and horse chestnut at the far end of the garden, now is the time to see that it is in position.

Planning for planting

Between bouts of digging, and while the soil is settling, make notes of what plants you intend to grow, and where they are to be placed in the garden. This will enable you to estimate the cost and order in advance.

First draw the shape of each of the planting areas onto separate sheets of graph paper, as this enables you to use a large scale. Then, with the aid of plant, bulb and seed catalogues, select your plants and list them on a sheet of paper. Alongside each plant put down what type it is (perennial, bulb, etc.), the variety, what height and width it will mature to, what colour its flowers and leaves are, when it is at its most colourful, whether it likes sun or shade, and any other points of interest about it. Armed with this information you are then ready to transfer your choice to each planting area graph.

In our Flower Garden, mixed borders of different types of plants predominate, giving variety, interest and plenty of colour all the year round, yet requiring the minimum of upkeep. The plant plan here shows how the border against the north wall (which faces south and is therefore sunny) has been planned, indicating the position of the selected plants and how many of each you need. Don't forget that the taller plants should be at the back and the smaller ones at the front of the border, with an intermingling zone in the centre.

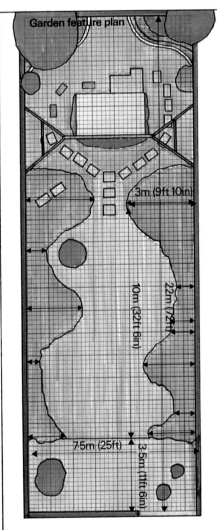

Garden feature plan

3m (9ft 10in)

10m (32ft 6in)   22m (72ft)

7·5m (25ft)   3·5m (11ft 6in)

Draw up your ground plan on graph paper, marking in essential features, and measure up the north border to help you work out your plant plan

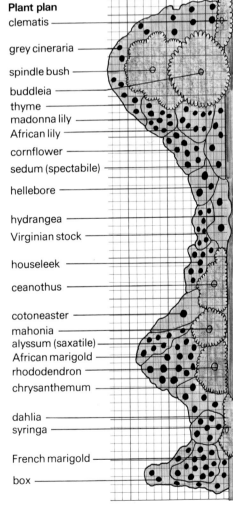

Plant plan

clematis
grey cineraria
spindle bush
buddleia
thyme
madonna lily
African lily
cornflower
sedum (spectabile)
hellebore
hydrangea
Virginian stock
houseleek
ceanothus
cotoneaster
mahonia
alyssum (saxatile)
African marigold
rhododendron
chrysanthemum
dahlia
syringa
French marigold
box

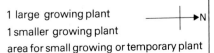

🌻 1 large growing plant
● 1 smaller growing plant
⬡ area for small growing or temporary plant

→N

SOIL CHART Recognize your soil type and make the best of it

TYPES	PROBLEMS	ADVANTAGES	HOW TO IMPROVE
CLAY Smooth, not gritty, often wet, sticky and slimy in winter and brick-like in summer	The very small particles stick together when wet, making a solid, almost airless mass. Heavy and difficult to dig and break down. Cold – takes a long time to warm up in spring. Dries out slowly, unevenly and in clods. Seeds germinate poorly (because of lack of air) and plant roots have difficulty in growing (because it is so heavy and solid).	Usually rich in plant food. Can hold water well in dry summers. Is receptive to the addition of plant and animal organic matter, which will decompose by physical, chemical and bacterial activity in the soil. This completely decomposed material is called humus. **Humus** is rich in plant foods, gives the soil 'body' and encourages the retention of food, water and air. In particular, it helps to make clay more workable by breaking down the mass.	Unless already alkaline (chalky), spread garden lime – 375g per sq m (12 oz per sq yd) – all over dug soil in autumn and let the weather work it in. Otherwise fork in during February. Lime makes it easier to dig and cultivate. For lasting improvement dig in large quantities of organic (animal and plant) matter in early spring for several years. This will rot down in the soil and gradually improve its structure and colour. Preferably use 'strawy' farmyard manure, otherwise plenty of peat and garden compost. Continue organic treatment every year, liming every 2–3 years. Do not mix lime with other fertilizers; apply 1 month before, or 2–3 months after, other soil conditioners. If clay is very heavy, artificial drainage may be required.
SAND Light and dry, gritty, crumbly and rough to handle	Poor in plant food. Unable to retain moisture; rainwater passes right through, leaching (washing out) plant foods into the subsoil out of reach of plant roots. Can be very acid due to leaching of lime.	Easy to work at any time of year. Warms up quickly after winter so cultivation can begin early in spring. Plenty of air in soil, allowing plant roots to grow strongly and deeply. Excellent for vegetables, especially root crops, when sufficient organic matter is added to retain water.	Manure, peat and compost must be dug in deeply to increase the soil's organic content. This will add plant foods and increase food- and moisture-retaining abilities. Treatment must be repeated yearly. Also add general fertilizer before sowing or planting in spring and autumn. A light sprinkling of lime should be added every other year if soil is acid. Watering with nitrogenous fertilizer is advantageous throughout the growing season. Artificial watering will probably be necessary during dry spring and summer periods.
CHALK OR LIMESTONE Variable, often shallow, topsoil with recognizable lumps of chalk or limestone, especially in lower soil	Lacks humus and plant food. Difficult to work when wet. Tends to dry out quickly in summer. The calcium in chalk or limestone soil inhibits plants from using many plant foods, and deficiencies may result. Chalky soil is alkaline, and not tolerated by most plants.	Generally light, easy to work, free-draining and warms up quickly in spring. Good for rock garden plants.	Add large quantities of farmyard manure, compost or other organic matter, preferably to the top layer of soil, each spring and autumn. This will break down (into humus) in the soil, improving its condition. Give top-dressings of general fertilizers throughout the growing season.
PEAT Dark brown or black, spongy to touch	Usually waterlogged and may need artificial drainage. May be very acid and sour. Often deficient in plant foods.	Contains plenty of organic matter as it consists mainly of organic material not yet fully decomposed. Easily worked. Too acid for most garden plants but very fertile when drained and limed.	If soil is waterlogged, then a soakaway or drainage pipes may be needed. Liming helps drainage and counteracts acidity. Add lime at 250g per sq m (8 oz per sq yd) every 2–3 years. Add regular, fairly heavy, dressings of general-purpose fertilizers in spring, summer and autumn.
LOAM Dark, crumbly, easy to clean from fingers	Should not be any problem as long as the drainage is satisfactory and the humus and plant food content is maintained.	Ideal garden soil, with a balanced mixture of sand, humus and clay. If humus content is maintained, a well-drained, well-aerated soil rich in plant food will result. Warm enough for early cultivation.	The improvements depend on the proportions of clay and sand in the loam. Sandy loam will require the regular spring and autumn addition of organic matter and fertilizers. Clayey loam may need regular addition of 375g per sq m (12 oz per sq yd) every 2–3 years. Heavy loams will benefit from being roughly dug over in autumn.

Getting your garden into shape

Once you have finalized your basic garden feature and plant plans on graph paper (as described on the previous pages), it is time to make more detailed lists of plants you want and to put your planning into practice.

Marking out borders and features
Clip your plans to a board and protect them with transparent plastic. With your garden feature plan worked out to scale, you already have your basic measurements. You now need to measure out these positions on site. For this you require a long measuring tape, canes and stakes, wooden mallet, and a large ball of string.

At each of the marked points you hammer in a stake. When you want curves (for the border) use canes at intervals of about 1m (3 ft) between the stakes. When these are positioned (see the north border plan here), take the ball of string and tie one end to one of the end stakes. Then twine string round all intermediate marking canes and main stakes until you reach the other end of the border.

Continue marking each of the edge lines of the borders, shed, pergola, trellis and raised borders in this way. These lines will be essential when turfing the lawn and other grassed areas. The final edges of the flower borders will be formed when you cut the turves.

Planning plants for the borders
You will have seen from the illustration of the Flower Garden ground plan on page 8 that we selected a wide variety of plants. To help you make your choice we list ours here under the following groupings: trees, shrubs, climbers, herbaceous perennials, bulbs including corms, tubers and rhizomes, annuals and biennials. Additional plants will, of course, be suggested later.

Trees
In our Flower Garden we were fortunate enough to have some mature trees *in situ:* aesculus (horse chestnut), *Betula pendula* (silver birch) and laburnum. To assist in breaking up the long, narrow plot we added three smaller trees, decorative in themselves.

Our selection: acer (small maple); *Euonymus europaeus* (spindle tree); syringa (lilac).

Shrubs
Be they evergreen or deciduous, shrubs help to create perspective and depth in mixed borders. They also make attractive features throughout the year when tub-grown, and add to the overall design of the garden while generally needing little care and attention. The lower-growing types also help to control weeds.

Our selection: aucuba; azalea; berberis (barberry); buddleia (butterfly bush); buxus (box); camellia; ceanothus; chaenomeles (quince); choisya (Mexican orange blossom); cotoneaster; cytisus (broom); erica (heathers and heaths); euonymus (spindle bush); garrya (in area reserved for a lean-to greenhouse); hamamelis (witch hazel); hydrangea; hypericum (St John's wort); lavendula (lavender); mahonia; olearia; pyracantha (fire-thorn); rhododendron; skimmia; viburnum; vinca (periwinkle).

Climbers
Both climbers, and shrubs that can be treated as climbers, are ideal for clothing bare walls or helping to hide unsightly objects as well as being highly decorative. In our garden they cover the trellis and pergolas that help to break up the length of the site and give it a broader appearance.

Our selection: clematis; jasminum (jasmine); lonicera (honeysuckle); polygonum (Russian vine); rosa (rose).

Herbaceous perennials
In a mixed border herbaceous perennials give colour at different periods in spring, summer and autumn, and provide cut flowers for the house. Unfortunately, they die down during the winter months, so use shrubs to help hide the bare patches.

Our selection: agapanthus lily (African lily); *Alyssum saxatile*; *Anemone japonica* (wind flower); campanula; chrysanthemum; grey cineraria; dianthus (pinks); helleborus (hellebore); *Helleborus niger* (Christmas rose); hosta (plantain lily); nepeta (catmint); pyrethrum; sempervivum (houseleek); thymus (thyme).

Bulbs
The bulb area (to be at the far end of our garden) should be a riot of colour each spring and provide plenty of flowers for early picking. Allow space for bulbous plants, including corms, tubers and rhizomes, in a mixed border as well, as they give long seasons of flowering.

Our selection in the mixed borders: *Lilium candidum* (madonna lily); gladiolus (sword lily); dahlias; iris.

Annuals
To give splashes of colour during the summer months, and to fill gaps in the borders, annuals are ideal plants – either the hardy forms sown straight into their final positions, or half-hardy ones planted out in late spring. Both forms will be discussed in more detail later.

Our selection: centaurea (cornflower); convolvulus; iberis (candytuft); malcolmia (Virginian stock); papaver (poppy); tagetes (African and French marigolds); tropaeolum (nasturtium).

Biennials
Raised from seed one year to flower the next, biennials have a useful part to play as temporary gap-fillers. In some cases, as with lunaria (honesty) plants, they will seed themselves each spring, flower in summer, and produce unusually decorative seed pods to enliven your winter flower arrangements.
In situ: althaea (hollyhock); lunaria (honesty).

Border measuring plan

■ main stakes

● intermediate marking canes

3m (9ft 10in)

10m (32ft 6in)

Turfing a lawn

For turf to flourish and produce a successful lawn, thorough soil preparation is necessary and if possible the ground should be prepararead a few weeks beforehand to allow for settlement. It is equally important to purchase good, weed-free turfs that are of the same thickness and have them delivered as near as possible to the date you intend to lay them. If they arrive 48 hours before laying, stack them without unrolling; if there is to be a longer gap between arrival and turfing, unroll each turf and lay it flat.

Marking out curved edges

There has, in recent years, been a breakaway from the traditional square or rectangular lawn in favour of ones with gently curving edges. An irregular lawn site is a bit more difficult to mark out, but the easiest method is to lay out a length of string or rope to mark the outline, then drive in canes or wooden pegs against the string at intervals of about 60–90cm (2–3 ft), and twist the string around them. You will then have quite a durable outline of the lawn to which you can work.

Preparing the site

Thoroughly dig the lawn site to the depth of a spade (single-digging), or, if the subsoil (lower soil) is compacted, to two

depths of the spade (double-digging). Be careful not to mix subsoil and topsoil – keep them in their correct layers. A hard subsoil could result in a badly drained or waterlogged lawn if it is not well broken up. During digging incorporate plenty of bulky organic matter in the bottom of each trench, such as well-rotted farmyard manure, garden compost, leaf mould, peat, spent hops or even decomposed straw. This will help to retain moisture in light, sandy or chalky soil during dry weather and will encourage better drainage of surplus water in heavy clay soils.

If you have such a heavy clay soil it would be advisable to incorporate plenty of coarse sand or grit during digging to assist further in drainage of surplus moisture. A good lawn can never be achieved if the soil holds too much water in the winter. If your site does become very seriously waterlogged in winter, the only satisfactory answer is to have a proper drainage system installed, consisting of tile drains sloping into a soakaway.

Levelling and raking

Once you have completed digging it is best to allow the soil to settle naturally for a few weeks. This is a good time to carry out any general levelling that may be necessary. Then, shortly before laying the turf, final preparations can be undertaken, when the surface of the soil is reasonably dry. Never work on the site

when it is wet and sticky or you will end up with a mud patch.

Break down the roughly dug soil with a fork or rake to produce a reasonably fine surface. Then firm the soil by treading systematically over the entire site with as much weight as possible on your heels. At this stage you may apply a general-purpose fertilizer or sterilized bonemeal at 135g per sq m (4 oz per sq yd), which can be incorporated into the surface during final raking.

This raking is to provide a fine, level surface on which to lay the turf, and you should take this opportunity to ensure the site is really level, with no hollows or bumps. Rake the soil from any high spots into the hollows and firm it well with your heels. The smoother and more level the site, the better the finished job will be.

Laying the turfs

The actual turfing should be done when the surface is reasonably dry. If you have a paved area with a straight edge, this is a good place to start. Lay one row of turfs along, and hard up to, this straight edge. The turfs will generally be 30cm ×

1 *Begin to lay the turf along one side of the lawn. Be sure the edges are straight*
2 *Turf should be cut with a sharp half-moon edging iron or a sharp knife*
3 *When filling in the turfs, lay them as close together as possible*
4 *Be sure that the turfs are level with the ground or following the slope of the chosen site*
5 *Place more soil under turfs which are too low or remove soil from under those which are too high*
6 *Tamp down the newly-laid turfs to firm them in place*
7 *A newly-turfed lawn has a brickwork pattern which later knits together*
8 *Use a stiff broom to lift the flattened grass and brush in the top-dressing*

1m (12 in × 3 ft) and should be laid lengthways across the site. Allow the turf to overlap your string outline so that when you finish laying you can go round the edges with a knife or half-moon edging iron, cutting them to the required shape, using the string as a guide.

When laying the second row of turfs remember that the joints should be bonded or staggered like bricks in a wall. In other words, the joints of the second row should fall in the centre of each turf in the first row. You should always work over the turf which has already been laid, so it is advisable to stand on a plank to stop your heels sinking into the new turf, especially if it is fairly moist.

Butt the turfs hard up against each other so there are no gaps in the joints. You can push them close together with the tines of a fork used back to front. If the turfs have been well cut and are all of the same thickness they will require little firming. Patting them down with the back of the fork is generally sufficient. If levelling is necessary, do it by adding or removing soil beneath the turfs during laying. Continue turfing the whole site in this way, ensuring that all joints are staggered. To achieve this bonded effect you will need to cut some of the turfs in half at the edges of the lawn.

After turfing, the lawn can be given a light roll if you have a small garden roller. If not, walk up and down the plank, moving this evenly so that the whole lawn is covered eventually.

Adding a top dressing
For a really good finish, brush in a top dressing with a stiff broom. This can be either good, fine topsoil or a mixture of topsoil, coarse sand and fine peat. Apply a 13mm ($\frac{1}{2}$ in) layer over the lawn and work it really well into the grass and joints. Remove any surplus, to ensure the grass is not smothered. This will fill in any gaps there may be between the joints and will also encourage the grass to grow and the turfs to knit together well.

Watering programme
In mid spring it will probably not be necessary to water the turfs after laying as the ground should be moist. But as late spring and early summer approach, with drier weather, you must undertake a regular watering programme. If the turfs are allowed to dry out before they become established or well rooted into the soil, they will shrink and the joints will open up, producing ugly cracks. In addition, the turf will take a long time to become established if it is not watered during dry spells in the spring and summer and it is quite likely the grass will turn brown. It will take a considerable time to recover from this, and weeds may start invading the dried-out patches.

The most thorough way of watering a lawn is to use a sprinkler on the end of a hosepipe, and leave this for at least one hour on any one part of the lawn. This will ensure the water gets well down to the roots.

15

Sowing a lawn

Although it is far cheaper to sow grass seed than to lay turfs, you will not be able to use the lawn for a few months. Also grass seed and seedlings are prone to damage by bad weather and birds, so a good deal of early care is needed.

The best time to sow is from early to mid autumn (August to September), but late spring (April) is also suitable. In spring you will have to pay more attention to watering as the ground can dry out rapidly, resulting in poor or delayed seed germination.

Preparing the ground

So that it has a chance to settle, prepare the soil several weeks before sowing. Dig and manure the site thoroughly and level it by raking the soil in various directions, breaking down any clods of earth and removing stones, weeds and other rubbish.

If the surface is particularly rough you may have to do a more thorough job. Use levelling pegs, a straight 2·50m (8–10 ft) plank of wood and a spirit level. Hammer in one levelling peg to a suitable height and put in the others at 2–2·50m (6–8 ft) intervals. Place the plank on top of the two pegs and check how straight it is with the spirit level. Hammer the pegs in as necessary until the plank is level. Repeat this procedure until all the pegs are at the same height.

Rake the topsoil until roughly the same amount of each peg is showing above the ground. If there are bad bumps or hollows remove some subsoil from the higher to the lower areas, but make sure the topsoil always remains on top.

A few days before sowing, break down the roughly-dug ground with a fork and then firm it by treading over the entire site systematically with your heels. Apply a general-purpose fertilizer, or lawn fertilizer, at 70g per sq m (2 oz per sq yd). Next, rake the site with an iron rake making the soil as fine as possible and removing any large stones and other debris. Then firm and rake the soil again, this time working 'across the grain' of the first raking. Remove any more stones that have reached the surface.

Just before sowing, go over the entire site in every direction very lightly with a rake, drawing it along the surface to produce mini-furrows. This will be a help when you come to cover the seed.

*To sow new lawn: **1** remove all debris from site, then dig and manure; **2** break down surface with fork; **3** tread over to firm, then rake; **4** sow seed evenly, releasing slowly; **5** divide ground, and seed, into equal parts for accurate sowing; **6** rake seed in – across previous furrows*

Utility lawn mixtures

Next choose your grass seeds: there are mixtures to suit all purposes.

If you require a utility lawn that is very hardwearing and suitable for games and a good deal of foot traffic, choose a utility-grade mixture which includes some really tough grasses. A typical mixture would contain 4 parts Chewing's fescue, 3 parts perennial ryegrass, 2 parts crested dog's tail and 1 part rough-stalked meadow grass.

Chewing's fescue is a fine-leaved dwarf grass which is very drought-resistant and is included in the mixture to help give the lawn a finer appearance. But it will eventually die out and be overtaken by the perennial ryegrass. This is a true utility grass, coarse-leaved, very hardwearing, and especially good on heavier types of soil. It will not stand really close mowing – and indeed a utility lawn should not be closely cut.

Crested dog's tail is another coarse, hardwearing species; it is good on light soils and withstands drought. Rough-stalked meadow grass is of creeping habit and clothes the soil with foliage. It is also a coarse-leaved type and is good on moist, heavy soils.

Luxury-grade mixtures

However, if you prefer a really fine lawn you must choose a luxury-grade mixture containing only fine grasses. Such a lawn is unsuitable for heavy use, but it will provide a beautiful setting for your flower beds and borders. You will have to give it much more attention and more mowing than a utility lawn. Mow it closely: this generally means mowing twice a week in the growing season (spring and summer). You must also feed and water it if you want to keep it looking really good, for it will soon deteriorate if you neglect it.

For a fine lawn mixture, choose 7–8 parts Chewing's fescue and 2–3 parts browntop bent. Both are very fine-leaved grasses. Chewing's is a tufted species, while browntop is creeping and covers the surface of the soil with foliage. It is a very drought-resistant species, like Chewing's, but this does not mean that you should neglect to water it in dry weather. This mixture will produce a dense, dark-green sward.

For shaded areas

Normal grass-seed mixtures are unsuitable for shaded areas under large trees or places overshadowed by tall buildings and walls. The grass simply would not grow well and would be thin and patchy. Fortunately, however, it is possible to buy mixtures specially developed for shaded areas. A typical mixture consists of 5 parts rough-stalked meadow grass, 3 parts wood meadow grass and 2 parts creeping red fescue. Wood meadow grass is very shade-tolerant and is often found

growing wild on the edges of woodland and forest clearings. Creeping red fescue is an adaptable species, that is highly drought-resistant and has a creeping habit of growth.

Calculating the quantity

Having decided on a mixture, you must then calculate the quantity of seed you require. You will need to know the sowing rate. For fine lawns this is 35–45g per sq m (1–1¼ oz per sq yd); for others increase the rate to 50–70g (1½–2 oz). Measure the length and width of your site and multiply to calculate the area. It should then be an easy matter to work out the quantity of seed required: multiply the area by the sowing rate.

How to sow

Ideally you should choose a fine, calm day for sowing, when the soil surface is dry. Be sure to sow the seed evenly, otherwise you will have a patchy lawn. Divide the entire site into strips 1m (1 yd) wide by marking out each strip with string, secured by canes at each end.

Then calculate the number of square metres (square yards) in each strip and weigh out sufficient grass seed for each one. Sow half the seed up and down the strip, and the other half across it. This should ensure even sowing at the correct rate. Repeat the procedure for all the strips until the whole site has been sown.

If you wish to be even more precise you could divide each strip into square metres (square yards) by laying bamboo canes on the soil. Then weigh out the seed into the required number of small lots, sufficient for each square.

When sowing seed by hand, hold it well above the soil, say at waist height, and slowly release the seed as you walk the length and breadth of the area, moving your hand fairly rapidly from side to side. This 'broadcast' method usually ensures very even sowing.

You can also sow the seed with a fertilizer distributor, but only if the machine is adjustable. Obtaining the correct sowing rate is a matter of trial and error. Make practice runs over a sheet of polythene until you find the right setting. Measure out sufficient seed for a given number of square metres (square yards), put this in the distributor and make one run over the measured area of polythene. If the machine runs out of seed before the area is completely sown, or if there is still seed in the machine after running once over the area, then you will need to try other settings. It will only be worth your while using a distributor if you have an exceptionally large lawn; for small gardens, hand sowing is just as quick.

Care of new lawns

After sowing, lightly rake the lawn to cover the seed. Rake across the tiny furrows you made before the seed was sown. You will find that most of the seed is then covered with soil. Don't firm the surface as it may become caked after rain or watering and so inhibit seed germination.

Birds can be a nuisance as they relish grass seed. Some seed is treated with a bird repellent; otherwise discourage them by stretching black cotton between sticks over the lawn in a criss-cross fashion about 8–10cm (3–4 in) above the soil.

It is very important to water whenever the surface of the soil starts to dry out, both before and after the seeds have germinated. If the soil is allowed to become dry germination will be patchy, and the seedlings can quickly die and wither away. In fact it is essential to carry on watering throughout the summer if you are sowing in spring, or well into the autumn if sowing during early or mid autumn (August or September). Apply the water gently and evenly using a lawn sprinkler on the end of a hosepipe. Always water thoroughly; dribs and drabs do more harm than good, so stand the sprinkler on each portion of the lawn for at least an hour.

The seedlings should appear in two to three weeks if you sow in late spring (April), or within one to two weeks after an early or mid autumn sowing.

Rolling and mowing

Once the seedlings are about 2·5–4cm (1–1½ in) high lightly brush the lawn with a brush or besom to remove any wormcasts. Carry out this task when the lawn is dry. Then you can give the lawn a light rolling – using either a small roller or, preferably, the rear roller of a handmower. This is to firm the surface of the soil which was loosened as the seeds germinated. It also presses into the soil any small stones which might otherwise damage the mower blades. Light rolling induces the grass seedlings to produce new shoots and so speeds up the lawnmaking process.

Start mowing when the grass is 5cm (2 in) high. Sharpen the mower blades well as they may tear out the seedlings or severely damage them. Set the blades high so that only the tops of the seedlings are removed.

Weeds usually appear with the new grass but annual weeds soon die out once you start mowing. You can handweed a new lawn, but make sure you hold down the grass seedlings with one hand while you pull out the weeds with the other, or you may also pull out the young grass.

On no account should you use the normal hormone lawn weedkillers on a new lawn as they could severely damage or kill the young grass. It is necessary to wait 12 months after sowing before starting to apply them. But there is a special weedkiller (containing the chemical ioxynil) which is suitable if applied according to the maker's instructions.

The trees in your garden

There are two types of trees: evergreen or deciduous; they may be tolerant of acid or alkaline soil. The varied shapes include widespreading, weeping and columnar.

In addition to contributing height and interest to a garden, they can be put to many practical uses, from providing shade or acting as a windbreak to hiding an obstinate eyesore. It is a pity to remove existing trees unless absolutely necessary, as they may have taken years to mature.

Making the right choice

The majority of trees will grow happily in a soil that has an almost neutral pH or is slightly acid. Some, such as birches, trees of heaven (ailanthus), elms and some poplars, have a definite preference for acid soils. Others, for example the decorative members of the apple and cherry genera, maples and crataegus (thorns), prefer some free lime.

Waterlogged or boggy ground suits very few trees, such as weeping willows and alders; dry or shallow soils do not worry many except the moisture-loving ones, provided the lower soil is not composed of solid chalk. (If chalk is a problem dig it out as deeply as possible and replace with good topsoil.)

For the best results with all varieties make sure the soil is deep, friable, well-drained and well-manured. A specific tree may prefer acidity or alkalinity and either can be provided for when preparing the ground for planting. If necessary, top dressings or feeds of special fertilizers can be given each year.

When to plant

It is best to buy and plant trees during the autumn and spring months when the weather is reasonably mild and the soil is not too wet or frozen. Some can be planted in winter if conditions are suitable, but generally trees do not pick up and grow as well in the first season, as their roots are in their most active state during that period.

The Common Laburnum
that was already
in existence in our Flower Garden

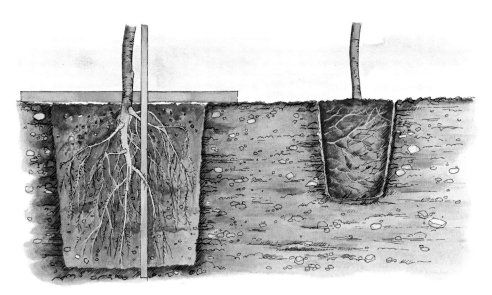

Trees must be planted to the correct depth and their roots well spread out; damaged or broken parts must be removed

Trees for planting in autumn and spring are often in the 'bare-rooted' state. This means there is little or no soil on their roots, or that the roots are in polythene or sacking containing a little loose soil. Bare-rooted trees are ideal for planting during their dormant period of non-active growth but *not* at any other time of year.

'Container-grown trees' – most nurseries and garden centres supply them – have been grown in soil-filled plastic, metal, whalehide or polythene containers from an early age, and their roots are well-established in the soil. The object of container-grown trees is to lengthen the planting season, so that they can be set in the garden at any time of year.

In theory this seems to work quite well, but in practice, after planting during the summer months, you must be especially careful to ensure that the roots get plenty of water during a dry spell and the leaves are sprayed every day for four to six weeks to help overcome any possible transitional shock.

If both bare-rooted and container-grown trees are available, you can plant at virtually any time of year, and have no excuse for a bare area. It also allows for impulse-buying should you see a specific tree you have not been able to obtain previously.

You will have to pay rather more for container-grown trees or plants of any kind, as they are more expensive to raise and transport to retailers.

Considering the many years a tree spends in the ground, it pays to prepare its site thoroughly. Begin by digging out the soil to the depth of a spade or the fork tines, and make a hole 1–1·5m

(3–5 ft) in diameter. Then dig over the next layer to the same depth and add to this as much well-rotted manure or compost as you have available. Tread it firm and follow this with a light scuttling of the top 5–7cm (2–3 in) of soil with the fork or a large rake.

During preparation remove any large stones or weeds.

Planting bare-rooted trees

Trees must be planted to the same depth as they were previously growing; this is shown by the soil mark on the stem above the roots. Place the tree in the hole and check the depth by the level of the soil mark. If the hole is too shallow remove more soil; if it is too deep, put back some topsoil and lightly firm it.

Then get a wooden stake, about 4cm (1½ in) square, preferably with a sharpened end, and firmly hammer it into the centre of the hole. It should be long enough to reach as high as the first set of branches.

Put the tree back in the hole, carefully placing the roots around the stake. If there are any broken roots cut off the damaged portions with a sharp knife or secateurs. Make sure all the other roots are spread out.

If you can get someone to hold the tree in position the planting will be easier. If not, tie the tree to the stake. Shovel the topsoil back into the hole so that it gets well round the roots (slightly shaking the tree will help). Return all the soil, firming it from time to time, and make sure the tree remains upright.

Planting container-grown trees

First water the soil in the container and leave it to drain. Then place the tree, in its container, into the prepared hole to ensure the correct depth.

Next remove the container either by

slitting the sides or tipping out the soil-ball round the roots. Hold the tree in position, return the topsoil and firm it. A stake of suitable length is again required, but in this case it is advisable to hammer it in *after* planting, taking care not to disturb the soil ball.

Caring for young trees

First tie the trunk of a new tree to its stake. Use one of the proprietary tree ties available or, if that is not possible, a nylon stocking. Don't use coarse string as it may chafe the bark. Fix a tie about 10cm (4 in) above soil level and another at about the same distance from the top of the stake.

After planting, a good watering is advisable and, especially in spring, the plants should be sprayed daily for about a month. A layer of mulch over the whole planting area will help to conserve moisture and provide food for the roots.

Until the trees are established, which could be up to three years after planting, keep the soil area free of weeds and grass that might inhibit healthy growth.

IN OUR FLOWER GARDEN

We 'inherited' two large and mature trees – silver birch (*Betula pendula*) and an Indian horse chestnut (*Aesculus indica*) – at the far end of the garden. They are both deciduous and, mainly because of their size, commonly associated with woodlands or parks. They can, however, look equally right in a garden, provided they are carefully sited (if being newly planted) or incorporated into the landscaping as in this instance – where they form features with underplanting for added interest.

Birches

Silver birch trees are most elegant in form with golden-yellow diamond-shaped leaves in autumn and white peeling bark, which develops as the trees mature, the final height being about 8m (25 ft).

Because of the tracery framework of their branches, silver birches do not cast dense shade, but they are rather shallow-rooting and plants set beneath them should not have roots that penetrate too deeply (hence our choice of azaleas). The only soil they don't like is a chalky one (again, like the azaleas).

There are a number of other fine birch trees. For example, *Betula costata*, with white peeling bark in summer that turns orange in winter; *B. pendula* Tristis, tall and slender with hanging branches; *B. pendula* Youngii, a smaller tree with weeping branches of delicate leaves that reach the ground; and *B. utilis*, with its greyish trunk and russet-brown branches contrasting with each other.

Horse chestnuts

Among the horse chestnuts, *Aesculus indica* is one of the most attractive, with its 'candles' of white, pink and yellow flowers in mid to late summer (June to July), followed by smooth-coated 'conkers' later in the year.

Other horse chestnuts are *A. flava* (sweet buckeye) which has yellow flowers and finely toothed, smallish leaves that colour attractively in autumn; *A. carnea* Briottii with deep rosy red flowers and smooth 'conkers'; and *A. hippocastanum* (common horse chestnut) with its summer 'candles' of white flowers up to 30cm (12 in) high followed by the 'conkers' loved by children. All horse chestnuts grow freely in most soils, except very chalky ones, and they create dense shade beneath, so underplants have to be carefully chosen.

Laburnums

We also inherit a laburnum sited on the south edge of the lawn. There are few smallish, drooping-shaped trees – they grow to about 6m (20 ft) – that are more attractive. They beautify a garden in late spring to mid summer (April to June) by their long, pendulous yellow pea-like

Right: slow-growing Japanese maple, Acer palmatum, *with glorious autumn foliage*
Below left: common horse chestnut, Aesculus hippocastanum, *bears 'candle' blooms and conkers. Below right: spindle* Euonymus europaeus, *has flowers and fruit*

flowers, followed in autumn with brown seed pods and in winter with green twigs.

All parts of the plant are poisonous, particularly the seeds, so obviously care should be taken where there are children.

The most common laburnum is *L. anagyroides* with various forms, such as *L. anagyroides* Aureum, with golden yellow leaves; and *L.a.* Autumnale, which often flowers for a second time in autumn. *L. vossii*, also very popular, is later-flowering than most, has darker glossy green leaves and is more erect in habit.

In our mixed flower border we added three small garden trees: a spindle, miniature maple, and a lilac.

Spindle tree

The spindle is one of the few trees among the Euonymus family of shrubs and is correctly called *Euonymus europaeus*. It grows to about 6m (20 ft), and its inconspicuous yellow-green small flowers are followed by a wealth of clusters of pinkish-red fruits, which open to reveal orange-coloured seeds. In autumn the leaves turn beautiful yellow and red hues. It is one of the easiest of trees to grow in almost any position.

Maples

The small maple, *Acer palmatum*, slowly grows to a height of about 4m (12 ft). We chose it for its attractive lobed leaves, which are pale green in summer and gorgeous orange and red tones in autumn. It is sometimes commonly called the Japanese maple and there are many cultivars of it, all equally attractive and easy to grow, if the soil is not too chalky.

There are several other forms of maples which are mainly much larger trees and more suitable for bigger gardens, or for planting in a far corner for shade or to hide an unpleasant view.

Syringas

Our lilac tree is more correctly called Syringa. The many trees and shrubs in this genus produce a mass of fragrant flowers in early to mid summer (May to June), and remain shapely green-leaved plants from early spring to late autumn (February to October).

Lilacs grow well in all but the most chalky soils, and they give their best in a sunny position. The most common varieties grown in gardens are those of *Syringa vulgaris*. They provide a wide colour range of flowers – from white, pale pink, dark red, mauve, purple, yellow to greenish-tinged – and can be either single or double flowered. There are so many that it is advisable to choose a colour to harmonize with other blooms in the immediate vicinity.

Some good ones are *Syringa vulgaris* Clarke's Giant (lavender-pink); Olivier de Serres (mauvish-pink); Esther Staley (carmine-pink); Charles Joby (purple-red); Mrs. Edward Harding (red); Maud Notcutt (white); and Souvenir d'Alice Harding (alabaster – off-white).

Left: the graceful birch, Betula pendula, has attractive leaf shapes, such as heart or diamond, as well as some splendid stem colours. Below: the lilac tree, Syringa vulgaris, has many varieties which happily mix with other surrounding plants.

Shrubs and climbers

Planning ahead

Apart from varying shapes and sizes, shrubs can be evergreen or deciduous and have a variety of features such as variegated or different-coloured leaves, colourful and/or fragrant flowers, decorative bark or aromatic leaves. They can change leaf colours in autumn, produce interesting and colourful fruits, and be suitable for planting in all types of soil, sun or shade.

Always remember to keep down the number of shrubs and climbers in your garden and not plant too many, otherwise they grow into a tangly mess and swamp other plants in the border. The best policy is to put young plants close together and then, when the selected ones are reaching maturity, pull out and discard the remainder; but this is expensive and unnecessary with mixed flower borders.

As with all plantings it is wise to plan the borders on paper beforehand and draw them out on graph paper, as we described on pages 10-11.

List your choice of shrubs and climbers—most good plant catalogues describe them in detail—and alongside each add its ultimate height and diameter, the colouring of leaves, flowers and fruit, their timing, whether evergreen or deciduous, soil preference, sun-or shade-lover, and any other specific requirement.

When and how to plant

As with trees, deciduous shrubs and climbers are best planted in autumn or spring, and evergreens in spring. Both types are available in bare-rooted and container-grown forms, the latter being suitable for planting at more or less any time of year provided the necessary precautions are taken. The preparation for, and the planting of, shrubs and climbers are essentially the same as for trees. After-care of the newly planted shrubs is also similar to that of trees.

Flower Garden ground plan key

1 azalea	**10** erica	**19** rhododendron
2 berberis	**11** euonymus	**20** vinca
3 buddleia	**12** garrya	**21** clematis
4 buxus	**13** hamamelis	**22** jasminum
5 camellia	**14** hydrangea	**23** lonicera
6 ceanothus	**15** hypericum	**24** polygonum
7 chaenomeles	**16** lavendula	**25** rosa
8 cotoneaster	**17** mahonia	
9 cytisus	**18** pyracantha	

IN OUR FLOWER GARDEN

We selected a variety of shrubs for different purposes here and, after the initial planting as shown in the ground plan (page 8), we added shrubs that can be planted almost anywhere in the mixed borders—aucuba, choisya, skimmia and viburnum—and olearia, which likes a sunny position. They are described in alphabetical order.

Aucuba

Really hardy and versatile evergreens that grow to about 1·5m high and spread to 1·5m (5 × 5 ft), in sun or shade, town or country, and any type of soil. *Aucuba japonica*, the common form, has glossy, oval leaves and brilliant scarlet berries on the female plants.

Aucuba japonica Crotonifolia (male) and *A.j.*Variegata (female) are both variegated forms.

Azalea

Here there is a wealth of hybrids from which to choose including some deciduous ones that are 2–3m (6–10 ft) tall, and evergreens 1–1·5m (3–5 ft) tall. In many catalogues these are listed under rhododendron as they belong to the same family and have the same requirements, of which an important one for both types is that the soil should have an acid pH and contain no free lime. If your garden does not have a naturally acid soil you must prepare the ground before planting by giving it thorough treatment. that is either providing lime-free topsoil with plenty of peat, or forking in adequate quantities of peat and leaf mould.

As the azaleas in our Flower Garden are growing under the shade of the deciduous silver birch, we have selected a mixture of evergreen cultivars (varieties) to give interest all year round, with the emphasis on different coloured flowers in early summer. A few popular evergreen ones from which to choose are:

Addy Wery	vermilion
Blue Danube	purple-blue
Hinodegiri	bright crimson
Orange Beauty	salmon-orange
Rosebud	pink
Palestrina	ivory
Mother's Day	rose-red

The deciduous forms of azalea, although without the advantage of being

Top left: silver-flowered azalea
Above left: Aucuba japonica *Variegata*
Left: blue berries of Berberis darwinii
Above: sweet-scented Buddleia globosa

orange, and the autumn fruits are very showy. Many berberis species also produce brilliant leaf tints in autumn and winter; all of them are more or less spiny, so you will need your gloves when clipping back.

In our garden we needed a low-growing form that would help visually to break the edge of the paved area near the house, but would also blend well with both the mixed border and the paving stones. For this purpose we selected *B.candidula*, an evergreen variety.

Berberis candidula Leaves with silvery undersides, yellow flowers and purple oval-shaped berries. Grows only about 45cm (18 in) high, 1–1·5m (4–5 ft) spread.

B. darwinii and *B.stenophylla* Bear their flowers and berries on arching stems and make ideal, unusual hedging plants.

B.verruculosa White undersides to evergreen leaves that colour well in autumn; golden yellow flowers on arching branches followed by rich purple berries. Grows to about 1m high, 1m spread (4 × 4 ft).

Two attractive deciduous types are:

B.thunbergii Brilliant leaf colours and scarlet fruits in autumn; mainly compact bushes.

B.wilsoniae Almost evergreen leaves that turn rich red and orange in autumn, and blend well with the clusters of coral-coloured berries. Smallish in size, tending to form mound-shaped bushes.

Buddleia (butterfly bush)

Quick-growing deciduous shrubs producing panicles (elongated branches) of flowers in late summer and mid autumn. As their common name indicates, they are much loved by butterflies for the sweet fragrance produced by most species. They thrive in any soil, and particularly love sun. For our garden we have chosen the very popular *B.davidii*.

Buddleia davidii Grows quickly anywhere to a medium size and flowers freely even in its second year. There are many varieties of this shrub with flowers colours varying from the usual bluish purple to white, rose, lavender and shades of purple.

B.alternifolia Almost tree-like in form, with fragrant lilac flowers in long, thin sprays. Grows freely, particularly against a warm wall.

B.globosa Virtually evergreen buddleia that produces in early summer sweetly scented flowers, round and orange in colour, on short stems; long tapering leaves that are grey underneath.

B.fallowiana Silvery-leaved with sweet smelling lavender-blue flowers in late summer. Alba is a white-blooming form.

evergreen, do have special attractions in that they produce an even wider range of flower colours and are usually fragrant, and the leaves turn to beautiful red tints in autumn. They are, however, rather larger than the evergreens and so require more planting space. Among the best deciduous ones to choose are:

Knap Hill Exbury hybrids	single colours or mixed
Directeur Moerlands	gold and orange
Coccinea Speciosa	orange-red
Aida	peach-pink
Koster's Brilliant Red	orange-red
White Swan	white
Narcissiflorum	pale yellow

Berberis (barberry)

Another family of plants with both deciduous and evergreen forms that can vary enormously in habit from horizontal ground cover growth to dwarf bushes 60cm high, 60cm spread (2 × 2 ft) or medium ones 1·5m high, 1·5m spread (5 × 5 ft). They can be planted as individuals or hedges, are easy to grow in any soil and tolerate shade; the evergreens will thrive in the shade. The flowers in spring and summer are usually yellow or

Buxus (box)

Very useful shiny green evergreens that are ideal for hedging, edging borders and paths or, as in our garden, forming a link between the north side mixed flower border and the paved area. They grow anywhere and withstand hard treatment. The larger boxes can be used for hedges or topiary (clipping of trees or hedges to make 'sculpted' designs). For our garden we chose *B.sempervirens*.

Buxus sempervirens Often sold as a low-growing shrub, 60cm high, 60cm spread (2 × 2 ft). Other popular boxes are:

*B.s.*Aurea Variation of *B.sempervirens*, with yellow-edged leaves. This dual coloration does not always make a good contrast to other plants.

B.s.suffruticosa Common edging box normally seen in small formal gardens. Its medium-sized leaves of bright green set off other plants to advantage.

Camellia

These beautiful shiny-leaved evergreen winter- and spring-flowering plants are not nearly as difficult to grow as is frequently thought. They are, in fact, as hardy as the common laurel. However, they do like the same acid, peaty soil conditions as azaleas, rhododendrons and heathers, hence in our garden we have planted them by the azaleas and heathers on the north-facing side, so all

these plants can have the same treatment. They like protection from north and east winds and not too much direct winter and early spring sun, which can damage the flowers following a frosty night. An ideal position, if you have it, is a lightly wooded part of the garden that offers frost protection. Camellias grow from 1·5 to 3m (5 to 10 ft) high 1·5m (5 ft) spread.

There is a vast range of camellias from which to choose, many with different flower shapes, and we have selected one of the early-flowering *C.williamsii* hybrids to grow by itself at the far end of the garden, and two of the later *C.japonica* hybrids to complement the heathers at the lower end of the flower border.

Camellia flowers may be in any shade of white, pink, red, peach or multi-coloured and some of the best to select from are:

Camellia williamsii Donation	orchid pink
C.w. J. C. Williams	pale pink
C.w. November Pink	pink
C.japonica Mathotiana	crimson
C.j. Elegans	salmon-rose, splashed white
C.j. Adolphe Audusson	blood-red, yellow centre
C.j. Lady Vansittart	pink and white striped
C.j. Mercury	light red
C.j. Lady Clare	pale pink

Ceanothus

Sometimes called California lilac. The most appealing feature of these evergreen or deciduous shrubs is that they are among the best hardy blue-flowering ones available. They vary in size, and do best in a sunny position where the soil is well-drained and not too chalky. Gloire de Versailles, a popular deciduous type, is the one we have selected for our south-facing wall and we suggest a few others: Gloire de Versailles, with sky-blue flowers borne on arching branches in late summer or late autumn.

Topaz (deciduous), with deeper blue flowers.

C.thyrsiflorus (evergreen) is one of the hardiest, with bright blue blooms in early summer.

C.thyrsiflorus repens (evergreen), a very attractive weed-suppressor, growing only up to about 1m (3 ft) high, but spreading to 2·5m–3m (8–10 ft).

Far left: well-trimmed Buxus sempervirens
Left: ceanothus Gloire de Versailles
Below left: camellia D. Olga Anderson
Bottom left: Camellia japonica *C. M. Wilson*
Right: chaenomeles bears edible berries
Below: C. japonica *Hearn's Pink Dawn*

Chaenomeles (quince, japonica)

Sometimes called *cydonia*. Very easy deciduous shrubs to grow either in natural form or to train as a climber. They do well in any soil and any position, regularly produce a mass of flowers from mid spring to early summer and tend to produce further blooms intermittently all year round. After saucer-shaped flowers in shades of red, pink, orange or white, they all bear edible quince fruits.

To grow up the north-facing end of our garden shed, we selected the crimson-flowering variety, *Chaenomeles superba* Rowallane. Other varieties worthy of note are:

C. superba	
Knap Hill Scarlet	orange-scarlet
Pink Lady	rose-pink
Crimson and Gold	crimson with gold centres
Boule de Feu	orange-red
C. speciosa	
Moerloosii	pink and white in clusters
Nivalis	pure white
Umbilicata	deep salmon-pink
Rubra Grandiflora	extra large, crimson
Eximea	brick-red

Choisya (Mexican orange blossom)

Choisya ternata, the only species in this small genus of evergreens, is virtually essential for all gardens. As its common name implies, it comes from Mexico and has sweetly fragrant, white flowers of orange blossom: its foliage is also aromatic when crushed. Useful on most soils and in sun or shade, it flowers spasmodically throughout the year, but most profusely in summer. It forms a rounded bush of about 2m (6 ft) spread and can be grown against a wall.

Cotoneaster

A large genus of plants that can be evergreen or deciduous; low-growing creepers, bushes or trees. They survive well in varying soils and positions, and they all produce white or pink-tinged flowers in summer, attractive autumn leaf colours and brilliant fruits. The ground covering plants are excellent weed-smotherers. For our purpose we selected a prostrate-growing evergreen form, such as *C.salicifolius*, for the front of the south-facing mixed border. *C.s* Autumn Fire, has longish, willowy leaves and orange-red berries. Other good examples are:

Cotoneaster dammeri	scarlet berries
C.microphyllus	crimson berries
C. Skogholm	coral-red berries
C.conspicuus	bright red berries carried on arching branches

A popular deciduous form for low-growing or training up walls is *C.horizontalis*, the 'fish bone' cotoneaster (its branches grow herring-bone fashion), whose berries and leaves produce a riot of colour in autumn and look very effective.

Most of the taller-growing varieties are semi-evergreen; *C.lacteus* is one of the popular, though few, fully evergreen forms for hedging or screening, with its fruits lasting well after mid winter. Other good taller types are:

Cotoneaster bullatus	red cherry-like berries
C.divaricatus	superb scarlet in autumn
C.rotundifolius	upright, small-leaved, berries last until late spring
C.franchetii	sage green leaves, scarlet berries

Cytisus (broom)

Varying in size from low-growing plants to small trees, all cytisus have pea-shaped flowers (usually yellow) and most of them like a sandy, rather acid soil and plenty of sun. In general they flower in spring and summer but some produce blooms in early autumn thus providing a long season of colour and interest.

For the planting space in the paved area of our garden we selected *C.purgans*. This dense, almost leafless shrub with fragrant yellow flowers in spring will give colour and fragrance near the house in the early part of the year. It grows to about 1·2m (4 ft) high maximum, and 45cm (18 in) spread. Other pretty low-growing species are:

Cytisus purpureus	lilac-purple flowers in summer
C.×beanii	golden-yellow, early summer

Others of note are the hybrid forms with flowers of yellow, red, white or pink, and species such as:

Cytisus×praecox	very floriferous
C.battandieri	beautiful leaves, pineapple scent
C.nigricans	late summer and early autumn
C.grandiflorus	grey woolly seed pods

Opposite page, far left: Cotoneaster
conspicuus bears bright red berries in
autumn. Opposite page, left: glossy-
leaved evergreen Cotoneasta microphyllus
This page, left: dwarf Cytisus × beanii
Above: low-growing Cytisus purpureus,
known as purple broom
Below left: the common broom, Cytisus
scoparius Canary Bird
Below: the tall Cytisus battandieri has
unusual pineapple-scented flowers

Erica (heather and heath)

Provide colour in flower or leaf form all year round, and are easy to grow. We chose cultivars of *Erica carnea*.

Euonymus (spindle)

Mainly evergreen and deciduous shrubs, but *E. europaeus* and its forms make attractive small trees for gardens. Spindles are easily grown and especially useful where the soil is chalky. Special attractions lie in their autumn leaf tints, the colours of the berries on the deciduous forms and the fact that they tend not to grow too large.

In our Flower Garden we wanted a spindle bush that would harmonize with the buddleia behind it and the grey cineraria alongside, and also give colour throughout the year. For this we chose the pretty evergreen *E. fortunei* Silver Queen variegata. Most of the *E. fortunei* forms are very hardy, trailing or climbing evergreens with a variety of uses.

Euonymus fortunei Silver Queen variegata Compact with silver variegations to the leaves and attractive rose tints in winter.

E. japonicus Another hardy type; does well in town, country or by the sea. There are a number of variegated-leaved forms.

E. alatus Superb deciduous spindle with corky bark, feathery leaves in spring turning to rich red in autumn, and purple berries with orange seeds.

E. sachalinensis Handsome shrub that is also highly colourful in autumn.

Garrya

A fascinating and decorative, quick-growing evergreen that we have planted to be trained as a climber against the north wall of our garden (unless you plan to put up a lean-to greenhouse here). It is available in male and female forms; the latter are the more popular for their long-dangling, grey-green silky catkins produced during winter.

Garrya elliptica Most common species; does well in all soils provided they are not heavy and are well-drained. It does not need a sunny site.

Hamamelis (witch hazel)

Produce the most fascinating winter and early spring clusters of flowers that withstand the coldest weather; and they enchant with fragrance and curious strap-like bright yellow and red petals borne on leafless branches. As a genus they are shrubs or small trees, and we have put one against the house wall in the south-east corner, but it can be grown in almost any position. Being deciduous it is a useful plant as it produces hairy, hazel-like leaves during spring which turn golden yellow in autumn, thus giving the plant a second season of attraction. *H. mollis* is the best and most popular of all the witch hazels, other species, such as *H.* × *intermedia*, *H. japonica* and *H. vernalis*, are not so frequently found in catalogues:

Hamamelis mollis Pallida Dark yellow flowers.

Top: Hamamelis mollis *(witch hazel) flowers throughout winter and spring*
Above: Hydrangea paniculata *flowers through summer and early autumn*
Left: Euonymus alatus *deciduous spindle*

Hydrangea

Highly prized plants in many gardens for their prolonged display of flowers during summer and early autumn. All of them like a sunny position, but not where the soil dries out round their roots, so it pays to give them a deep, well-manured site and regularly mulch them every spring. They are all deciduous, but grow in a variety of forms from small to medium-sized bushes, 60cm–2·5m (2–8 ft) high, and some are genuine climbers, such as the one we have growing on the north-facing wall:

Hydrangea petiolaris Climber with flat heads of white flowers.

Hydrangea flower-heads are of three types: large and rounded (known as hortensias or mop-heads); large and flat or dome-shaped (known as lacecaps); and species (with heads of various shapes). These last are easy and reward-

Top: Hypericum calycinum *(St John's wort) in flower, a semi-evergreen plant*
Above and above right: Mahonia aquifolium—*its berries are good for jam*
Top right: Hypericum Elstead *in fruit*

ing shrubs to grow, and we have chosen *H. involucrata* for the south-facing wall:
Hydrangea involucrata Late-flowering dwarf bluish-purple and white blooms.
H. arborescens Grandiflora Greeny-white flowers that turn bronze-brown in winter.
H. villosa Pale blue flowers, grey-green leaves.
H. paniculata Grandiflora Creamy white to pink semi-arching branches of flowers.

As their name implies, lacecaps have flat, lacy flower-heads with pink or blue flowers and among the most popular are: Bluewave, Mariesii, Veitchii and White-wave.

The hortensias are the hydrangeas most frequently seen as pot-grown specimens in florists' shops, and there are a large number of cultivars, mainly with shades of pink or blue globular flowers. It is an interesting fact that on acid soil blue flowers will appear, whereas on chalky alkaline soil pink blooms will be produced. (This is thought to be due to the 'locking-up' of certain chemicals in different soils which affect the flower coloration.) These hardy hortensias grow to medium-sized shrubs and their dead flower-heads are much sought after for dried flower arrangements.

Hypericum (St John's wort)

Semi-evergreen shrubs. Some are low-growing, and have mat-forming and weed-suppressing growth; others have a delicate, and more branching habit, growing to about 1·2m (4 ft) high. They grow easily in any soil, sun or shade, and have attractive brilliant yellow flowers lasting from mid summer to late autumn. Some, too, have the added advantage of autumn leaf tints or coloured berries. One of the most popular is *H. calycinum* as a spreading plant that keeps weeds under control. It forms a dense mat and the leaves turn a purplish colour in autumn.

For our garden we have chosen a beauty: *Hypericum* Hidcote (*H. patulum* Hidcote). Forms a delightful bush with saucer-shaped golden flowers that blend well with surrounding catmint and iris. Other good species are:

Hypericum elatum	rose-red berries
H. androsaemum	red and black berries, autumn leaf tints
H. × *moseranum* Tricolor	pink, cream and green variegations

Lavandula (lavender)

Much favoured, mainly for their soft grey permanent foliage and delightful fragrance. We have planted a whole border of this in front of the shed trellis so that it makes an attractive spot throughout the year. Lavenders also have a long season, providing their flower spikes from summer to autumn, and they enjoy any well-drained soil and as much sun as possible. They are excellent by the sea and for making dwarf hedges. Forms of *Lavandula spica* are those most commonly grown and in our garden we have a mixture of:

Hidcote	deep purple-blue flowers
Nana Munstead Dwarf	lavender blue
Twickel Purple	purple
Loddon Pink	pinky-blue
Vera	soft blue

Mahonia

Often confused and listed with berberis, but the essential difference is that they have compound leaves (leaves with several lobes) and no prickly spines on the stems. They are all evergreen, grow about 60cm–1m (2–4 ft) high and produce flowers in winter or spring followed by berries which are usually blue-black. They grow in almost any soil, but prefer a well-drained one, and are happy in the shade. We chose *M. japonica* for our garden against the south-facing wall:
Mahonia japonica is similar to *M. bealei* but bearing clusters of two flowers during winter and early spring.

Two of the most popular species are:
M. bealei Scented like lily of the valley.
M. aquifolium Holly-leaved, of bronze colour in spring, purple-red in winter and berries that are excellent for making jam.

Olearia

Attractive and easy to grow when on chalky soil in sunny position, these evergreens (often called daisy bushes) have daisy-like flower-heads usually of a whitish colour, and grow between 1–2m (3–6½ ft) high. They flower from early summer to early autumn and are excellent by the seaside. Our choice is *O.* × *haastii*, one of the hardiest forms:

Olearia × haastii. Also good by the sea or in industrial areas. Has delightful fragrant flowers and is ideal in a mixed border.

For olearias with pink, lavender or blue flowers, choose forms of *O. stellulata* Splendens.

Pyracantha (firethorn)

True shrubs but frequently trained as climbers up walls and garden supports so that they are very often listed in the climbing plant section of catalogues. They are the most useful of hardy evergreen, berrying shrubs, growing freely in all positions and soils. They can reach a height of about 4·5m (15 ft), though only half this, particularly if the long shoots are kept cut back, is more customary. Firethorns bear masses of hawthorn-like white flowers in early summer, and clusters of berries in autumn that often last through to spring.

We selected a free-fruiting hybrid, *P. Watereri*, which has dense clusters of bright red berries, to grow against the south side of the garden shed. Other fine varieties are the free-branching:

Pyracantha rogersiana	red berries
P.rogersiana Flava	yellow berries
P.atlantioides Aurea	yellow berries
P. Orange Glow	orange-red berries

One of the most popular, *P. coccinea* Lalandei, has rather broader leaves and bears clusters of orange-red berries throughout autumn and winter.

Rhododendron

One of the largest and most varying groups of shrubs and, as mentioned on page 22, these include azaleas. They both need the same type of acid soil and general treatment. Most are evergreen, they can be prostrate, shrubby or tree-like in habit and usually flower from late spring to late summer. Broadly, they can be classified into hardy or pedigree hybrids and species. We wanted a rhododendron in our garden to go between the mahonia and syringa, but were restricted for space. We therefore selected the hardy hybrid Britannia with its glowing crimson flowers for good contrast and its semi-dwarf habit as it grows only to about 1·2m high and spreads to 1·2m (4 ft × 4 ft). Other hardy hybrids which grow to less then an average height of 3-4·5m (10-15 ft) are also available.

Above left: Viburnum betulifolium *with berries that last through into winter*
Far left: Lavandula *Nana Munstead, dwarf fragrant lavender, good for hedges*
Left: Viburnum davidii, *low-growing evergreen with bright berries contrasting well with rich-toned branches*
Below, far left: Olearia × scilloniensis, *profusely flowering, evergreen daisy bush*
Below: Viburnum tomentosum, *whose leaves turn plum-colour in autumn*
Above, and below right: pyracantha *(firethorn) in fruit and flower. This evergreen shrub trains well as a climber*

Skimmia

Small evergreen shrubs with aromatic, long, glossy leaves and fragrant flowers in late spring and early summer. If male and female plants are grown together (as these shrubs bear all male or female flowers on separate plants) then you can expect a profusion of coloured berries on the females in the autumn.

Skimmia japonica Most popular and hardy anywhere and in almost any soil. It is available in a variety of forms and the male Rubella (red buds in winter, white flowers in spring) grown alongside the female Foremanii (brilliant red berries in autumn) make an attractive combination.

Viburnum

Large genus of shrubs in evergreen or deciduous form. Most produce white, often sweetly scented, flowers followed by autumn leaf tints and/or coloured berries. They can be grown in almost any position. The plants grow about 1–3m (3–10 ft) high. As they vary so much in their season of attraction, the easiest way to describe them is to divide them into three groups: winter-flowering. spring/early-summer flowering, and autumn colour:

WINTER-FLOWERING

Viburnum tinus (Laurustinus) Highly sought after, has pink-budded white flowers from late autumn to early spring among evergreen dark glossy leaves, and blue-black berries from late summer.

Another good variety is *V. fragrans* with bronze-coloured young leaves, fragrant winter flowers and scarlet berries.

SPRING- AND EARLY SUMMER-FLOWERING

V. tomentosum Very popular with its large clusters of snow-white flowers and pendant green leaves that turn plum-colour in autumn.

V. × burkwoodii (evergreen) Large fragrant white flowers opening from pink buds and leaves that are dark shiny green above with brownish-grey 'felt' beneath.

AUTUMN COLOUR

V. betulifolium One of the best of all the berrying shrubs, producing berries in redcurrant-like form after small white flowers in spring.

V. opulus (guelder rose) White flowers in mid summer followed by autumn leaf colour and translucent berries.

V. davidii (low-growing evergreen) If male and female forms are planted together, the female produces exceptional turquoise-blue berries.

Vinca (periwinkle)

Most popular of low-growing glossy, evergreen shrubs for planting as weed-suppressors, in shady or sunny sites, on banks, or any difficult spot where nothing else wants to grow.

Vinca major These forms flower in early summer; *V. m.* Maculata has yellow-blotched leaves and *V. m.* Variegata creamy-white ones that set off the blue blooms to advantage.

V. minor Its forms are smaller versions of
V. major, flowering in late spring and
early summer and intermittently until
autumn, in various shades of blue or
white and some with variegated leaves.

CHOICE OF VINE CLIMBERS

Climbing plants are ideal for adding an
extra dimension to the back of mixed
flower borders or for growing naturally
up trellis or other supports, to give
additional height, or to act as a screen to
partition the garden into interesting
sections. Here we have chosen various
popular vine climbers for our garden in
addition to the shrubs that can be grown
as climbers, as already mentioned.

Clematis

Among the most versatile of climbers. As
long as the soil is well-drained and the site
sunny, but with a shady root area,
clematis rarely fail to give endless plea-
sure. They support themselves with
curling leaf stalks and except for pruning
need little attention.

Clematis are a large genus and for easy
distinction you can divide them into the
species and large-flowering groups. Of the
species we suggest the following:
Clematis tangutica Mass of yellow flowers
in mid summer, followed by silky old
man's beard berries (superior form of
those seen in hedgerows).
C. montana (white) and *C. m. rubens*
(rose-red) have scented flowers which

smother the plant in early summer.

If you want an evergreen clematis, two
good species are:
C. armandii White.
C. balearica Pale yellow with bronze
fern-shaped leaves.

Of the large-flowered group we suggest
the following:

Nelly Moser	pale mauve and carmine
Barbara Dibley	bright violet
Comtesse de Bouchaud	rose pink
Gravetye Beauty	cherry red
Lasurstern	lavender blue
Marie Boisselot	white
The President	purple-claret

Right: Clematis montana, *favoured for its
scent. Below:* C. patens Barbara Dibley
Bottom: Jasminum officinale, *common
white jasmine, a fragrant semi-evergreen*

Jasminum (jasmine)

Always popular, especially the winter-flowering one *J. nudiflorum*.

Jasminum nudiflorum Bears yellow trumpet-shaped flowers from early winter to late spring on naked green branches. During the remainder of the year it is clothed with small, shiny green leaves.

J. officinale Common white, summer-flowering jasmine that is sweetly scented and opens from pale pink buds; it has many-lobed leaves.

J. × stephanense Another summer-flowering hybrid that requires plenty of space to show off its sometimes variegated leaves and pale pink flowers followed by glossy black berries.

Lonicera (honeysuckle)

Love to ramble over pergolas, arches or old tree trunks and are best given their freedom rather than trained against walls or other supports. Most flower in summer, but some continue blooming until late autumn; they all grow in almost any soil and aspect but, like clematis, prefer to have their roots in the shade. With the exception of *L. japonica* and its forms (which are evergreen), the remainder are all deciduous, though *L.×purpusii* is winter-flowering.

Among the most popular are the early and late blooming Dutch honeysuckles:

Lonicera periclymenum Scented tube flowers of rose-purple and yellow.

L. tellmanniana Produces 5cm (2 in) long trumpet flowers but no perfume.

L. × americana Spectacular hybrid with large trusses of white to yellow, sweetly fragrant flowers.

Polygonum (Russian vine)

Sometimes known as mile-a-minute vine, this rampant climber grows rapidly in any position and will completely smother a wall or building in one year. The most commonly grown is:

Polygonum baldschuanicum Often confused with *aubertii*, its pale heart-shaped leaves and froth of creamy-pink flowers make a wonderful sight each year from late summer to late autumn.

Rosa (climbing rose)

Some suitable climbers for covering the trellis and pergolas are listed in our Roses section on page 63.

Left: Jasminum nudiflorum, *Chinese winter jasmine, even blooms well in hard winters*
Right: Lonicera sempervirens *(honeysuckle), is better as a rambler than trained climber*
Above right: Vinca major Elegantissima *(periwinkle) a good weed-suppressor*

Herbaceous plants

All annuals and biennials are strictly speaking herbaceous – all the word means is that the stems are of only annual duration and die down each autumn, so that in that sense even bulbs are herbaceous – but the term is usually used of herbaceous perennials. Perennials are plants that go on growing for many seasons, increasing in dimensions as they do so. They are normally planted either in the autumn or in the early spring, although there are one or two exceptions.

When to plant
Ideally autumn is the best time to plant, if you do so early enough. This enables the plants to root into the fresh soil before winter comes, so that they will be in a good condition to grow away as soon as the days lengthen and the air warms up. Plants that are transplanted in the spring have to start to grow away at once, so that if the spring is exceptionally cold or exceptionally dry their initial growth can be checked quite considerably. However there are one or two plants which seem to make very little growth after being transplanted in the autumn, with the result that they often die during the first winter and for these spring planting is obviously better. The most well-known of these is that large scabious, *Scabiosa caucasica*, one of the best herbaceous plants to grow for cutting.

When to transplant
There are a number of plants that really loathe any root disturbance, either because they have long tap roots, which may cause the death of the plant if they are damaged, or for less recognizable reasons. There seems no obvious reason why hellebores should dislike being moved, but they certainly do and may sulk for a year or so after they are transplanted. We find the same thing with paeonies, but this may be because they have such a vast amount of tubers underground that it is almost impossible to move a good-sized plant without seriously damaging the root system. Plants with long tap roots, such as lupins or oriental poppies, should only be moved as young plants and once planted should be left.

In any case it is always best to start off with small plants, whether they be seedlings or divisions from other plants.

Such plants usually arrive with their roots more or less undamaged and soon grow on to make vigorous specimens.

Caring for herbaceous plants

You can find herbaceous plants to fit any soil or situation, but the majority will be perfectly happy in a soil that is reasonably deep and not inclined to water-logging. Most like full sunlight, although it is possible to grow bog plants and shade-lovers where conditions allow.

After a time some herbaceous plants may become very large, in which case they should be lifted and divided up: Some plants get their roots so interlocked that it is by no means easy to divide them; the answer is to get two garden forks and insert them back to back in the clump and then lever them apart. The centre of the clump is probably impoverished, due to the fact that it will have exhausted the soil where it was originally planted; also the centre tends to get overgrown by the stronger outside parts which are in fresh soil; so when clumps are split up the centre is usually discarded and the plantlets on the outside are preserved.

There are many hundreds of herbaceous perennials to choose from, so for our Flower Garden we have selected a number of plants which are easy to grow and which will establish themselves in the border quickly.

Hellebore

Helleborus niger (the Christmas rose) is the earliest-flowering of our selection. It grows on the edge of woodlands in the wild, so a position giving dappled shade is ideal. Almost all the hellebores are somewhat greedy plants, so the soil cannot be too rich. The white flowers will emerge from the ground at any time from early winter to early spring (November–February) and the new leaves start to emerge at the same time. Later the leaves are going to be quite large, so a position among or just in front of shrubs should prove very suitable. Some Christmas roses have the unfortunate habit of producing only very short stems, so that the flowers easily become splashed with mud in bad weather. If you are ordering plants by mail there is not much you can do about this; but if you go to a nursery, pick out the long-stemmed plants.

Otherwise you might prefer to grow one of the hybrids of *H. orientalis* (the Lenten rose). These all have long-stemmed flowers, which usually do not open before early spring (February). There are a few whites among them, but most are some shade of pink or greenish-pink, while a few are a very deep maroon. They require the same treatment as the Christmas rose, but have very much larger leaves, which take up a lot of room later in the season. There are also a number of hellebores with green flowers.

Hellebores may be transplanted in the autumn (September), and the earlier the

better. The old leaves of the Lenten rose often persist while the flowers are opening, but the plants seem to come to no harm if you cut these off before the flowers open: the leaves begin to look rather tattered by that time. This is not a problem with the Christmas rose.

Alyssum
Our next plant is *Alyssum saxatile*, which flowers in late spring (April). Strictly speaking it is not herbaceous at all, but a small shrub, which carries its grey leaves throughout the winter and makes the border interesting during the dreary season. In the spring it covers itself with golden, sweet-smelling flowers. It likes full sun and has no objection to rather

poor soil. After about four years it gets somewhat leggy, but it is very easily propagated by cuttings or by seed.

Senecio cineraria
The grey-leaved cineraria (which you might otherwise know as *Cineraria maritima*) is a good example of the sort of

Above: double dianthus. Pink Diane
Top: Helleborus niger, *the Christmas rose*
Above left: delicate Scabiosa caucasica *is best planted in the spring*
Left: the leaves of Alyssum saxatile *give winter interest, the flowers appear in late spring. Right:* Hosta albo-marginata, *the plantain lily, thrives in shade*

plants that are grown for their foliage colour rather than for their flowers. Such plants are very valuable since they remain attractive for more than six months; this is more than can be said for most flowering plants, which seldom carry their flowers longer than three weeks and often considerably less. The grey (or, in the variety White Diamond, the silvery-white) leaves are very attractive, and they gain much of their appeal from their contrast with more usual green leaves. Don't try to overdo this effect, because unfortunately the cineraria bears rather crude yellow daisy-like flowers which are not very appealing.

Most grey or silver-leaved plants will not survive in soils that retain too much wet and our grey cineraria is also liable to perish during particularly severe winters. Fortunately cuttings root very easily, so it is always a good idea to root a few in late summer (July) and keep them in pots under cover during the winter, in case disaster strikes. In any case, the plants become rather gaunt after a few years and are best replaced.

Hosta

Another plant with unusual foliage but also with quite attractive lily-like flowers, is the plantain lily, a species of hosta (sometimes known as funkia). This vanishes completely during the winter and the new shoots can often be wrecked by slugs, so it is as well to mark their positions and put down bait in late spring (April) when young leaves are emerging.

The leaves vary in size and in colour and some are variegated with ivory, but they are all handsome plants, which get more effective as they get larger. There is really no need to split up their clumps at any time, as they can go on getting larger and larger without any ill effects. In summer (June–July) they send up spikes of lily-like flowers, usually about 5cm (2 in) long, trumpet-shaped and white or mauve in colour. These plants thrive in dense or partial shade.

Dianthus (pinks)

These plants also have pretty grey leaves, but they are grown mainly for the sake of their small, fragrant, carnation-like flowers. They prefer a limey soil and, if you have the sort of soil that will grow rhododendrons, you will probably have to add some lime before you plant your

Above: peach-leafed Campanula persicifolia Telham Beauty *is easy to grow*

dianthus. These again are evergreen and look interesting during the winter, but they very soon become gaunt and need frequent replacing. This is done by means of cuttings, usually known as pipings, which are ready in late summer or early autumn (July and August).

Dianthus are not particularly showy flowers, but their heady scent makes them worth all the trouble. They look attractive massed together or along the front of a border. The flowers are usually white, pink or crimson, and popular varieties are Mrs Simkins, Red Clove, and the newer Imperial Pink.

Campanula

Two species of these nice trouble-free plants are generally grown in borders. One is the peach-leafed *Campanula persicifolia*, which grows about 45cm (18 in) high and has flat blue or white flowers in mid summer (June). These are only slightly bell-shaped and reach about 5cm (2 in) across. The other is the tall *C. lactiflora*, which can grow to 1·2m (4 ft) and has a huge head of small mauve, rather spidery flowers in late summer

(July). Although the individual flowers are only about 2–3cm (1 in) across, they are borne in large numbers and a plant in full flower is a wonderful sight. There are shorter forms of *C. lactiflora* and also some pinky-purple ones.

Agapanthus (African lily)
An attractive plant flowering in late summer (July and August). The plants to obtain are called Headbourne hybrids and are all hardy, whereas the larger *A. africanus* generally requires wintering under cover. The Headbourne hybrids have quite small strap-shaped green leaves, but throw up stems to 75cm (2½ ft), bearing at their tops heads of blue

trumpet-shaped, lily-like flowers about 5cm (2 in) long. They like as warm a position as you can give them and full sunlight, but they are very tolerant about soil, so long as it is not waterlogged.

Chrysanthemum
For late autumn (October) we have chrysanthemums. The cut flower types, *C. maximum*, are not the most beautiful plants and are best raised each year from cuttings, but the Korean chrysanthemums are excellent for the border.

Top: pompon chrysanthemum London Gazette, give welcome autumn colour
Above: mixed lupins, including Harlequins, give a good massed colour effect

These bear daisy-like flowers in the greatest profusion, usually some shade of red in colour, and are completely trouble-free. The little pompon chrysanthemums add needed colour in autumn (early October) and are now available in various pastel shades which are preferable to the rather dull colours which they used to be.

The ordinary chrysanthemum can be grown as a border plant, if the flowers are not disbudded, but it is less attractive than either the Korean or the pompon types.

Japanese anemone (wind flower)
The Japanese anemone, in pinky-purple or in white, is a marvellous plant, being completely trouble-free and increasing with ease, and always flowering well in mid to late autumn (September–October). It does not really like being moved, so it is best left undisturbed as long as possible.

Pyrethrum
Botanically derived from *Chrysanthemum roseum*, these are invaluable for their single white, pink or carmine daisy-like flowers on long stems in early and mid summer (May–June). They like a sunny position and deep well-drained soil.

Above: pyrethrum chrysanthemum with daisy-like flowers in early and mid summer

Lupins
Excellent companions for the pyrethrums are *Lupinus* (lupins) which like the same conditions and produce their spires of pea-like flowers above decorative leaves about the same time. They are available in a wide range of colours of white, pink, yellow, red and lavender-blue, and are often bi-coloured. The Russell hybrids are a good strain but there are many varieties from which to choose. If you remove the old flower-heads as they fade, you will encourage a second season of blooming.

Oriental poppy
A third perennial to plant with the two foregoing is *Papaver orientalis* (the Oriental poppy), which also likes the sun and flowers at about the same time. It is available in pink, white, scarlet or

crimson flower shades. Incidentally, it likes water if there is a drought period immediately prior to its flowering season in early to mid summer (May–June).

Thyme

This, the first of our two dwarf plants, is the creeping *Thymus serphyllum*, which makes a mat of aromatic foliage covered with crimson or purple flowers in mid summer (late June). These are also fragrant. Thyme spreads rapidly and the plants should be at least 30cm (12 in) apart to avoid congestion.

Papaver orientale, the poppy with pronounced colour contrast in its markings

Sempervivum (houseleek)

Looking like a little cactus with rosettes of fleshy leaves, which are often attractively coloured, this dwarf plant has rather odd looking daisy-like pink flowers on 10cm (4 in) stems. The houseleek produces numerous offshoots each year, so do not place new plants too closely together. The cobweb houseleek has its leaves covered with cobwebby grey hair.

Nepeta (catmint)

A spreading plant, catmint has feathery masses of small, grey-green fragrant leaves, with lavender-coloured feathery flower spikes in summer and autumn (June–September).

These last three plants like rather gravelly soil and it is worthwhile incorporating some gravel if the soil is rather slow-draining.

Bulbs

It is at the far end of our Flower Garden that we have decided to make a special feature of bulbs. The word 'bulb' is, of course, used here rather loosely, as the term is intended to cover also corms and tubers.

The function of the bulb itself (or corm, or tuber) is to be a form of food storage, to help the plants survive not only the long cold winter, but also the hot dry summer that is common in the parts of the world where these plants grow wild. Most bulbs are found naturally in mountainous regions, where they are covered with snow for much of the winter. Directly the snow melts the leaves and flowers appear; and during this period, although they get plenty of water, the soil in which they grow drains quickly.

There are, of course, exceptions to this. The various members of the narcissus family often grow in alpine water meadows, and there are one or two bulbs that have no objection to quite marshy conditions, such as the spring and summer snowflake, *Leucojum vernum* and *L. aestivum* and the big summer-flowering Peruvian squill (*Scilla peruviana*).

Where to plant

Generally, however, it is safe to assume that bulbs do best where the soil is reasonably light and well-drained. In practice, they will thrive in most gardens. And since bulbs will have made most, if not all, of their growth by early summer (mid May), they will be perfectly happy under deciduous trees and shrubs, where they can get enough light for their growth before the leaves have developed too much. They should not be planted beneath evergreens, however, as they will not get enough light to produce food to store for the coming year.

How to plant

There are a lot of old gardeners' tales about the correct planting depth for bulbs: one of the favourites is that the top of the bulb should be the same distance from the surface as the length of the bulb. But in the wild, bulbs are almost always considerably deeper than this, and you can safely say that the tops of small bulbs should be at least 10cm (4 in) below the surface, while larger bulbs should be 15cm (6 in) below. If they are less deep there is always a risk that hoeing or some other operation will bring them to the surface. Small bulbs can be planted close together, say 5–8cm (2–3 in) apart, but the larger ones should have 15–20cm (6–8 in) between them.

Most spring bulbs should be put in the ground as soon after early autumn (August) as you can obtain them, and they will start making roots within a month. Narcissus, in fact, are scarcely ever without roots and must inevitably receive a slight check if they have been lifted and dried off, although it may be barely noticeable.

Tulips are an exception to this rule, and can be left until early winter (November) before planting.

Soil or sand?

If your soil is very damp and heavy there is probably some advantage in planting your bulbs on a layer of sharp sand, which drains fast and will prevent water from lodging immediately around the basal plate of the bulb, the part most susceptible to fungus rot. This makes con-

Above: the scented Iris reticulata
Harmony *has prominent gold markings*
Left: Galanthus miralis *(snowdrops), one of the earliest flowers of the year*
Below: crocus, easy-to-grow and free-flowering for several years
Right: Narcissus pseudonarcissus *(daffodil)* Penrose *and (above) narcissus* White Lion

siderably more work: it is fine if you are only planting 10 or 12 bulbs, but quite another matter if you are planting hundreds. Nevertheless, it is certainly worth doing with expensive bulbs.

It is of even greater importance to make sure that the base of the bulb is in contact with the soil (or the sand). With rather large bulbs it is only too easy to take out a trowel full of soil and put your bulb in so that it lodges halfway down the hole with its base suspended in air. When the roots emerge they are unable to find any nourishment, and they may well perish. There is enough nourishment stored in

the bulb to produce leaves and possibly even a flower, but the bulb cannot renew itself and will eventually die. Seeing that plants get off to a good start is one of the main secrets of success in gardening.

Dividing the clumps

If your bulbs are doing well they will, in the course of five or six years, form clumps. These will eventually get so crowded that flower production suffers. When this happens you must lift the clumps and divide them up. The best time to do this is in the early summer, when you see the leaves just starting to yellow. The bulbs should be good and plump by then and the new corms should have been formed. Some bulbs, most notably snowdrops, never seem to become overcrowded and there is no need to lift and divide them unless you wish to increase the area of these bulbs. To help you plan your 'calendar of bulbs' for the early spring we suggest a selection of winter aconite, snowdrops, iris, crocus, narcissus and tulips.

Winter aconite

The first to appear is usually the winter aconite *Eranthis hyemalis*. This has a tuber from which springs a little ruff of leaves, in the centre of which is a yellow flower not unlike a buttercup. The plant grows wild in woodland and does best in a shady position. If it is happy it spreads quite extensively and will also seed itself,

but it is not happy everywhere. It seems to like the sort of woodland soil that has plenty of leaf mould and if you have either a very sandy or a very clayey soil you may well find that it does not persist for more than two or three years. *E. × tubergenii* is a hybrid between the ordinary winter aconite and the larger species from western Asia, *E. cilicica*. It has larger flowers which, however, never set seed, and is somewhat more expensive.

Snowdrop

After the winter aconite come the snowdrops. There are many species of these, all looking rather similar and chiefly distinguished by the way their leaves emerge from the ground. The one most widely grown is *Galanthus nivalis*, that is available with either single or double flowers. We are always told that snowdrops should be moved when they are still in active growth. This is fine if you are moving them from one bed to another, or if you can get some from your friends, but firms only sell the dried-off bulbs and when you are buying new snowdrops you will have to make do with these. They seem to grow adequately, although the display the first spring after planting may not be quite as good as you would expect. However, do not lose heart, it will almost certainly be much more satisfactory the following year.

Among other species, *Galanthus elwesii* is supposed to be a much larger-flowered snowdrop, but the large flowers are seldom maintained for long in cultivation and after a few years you can only distinguish *G. elwesii* from the ordinary snowdrop by its broad glaucous leaves. If you can obtain *G. caucasicus*, particularly in its double form, you will find that it flowers earlier than *G. nivalis*, usually in late winter (January), and has the added advantage of increasing faster.

Iris

We come now to the dwarf bulbous iris, of which three are worth having. The most spectacular is *Iris histrioides* Major. This produces blue flowers up to 10cm (4 in) across, which usually open in late winter (mid January) and, although they look very exotic, are completely unmoved by the worst that the winter can unleash. They are often frozen and covered with snow without showing any ill effects. They are not, alas, cheap, but they persist and increase, although not very rapidly.

Then there is the charming little yellow *I. danfordiae*. In most gardens, after flowering, it splits up into several smaller bulbs which take a long time to flower again, so frequently they have to be

replaced each year. It is said that if the bulbs are planted very deeply, at least 23cm (9 in), they are less liable to split up.

The commonest of the early iris is *I. reticulata*, which flowers usually in early spring (February). It has rather narrow violet flowers (although purple or blue in some forms) with an exquisite violet scent. Provided they have well-drained soil all these bulbous iris are very easy to grow. An infection to be watched out for is the dreaded fungus disease known as ink-spot, which causes the bulbs to rot. There is no simple cure for this, if indeed there is any. It has been suggested that if the bulbs are lifted, dried off completely and then soaked for two hours in a very weak solution of formaldehyde (one part in 300), they can be protected, but this only applies to healthy bulbs, not to infected ones.

Crocus

Perhaps of all the spring bulbs the crocus is the favourite, and here we have an enormous choice. For many of us the first sign of spring is the Dutch yellow crocus. This is a sterile form of the eastern Mediterranean *Crocus aureus*, which has been known in gardens for nearly 300 years. Since it never sets seed it increases rapidly by producing extra corms, and soon makes large clumps. The true *C. aureus* flowers slightly earlier and has rather richer coloured flowers, as well as increasing by seed.

However, if you want a crocus that increases by seed the best is *C. tomasinianus*, a very slender plant with grassy leaves and a thin flower, which is nearly invisible until the sun opens the lavender

Three types of tulip: (above) the Darwin hybrid variety Apeldoorn, up to 75cm (2½ ft) tall, is good for display; (below) Tulipa kaufmanniana, the 'water-lily' tulip, an early species; (below right) Blue Parrot, easily recognized by its characteristic fringed petals

petals. There are also some darker purple varieties, such as Taplow Ruby, Barr's Purple and Whitewell Purple. *C. tomasinianus* increases at a prodigious rate, both from extra corms and from self-sown seedlings, which may flower the second year after germinating. Very similar, but with a larger flower, is *C. dalmaticus*.

C. chrysanthus has a large number of forms, all characterized by bunches of rather globular flowers, mainly in varying shades of yellow, but including some very good blues, which unfortunately are usually very slow to increase, while the yellow and cream forms are vigorous.

The Cloth of Gold crocus, *C. susianus*, is prodigal with its rather small yellow flowers which have dark brown stripes on their outside. A very attractive crocus is *C. etruscus*, that is usually only obtainable in the form known as Zwanenburg and that flowers in early spring (late February). The flowers are quite large and a very fine shade of lavender-mauve. Another very popular crocus is the deep mauve *C. sieberi*. Finally there are the huge Dutch hybrids, that flower in mid spring (March) but some people find rather gross. Best of these is the showy silver-lavender Vanguard.

Narcissus

Daffodils (with a trumpet centre) and narcissus (with flatter, cup centre) all belong to the genus *Narcissus* and they all like ample water when they are growing. They are exquisite in flower, but they have very long leaves, which persist until mid summer (June) and tend to look unsightly. They are probably best placed between shrubs, where their leaves will not be so noticeable. Whatever you do, do not cut the leaves off or plait them into dainty bundles, as that will wreck your chances of good flowers in the next season. You must just make up your mind that when you grow narcissus, you must put up with these disadvantages.

Tulip

Most tulips come rather late, but the water-lily tulip, *Tulipa kaufmanniana*, is usually in flower by mid to late spring (March–April) thus linking early and late spring displays. Many tulips tend to deteriorate after a year or so, but *kaufmanniana* is fairly reliable, although rather slow to increase. The wild plant has a flower that is long and pointed, cream outside, with a broad crimson stripe down each petal, and ivory inside. The flower opens nearly flat in sunlight. It has now been hybridized, producing blooms in deep yellow, pinks and even scarlets.

Above: Narcissus *Actaea makes an attractive show when massed*
Below: Eranthis hyemalis, *which prefers a fairly moist soil*

Hardy annuals

Annuals – hardy, half-hardy or tender – are old favourites that have a place in every garden. On these two pages we tell you how to sow hardy annuals and help you make your choice, but meanwhile there are certain things to be done in the garden at this time – mid spring.

First clear the mixed flower border of dead leaves and weeds. Then give a dressing of a general purpose fertilizer such as Growmore, at the rate recommended by the manufacturers, that will help new spring shoot and root growth. Hoe this in lightly, taking care not to disturb the roots near the plants. A layer of mulching material – peat, bark fibre, compost, hop manure and suchlike – will help to improve soil conditions, retain moisture during drought periods and suppress weeds; if any of the latter do appear, they are easy to pull out of the mulch layer.

Plant gladiolus corms now in warm parts of the border, where they will get sun and be protected by other plants. With a hand towel, dig out a hole 10cm (4 in) deep (or a little deeper if there is still danger of frost), put in a small handful of silver or coarser garden sand and then place the corm, root disc downwards, on the sand and replace the soil. For most effective results, plant the corms in clusters of 5–10, each about 12cm (5 in) apart. Mark each batch with a label or stake so you remember where they are.

While planting the gladiolus, take the opportunity to fork over the soil (to a depth of the tines) where chrysanthemums and dahlias are to be planted next month. Mixing in some bonemeal (at the manufacturer's recommended rate) will help the plants make a good start in life.

Creating an annual border

When making a new garden it is virtually impossible to produce a finished result in one year, unless you are going to spend a small fortune on buying container-grown plants of a fairly large size.

It is generally best to plan first for your major trees, shrubs and perennial plants and to get them into position. For the first year or two, while these are growing to their more mature size, fill up the gaps between with annual plants which will give welcome splashes of colour during the summer months. It

may even be that in your first year of a new garden you will not be able, for various reasons of timing, design and final selection decisions, to do much permanent planting. In such cases the borders can consist entirely of annuals for the first summer. Once established, these borders can be given more colour and variety the following year.

However, as there is going to be plenty of ground work to be done in the first year of preparation, it is not very practical to add to your chores by raising half-hardy and tender annuals yourself, as these need to be grown under heated glass (greenhouse, frame or propagation unit). Buy some packets of hardy annual seeds instead, and sow these from mid spring to early summer (March to May) directly into the borders where you wish them to flower. In addition, you can always purchase, quite cheaply, boxes of young half-hardy annuals for planting out in early summer when all danger of frost is over.

It is best to select from some of the more popular hardy annuals likely to be found in most seed catalogues, shops or garden centres. Choose ones that will give you a variety of heights and colours.

Above: Sweet pea Lathyrus odoratus
Below: Linum grandiflorum

Above: Mentzelia lindleyi

Sowing hardy annuals

When the soil is not too wet and sticky it should be dug over lightly with a fork, and weeds removed, then trodden down to firm it. To do this, simply walk up and down with your footsteps close together. Then rake it lightly backwards and forwards so that the surface soil is as crumbly and flat as possible. If the soil is not in very good condition (lumpy and hard, for instance) add a 13mm ($\frac{1}{2}$ in) layer of moist peat and a handful of a general fertilizer, such as Growmore, per square metre (or square yard) while raking.

The seeds are best sown in fairly bold patches, with the taller-growing annuals towards the back of the borders and the lowest along the front edges. An easy way to plan a layout is to get a stick and draw the outline of the clumps on the soil. Then scatter the seeds as thinly as possible over the soil in the designated areas. Very fine seeds will require a sprinkling of fine soil over them (some topsoil through a sieve is easiest) but the larger seeds can be covered by careful raking. The biggest seeds of all, like sweet peas and nasturtiums, can be sown separately by pushing each one down about 2–3cm (1 in) into the soil – each seed approximately 15cm (6 in) apart.

The seeds should germinate and start poking their noses through the earth any time in the next four weeks. When the seedlings are large enough to take hold of, thin them out by pulling some out completely – roots as well – so that those left behind are about 10–30cm (4–12 in) apart, according to the instructions on the packet and their ultimate height. After that, except for removing weeds, watering with a sprinkler in very dry weather and dealing with pests, there should be nothing to stop a fine display of colour through the summer. (Incidentally, removing the dead flowerheads promptly will help to encourage the plants to keep on producing more and more blooms.)

If you want to add *half-hardy* annuals, such as althaea (hollyhocks), antirrhinums, petunias, verbena, nicotiana (tobacco plants), nemesia, zinnias, tagetes (African and French marigolds), these should be planted out in early summer.

Down with slugs

These pests are the main enemy of your flower border. They must be destroyed or they will, in turn, destroy the plants. The small, grey slug loves to munch his way through the leaves, especially if the weather is warm. Operating mostly at night, slugs leave a tell-tale trail of white, mucous film behind them. This is the sign of all types of slugs, and snails too. Put down proprietary slug pellets; remember to carry out this eliminating operation regularly.

Beware birds – and cats!

Both birds and cats love newly seed-sown areas of the garden and to prevent them wreaking havoc among your annuals anchor down some nylon netting over the beds, and place a lot of twiggy sticks and branches, or gorse, over the areas. Remove these protective barriers when you thin out the seedlings. Alternatively, treat these areas with a proprietary animal repellent that will help to deter both birds and rodents.

Laying the stepping stones

York stone slabs were selected for the stepping stones here. Once the positions of the flower beds, trellis and pergolas have been marked out it is easy to estimate the number of slabs required. Laying them is also a simple matter and it is advisable to position them before making the lawn. See pages 14–15 for instructions how to turf the lawn area.

Stepping stones should be level and the best way to achieve this is to remove approximately 5cm (2 in) of soil, put down a layer of coarse sand to replace it and lay the paving slab in position. Then, using a spirit level, ensure it is level by raising or lowering it by adding or removing sand. It is particularly important to ensure the slabs by the shed door are all level, not only with the ground but also with each other, so there are no jutting-up edges to trip over. When the lawn turfs are laid, these should come slightly above the level of the slabs, thus making it easy to cut the grass with a lawn-mower. If the slabs are above the turfs, then it will involve the onerous task of cutting grass round the paved areas with hand shears. The turfs will be about 3·5cm (1$\frac{1}{2}$ in) thick and you can always adjust the paving slabs later so that they are at the correct height to the grass.

See pages 14–15 for instructions how to turf the lawn area.

POPULAR HARDY ANNUALS

alyssum (madwort)
amaranthus (love-lies-bleeding)
Anchusa Blue Bird
bartonia/*Mentzelia lindleyi*
calendula (pot marigold)
centaurea (cornflower)
chrysanthemum (annual varieties)
clarkia
delphinium, annual (larkspur)
dianthus (annual pinks)
eschscholtzia (Californian poppy)
godetia   gypsophila
helianthus (sunflower)
iberis (candytuft)
lathyrus (sweet pea)
lavatera (mallow)
linum (flax)
lupinus (annual lupin)
lychnis (silene)
malcolmia (Virginian stock)
nemophila (Californian bluebell)
nigella (love-in-a-mist)
Papaver rhoeas (shirley poppy)
Phacelia campanularia
reseda (mignonette)
Salvia horminum
tropaeolum (nasturtium)

Popular hardy annuals: (top) annual chrysanthemums and tropaeolum

Half-hardy annuals

Half-hardy annuals can be very useful in the garden, especially for summer bedding and filling up gaps in the border. The only conceivable objection to them is that they need some heat when the seeds are germinating, so that if you have no greenhouse, you will have to raise them in the home, or sow them outside rather late in the season, or buy plants in.

Why 'half-hardy'?

The reason we call a plant half-hardy is that it is liable to be damaged by frost. This means that in most parts of the United Kingdom, for instance, it will not be safe to put the plant out in the garden before the last week in early summer (May) or the beginning of mid summer (June). As the plant is also an annual it is in a great hurry to flower and set seed. Since, once its seeds are ripe, it is going to die in any case, it is not much concerned with making a large root system; the important thing is for it to flower and set seed before the winter comes.

Buying plants

What this means in practical terms is that once an annual starts to flower it has, almost certainly, ceased making growth, so do not choose any plants that show either buds or flowers. It is possible to encourage further growth by taking off all the visible flowers and buds, but they will never make really satisfactory plants.

Half-hardy annuals are liable to come into flower quickly if their root space is at all constricted, so you will be wise to avoid boxes of seedlings with a crowded mass of plants growing closely together. Look for a box where the plants are at least 5cm (2 in) apart in each direction. This gives the roots room to expand and so will stop the plant coming into flower prematurely. The point is that although annuals can come into flower with very few roots, if they are given the opportunity to make a sizeable root system they

Top: Cleome spinosa *need a warm spot*
Above, left: callistephus Milady Blue, a single species of half-hardy annual that likes a loamy soil; decorative as pot plants

Above, right: dimorphotheca, or African daisy, whose flowers do not open in the shade

will make larger plants and produce more flowers, and so continue flowering over a longer period. Thus, ideally, you want to purchase plants that are well-spaced in their boxes and not showing any signs of flowering.

The best time to buy
The next question is when to buy them. As you will probably not want to plant them out before mid summer (end of May), take no notice of anyone offering you plants in late spring (April). (This, of course, only applies to half-hardy annuals, since hardy annuals can be purchased at any time if you are unable to grow them from seed.)

The plants will probably have come out of the nurseryman's greenhouse and will be what some gardeners call 'lishy'. The leaves are very soft and practically irresistible to slugs and insect pests, and you will need to harden them off before you plant them out. This usually takes 10–14 days, so around the middle of early summer (mid May) is an excellent time to purchase the seedlings of half-hardy annuals. All you have to do is stand the boxes outside, preferably propped up on some support to keep the slugs away, water the soil if it gets at all dry (but not otherwise), and put the plants wherever you want them after 14 days.

Of course, if there is a risk of frost during this fortnight, you will have to bring the boxes indoors overnight. Anywhere in the house will be frost-free at that time of year, so it does not matter where you put the boxes, which can go out again during the daytime. If you have a frame you can, of course, harden your plants off in that, opening the lights at all times, except when frost is expected.

Raising from seed indoors
With the exception of *Begonia semperflorens*, most half-hardy annuals require very little heat to germinate. About 15°C (60°F) is quite adequate so, if you lack a greenhouse, you can probably germinate them on a windowsill indoors. In this case sow the seed in mid spring (towards the end of March) in a seed compost. When the seedlings have produced about two pairs of leaves, prick them out 5cm (2 in) apart in trays in a growing compost, either J.I. No 1 or a soilless mix, and put them in a slightly cooler place after ten days.

Then harden them off as already described. There is not much point in starting the seeds too early, as either the weather is too cold or the plants get too advanced by planting out time. The same routine applies if you have a greenhouse.

Sowing 'in situ'
One other possibility is to sow the seeds in position outside in early to mid summer (the end of May), for flowering in late summer and early autumn (July and August). This will not be possible with plants that flower in early and mid summer (May and June), as they will not have enough time to make their growth.

Care after planting out

Once they have been planted out – with tall plants about 30cm (12 in) apart and the shorter ones 15–25cm (6–9 in) apart – there is not much that needs doing. You should bear in mind that the annual's main object in life is to set seed, so if you can find the time to nip off all flower-heads as soon as they have finished flowering, you will encourage the plant to produce more flowers and so prolong the season. If, at the same time, you give a very light dressing of a balanced fertilizer or a foliar feed you will aid this process, although probably not very significantly.

Some plants to choose

The first four plants in the following list are all known as 'everlastings', that is, they can be dried and used for flower arrangements throughout the year.

Acrolinium, Helichrysum, Lonas and **Xeranthemum** have mixed colour, single or double, daisy-like flowers and grow up to 60cm (24 in). They can all be started early or sown direct out of doors, and flower from late summer to late autumn (July to October).

Ageratum These are usually low-spreading plants rarely more than 15cm (6 in) tall, although there are some taller ones. They bear heads of small bluey-mauve powder puffs over a long period, if regularly dead-headed. Seed sown outside in early to mid summer (the end of May onwards) produces good, autumn-flowering (August to October) plants.

Alonsoa A rather unusual plant about 30cm (12 in) tall with masses of small bright red flowers. Sow outside early to mid summer (late May) for late summer to late autumn (July to October) flowering.

Antirrhinum The popular snapdragon is not strictly half-hardy at all, but the plants need quite a long growing season, so seedlings must be raised early. There is little point, therefore, in sowing in early to mid summer (late May), but you can sow outside in early autumn (August) and let the plants overwinter *in situ*. In fact you can treat antirrhinum as a biennial.

Begonia semperflorens A marvellous little plant about 20cm (8 in) tall, sometimes with purple leaves and an endless succession of red, pink or white flowers from mid summer (the end of June) onwards. There is no objection to buying flowering plants as it is really perennial and can be kept through the winter in heat. Nor is it necessary to remove the faded flowers. It will also, rather unusually, grow in semi-shade, whereas most annuals require full sun. A temperature of at least 22°C (70°F) will be needed to germinate the dust-like

seeds, so most gardeners will have to buy plants at the appropriate time.

Callistephus (Chinese aster) This decorative plant is highly popular. The flower-heads, usually in various shades of pink and blue, yellow or white, come in a number of shapes – daisy-like blooms, doubles, quills, pompons or chrysanthemum shape – and are always interesting. It will grow to a height of approximately 15–60cm (6–24 in), and can be sown outdoors in early summer (May). Its flowering season lasts from late summer (May) onwards.

Celosia (cockscomb or Prince of Wales feathers) This plant possesses rather odd, feathery heads that are coloured crimson or yellow. It can grow up to 90cm (3 ft) tall, and it will flower from late summer (July) onwards.

Cleome (spider flower) This grows as a tall bushy plant with pink and white flowers. It can reach a height of 1·2m (4 ft), although usually it will grow to less than this. It produces flowers from late summer (July) onwards.

Cosmea (cosmos) This has fern-like leaves and dahlia-like flowers that come usually in some shades of pink or red. It will grow up to 75cm ($2\frac{1}{2}$ ft) in height, and its

Far left, above: Cosmos Sunset loves sun
Far left, below: helichrysum, in mixed colours, can be dried for winter display
Above left: celosia Belden Plume, a fiery tropical plant, thrives in warm conditions
Left: ageratum North Sea, its clusters of neat flower-heads last for a long time
Above: Mesembryanthemum criniflorum, or Livingstone daisy, does well near the sea

49

flowering season occurs in the autumn (August and September).

Dimorphotheca (star of the veldt) Probably best left until early summer (May) and sown where you want it to flower. It grows about 30cm (12 in) tall and has masses of bright orange, yellow or white daisies which appear right through summer and into autumn.

Felicia bergeriana (kingfisher daisy) Is again best left until near mid summer (late May) and sown *in situ*. It only reaches a height of 10cm (4 in) and has daisies of a brilliant kingfisher blue from mid summer to mid autumn (June to September).

Gaillardia The annual variety. Has large daisies in various shades of yellow and orange with almost black cones in the centre. Grows about 60cm (24 in) tall, and flowers from mid summer to late autumn (June to October).

Lobelia Has such tiny seeds that it is almost essential to start them in pots, although you will get nice plants from seed sown in early summer (May). Mainly blue flowers but some red or white, from late summer (July) onwards. The plants grow about 10cm (4 in) tall.

Mesembryanthemum (Livingstone daisy) Has fleshy leaves and daisy-like flowers in a bewildering assortment of colours. Grows only about 10cm (4 in) high, but spreads widely and flowers from late summer (July) until the frosts come. It also likes dry conditions. Seed sown outside in early to mid summer (late May) starts to flower rather later, but is quite satisfactory.

Nemesia Showy South African plants growing about 25cm (10 in) tall with clusters of flowers in varying shades of red, orange, yellow, and even blue. The flowering season is rather short, so late-sown seeds will provide you with a second display.

Nicotiana The popular tobacco plant, usually 45–90cm ($1\frac{1}{2}$–3 ft) tall has white or red night-scented flowers from late summer to mid autumn (July to September).

Perilla This is grown not for flowers, but for its dark purple, almost black, indented leaves. Grows to about 60cm (24 in).

Petunia Possibly the most reliable half-hardy annual for continuous display. It does require starting fairly early in the year, but is usually trouble-free, flowering through summer and autumn until the

first frosts. The flowers come in a wide range of single or bicolours and may be simple and bell-like or a mass of petals (multifloras). It grows to a height of 10–25cm (4–10 in).

Annual phlox A very attractive annual with heads of flowers from deep crimson to white and yellow. Can well be sown outside at the end of May. Grows to 15–20cm (6–8 in) and flowers from late summer (July) through the autumn.

Portulaca Rather rarely seen nowadays as

it can be unsatisfactory in wet summers, but gorgeous in a dry, warm one. Grows to 15cm (6 in) with large single or double red and yellow flowers from mid summer to mid autumn (June to September).

Ricinus (castor oil plant) Grown for its ornamental bronze, dark purple or green leaves and stately habit, it reaches 1·2m (4 ft). You will probably have to grow this yourself, as nurserymen rarely offer it in plant form.

Salpiglossis The plants are unpleasantly

Above right: Salpiglossis sinuata *blooms in profusion and has beautiful veined markings. It originally came from Chile*
Above, far right: Lobelia erinus, *a dwarf spreading plant, flowers from early summer*
Right: Phlox drummondii *should be planted out in a moist, sunny border*

sticky to touch but the flowers, which are trumpet-shaped and about 8cm (3 in) long in many rich colours, are amongst the most spectacular of all annuals. The plants grow to 60cm (24 in) and flower from late summer to mid autumn (July to September).

Salvia The bedding salvia, well known for its scarlet flowers, though there are now forms with the spiky flower-heads in purple or pastel shades. Grows between 23–30cm (9–12 in), flowering in late summer and early autumn (July and August).

Statice About 30–45cm (12–18 in) tall with large heads of everlasting flowers in a wide selection of colours. Can be sown outside, and flowers in late summer (July).

Tagetes French and African marigolds. The French makes perfectly good plants from seeds sown in mid summer (June), but the African, which is taller, needs a rather longer season, although it flowers from mid summer seeding in a good year. Usually yellow and orange flowers from late summer (July) onwards; the bushy plants grow to about 15cm (6 in).

Ursinia Another orange South African daisy, best sown outside in a sunny position. Grows to 23cm (9 in) and flowers from mid summer to early autumn (June to August).

Venidium (monarch of the veldt) Large daisy in pastel shades, with a dark blotch in the centre. Height-wise, it will grow up to 75cm (2½ ft), and its flowering season lasts from mid summer to late autumn (June to October).

Verbena (vervain) Still a valuable bedding plant with heads of bright flowers in pink, crimson, scarlet or violet from mid summer (June) until the first frosts. Height about 30cm (12 in).

Zinnia One of the showiest annuals for late flowering either in tall forms up to 60cm (24 in) or in dwarf forms not taller than 30cm (12 in). The flowers are multi-petalled in shades of orange, yellow, red or white. They should not be planted out before mid summer (mid June), long after most other half-hardy plants, and even so may prove unsatisfactory should the summer be either cold or wet.

Above, far left: Nemesia strumosa Suttonii, *whose cut flowers last well in water*
Above left: clarkia, used mainly as border decoration, or can be grown for cutting
Left: Zinnia elegans Envy, *a showy plant*
Above: statice, with its plume-shaped panicles, dry well as everlasting flowers

Biennials

True biennials are plants that grow one year, overwinter, then flower, seed and die in the following year. Among them are many of the popular garden plants such as Canterbury bell, honesty and foxglove, also a number of plants usually grown as biennials which are really perennials, such as wallflower, pansy and sweet William.

Some have such large seeds that it is possible to sow them in their flowering positions, but others will need to be sown in a part of the garden reserved for raising seedlings, such as in our seedbed in the north-west corner. They can be thinned out subsequently into rows where they can remain until it is time to plant them in their flowering positions in mid autumn (September). With very fine seeds, like those of foxglove, it is probably better to sow in a flowerpot left outside; once they have germinated they can be transplanted 15cm (6 in) apart into rows in the seedbed and then planted into their flowering positions in the autumn.

When to sow
The time for sowing depends to a large extent on when the plant will flower the following year. Plants that flower fairly early in the spring, such as wallflower, honesty and pansy, have to make all their growth before the winter so the longer they are given the better it will be. Later-flowering plants, such as hollyhock, stock, sweet William or Canterbury bell, will make some further growth after the winter before they start producing flowers so they can be sown somewhat later.

Annuals treated as biennials

There are also some hardy annuals that will produce much larger plants if they are treated as biennials and sown in the autumn (September). The plants that like this treatment include godetia, calendula, candytuft, echium (viper's bugloss), sweet pea, cornflower, larkspur, Shirley poppy, eschscholtzia and annual clary sage. Just sow the seeds in rows in drills and leave the young plants until the following spring, when you can transplant them to wherever you want them to flower.

Preparing to sow

Before considering sowing times, you should first think of preparing the ground. The most important things for a young seedling are plenty of light, so that it can manufacture energy, and a fairly light soil so that the roots can penetrate quickly and anchor the plant.

The light will normally be there, unless you sow in the shade of evergreens, but you will have to prepare the soil. It will need loosening up, even if it is a light, sandy one. A very stiff soil is hard for the

Far left: Echium plantagineum *Blue Bedder (Viper's bugloss); left:* Cheiranthus cheiri *(wallflower) with profuse showy blooms Below left: richly-coloured giant pansies Below and below right:* Lunaria annua *(honesty) flowering, and seeding in autumn to leave flat silver pods that can be used to make excellent winter decoration*

roots to get into so, if your soil is heavy, dig it, break it up and incorporate some sand or peat into this broken-up soil. If the soil is dry, give it a thorough soaking with water before you start your sowing. If the soil has been well soaked the young roots will soon get down to the moisture, even though it may be dry on top.

How to sow

Having got your soil prepared, make a small drill, not more than 2–3cm (1 in) deep and sow your seeds as thinly as possible. Rake some soil over them and sit back and wait.

After sowing, biennial seeds usually germinate rapidly enough and you should not have to wait more than a fortnight before you see the seedlings appear; usually you will get results even sooner.

With the large-seeded plants, which you can put where they are expected to flower, it is wise perhaps to put two seeds in every place and pull out the weaker of the two if both germinate. The distance between the plants when you line (plant) them out will vary according to type and the recommended distances are given below under each plant individually.

Thinning and transplanting

Apart from those seeds sown *in situ,* you now have two choices. If you do not want many plants, you can just thin the seedlings out and leave them where they are. Alternatively, you can transplant

them as soon as they are large enough to handle and leave them in rows until about the middle of autumn (mid September) when you lift them and put them where you want them to flower.

Be sure that the young plants do not dry out when you line them out. The simplest way is to puddle them. You dig a hole to the required depth with a trowel – the required depth will be such that the roots can be as deep in the soil as they were before you moved them. Then pop in the plants, fill the hole with water and then push the soil back around the roots. This enables your small biennials to get away without much check, and you want to keep them growing with as few checks as possible.

The plants should be in their final positions by mid autumn (mid September), to give them a chance to make a little growth and anchor themselves in the fresh soil before the onset of winter. However, this may not always be possible. You may, for example, want to put wallflowers where you now have dahlias. These will not be lifted before late autumn (the end of October), so it may well be early winter (November) before you put in your wallflowers.

The result will be that you won't get quite such a good display in the spring as you would have done if you could have moved the plants earlier, but, failing an absolutely appalling winter, you should still get quite good results.

Some plants to choose

Here we list some good biennials, in order of flowering.

Pansy Sow in late summer (July) and prick out 15cm (6 in) apart. They start to flower in late spring (April) and can go on until late summer (late July). The blooms come in a variety of rich shades, either single or bi-coloured.

Wallflower Sow either in mid or late summer (June or July). Line out 15cm (6 in) apart. In flower from late spring (late March) to mid summer (June) in reds, oranges and yellow colours.

Honesty Should be sown in mid or late summer (June or July), preferably where the plants are to flower. If you do prick them out they should be 25cm (9 in) apart. The purple or white flowers appear in early to late summer (May to July). The flat and round silver seed pods which follow are very sought after for winter flower decorations.

Sweet William Sow in late summer (early July) and prick out to 25cm (9 in) apart. They flower mid to late summer (June to July) in mixtures of red, white, pink or salmon colours.

Stock It is the Brompton and East Lothian strains that are biennial; the ten-week and the night-scented are annuals. Sow in late summer (early July), and prick out 30cm (12 in) apart. It is possible to leave them in the rows until the following spring, in which case they must be put

Far left: the familiar digitalis (foxglove)
Far left, below and bottom: two Papaver
nudicale *(Iceland poppies), suitable for
rock gardens as well as mixed borders*
Below left: Verbascum bombyciferum
(mullein)
Below: matthiola (Brompton stocks)
Left: Althaea rosea *(hollyhock)*
Above: Campanula media *(Canterbury
bell) a sturdy native of southern Europe*

in their final positions in mid spring (March). Flowers are shades of pink, red, lilac, yellow or white, with the Bromptons appearing in early summer (May) and the East Lothians during summer and early autumn (July and August).

Foxglove These digitalis seeds are so minute that they are best started in a pot. Prick out the seedlings to 30cm (12 in) apart and, again, they can be left in the rows until late spring (early April) if it is more convenient. The flower spikes of white, pink, purple and yellow appear in mid summer (June).

Canterbury bell Sow in summer (May or June). The seeds are very small, so it may be easier to start them in a pot. Prick out the seedlings at least 30cm (12 in) apart and once more you can wait to plant them in their final positions until the following late spring (April). They flower in summer (June and July) in white, pink, blue or mauve shades.

Iceland poppy This needs rather different treatment. All poppies (or papavers) dislike transplanting so you can either sow them where they are to grow, or start them in a pot, prick out or transplant about 5cm (2 in) apart into trays and then put them in their final positions the following spring (April). The trouble with sowing them *in situ* is that the seeds are very tiny, so it is not easy to differentiate between the young seedlings and weeds when thinning them out. Some people treat these poppies like any other biennials with complete success, but it can be a bit tricky. Sow in mid to late summer (late June or early July). They flower from mid summer (June) until the frosts come, in various shades of pink, orange, red or yellow.

Mullein The one you find catalogued most often is either called *Verbascum* Broussa or *V. bombyciferum*. It makes an enormous silver rosette of leaves the first year and the following year sends up a great golden spire 1·2m (4 ft) high. Sow in mid to late summer (June to July) and prick out 30–45cm (12–18 in) apart. These again can be left until the spring before being put in their final positions. They flower from mid summer to early autumn (June to August). There are other mulleins which are perennials, but they all want the same treatment.

Hollyhock These have such large seeds that you can put them where you want them to flower. Sow in mid to late summer (June or July) and, if you are pricking out, put the plants 30cm (12 in) apart. They flower in shades of pink, white, red, yellow or purple from late summer to mid autumn (July until September).

Roses:
Hybrid teas and floribundas

Anyone interested in roses will want to be able to recognize the various forms and to be aware of their advantages and disadvantages. Here we tell you about the famous hybrid tea and floribunda roses and on the following pages the climbers and ramblers.

Hybrid teas (HT) are the most popular roses in Britain because of the size, scent and beauty of their flowers.

It is often said that modern roses lack scent. This is true of floribundas, to a large extent, but they make up for this with their extra vigorous character and profuse flowering.

Provided proper care is taken, both can be grown successfully anywhere.

HYBRID TEAS

The first hybrid tea rose, raised in 1867, was the silvery-pink La France. This was the result of crossing the older hybrid perpetual roses with tea roses from the Far East, thus combining the greater refinement of shape and more recurrent blooming habit of the latter with the robust constitution of the hybrid perpetual. Few tea roses could survive the climate of the British Isles except under glass. Their name, rather a strange one, supposedly comes from the fact that they smelled like the newly-opened tea cases that arrived from the East.

Their colour range is probably only exceeded by that of the iris, for there are no blues among the roses, nor is it likely there ever will be, for they lack the necessary pigment – delphinidin. The lilac-mauve of the HT Blue Moon is the nearest approach there is. Unlike the floribundas, there is an abundance of HT varieties that are just as strongly-scented as any rose of the past. Several come to mind, such as Alec's Red, Blessings, Bonsoir, Ernest H. Morse, Fragrant Cloud, John Waterer, Lily de Gerlache, Mala Rubinstein, My Choice, Prima Ballerina, Red Devil, Wendy Cussons and Whisky Mac, and there are many more. The HT Peace, the most popular rose ever raised, seems scentless, although some people claim to detect a trace.

Advantages of the hybrid tea

Hybrid teas are most often used in the garden for bedding, and for this they certainly have advantages over other plants. They are permanent, or at any rate they should last for twenty years or more, so that you do not have to replant each year as you do with annuals. Their range of colour has already been mentioned, and they will bloom for five to six months with only the briefest of resting periods. Some varieties have coppery-red foliage when they first come out, so the beds can look appealing even before the first flush of bloom in mid summer (June). There is even a modern HT called Curiosity, a red and yellow bi-colour and 'sport' (chance variation) of the older Cleopatra, that has variegated leaves of deep green, splashed yellowish-white.

Finally, they make wonderful flowers for the house, though it is largely true that those lasting longest in water are often the most prone to rain damage outside. Gavotte, Red Devil and Royal Highness come into this category, but Alec's Red,

Right, and below: vigorous, upright HT varieties Alexander, and Fragrant Cloud

Fragrant Cloud, Gail Borden, Grandpa Dickson, Piccadilly and Troika are a few that can be recommended for both indoors and out.

Planting distances

It is impossible to be exact about how far apart HT types should be planted for bedding; 45cm (18 in) is a good average,

but some varieties, Peace for example, are far more vigorous than others and need fully 75cm (2½ ft). Others, like Perfecta, are strong growers but tall, narrow and upright, and yet others, like Josephine Bruce and Percy Thrower, tend to sprawl outwards. The important thing is that the roots should not be so close as to rob one another of nutrient and water, and there should be room between them for hoeing, mulching and proper spraying. The beds should not be so densely packed that air cannot circulate freely as this would encourage disease and probably insect pests as well. On the other hand, nothing looks worse than a rose bed with huge

spaces of bare earth between the plants.

If you have seen your chosen types of rose growing before you buy them, you will probably know their spacing requirements, but some people favour ground-cover plants between their roses and space must be left for sunshine to reach these. Violas and pansies, particularly the blue varieties, are the most frequently recommended, and there is no doubt that they can look very attractive. On the other hand, it is hard to reconcile the use of these with good rose cultivation. Roses need to be well mulched to give of their best, or, failing this, the beds should at least be hoed regularly to keep them free

of weeds, and neither of these activities would make violas or pansies very happy about their living conditions.

Plants for edging rose beds

The use of edging plants is another matter. Small, or smallish, grey or silver-leaved kinds like anaphalis (pearl ever-lasting), lavender, nepeta (catmint) and dwarf sage, most of which have reasonably discreet mauve flowers, are excellent for this purpose. They blend in beautifully with roses and there is no colour clash, but you may wish to use plants that flower earlier and so give colour to the bed before the roses are out. In this case, polyanthus and primroses are hard to beat.

You can also use miniature roses; many are almost evergreen in a mild winter and most start flowering before the HT. They are best suited to the edge of a south-facing border, or at least where their bigger neighbours will not overshadow them and keep the sun away. Even the greatest rose enthusiast could not claim that a newly-pruned rose bed was a thing of beauty and some form of edging does divert the eye from unsightly stumps.

Mixing varieties and heights

It is generally supposed that you should not mix several different varieties or colours of roses in one bed. It is really a matter of choosing what you like. The plants of one variety will be more or less uniform in height and can look marvellous in the mass, but with some roses there may be quite a long rest period in the middle of summer, when little or no colour is showing. A mixed bed can look spotty, with some varieties blooming and some not, but there will be long periods

Left: small mixed border with HT roses and a floribunda in the background
Below: Whisky Mac, a strong-growing HT

when all are out together and a spectacular riot of colour can result. Plant
mauve, white or cream roses between any
two colours that might otherwise clash.
You can divide a round bed into segments
like an orange, each one planted with a
different variety of rose, and possibly
add a standard or half-standard HT in
the centre to give height.

The question of height is an important
one, particularly if your garden is flat.
Trees and shrubs carry the eye upwards
and break up something that could
otherwise seem rather monotonous. Standard roses, either in the centre of a round
bed, or spaced out at about 1·8m (6 ft)
intervals along the centre of a long one,
can have the same beneficial effect. Use a
rose of a contrasting colour for these.

Varieties for hedges and shrubs
The standard HT can also be used to line a
path or a drive, which suggests another
use for the bush varieties. Not nearly
enough use is made of rose hedges, and
tall robust kinds, like the vermilion
Alexander, Peace, Chicago Peace, and
many others are first-rate for this. Some,
if not pruned too hard, can be built up
into fine specimen shrubs to stand on
their own, perhaps in the middle of a lawn
or by the corner of a patio.

FLORIBUNDAS
Most of the general principles outlined
for the hybrid tea rose apply equally to
floribundas, so with these it is enough to
point out where they are better or worse,
how they differ, and to recommend
varieties suited to different purposes.

The floribunda, as opposed to the HT,
grows with large heads or trusses of
comparatively small flowers. These are
often only single or semi-double, and
open to show their stamens. Modern
breeding tends towards larger, HT-shaped
flowers with fewer in a truss so that in
some instances it is difficult to say to
which class a rose belongs. Pink Parfait
and Sea Pearl are examples of this and
have the rather clumsy official
classification of 'floribunda – hybrid tea
type'. In Germany, its country of origin,
Fragrant Cloud is classed as a floribunda,
though it is rather difficult to see the
justification in this case, as the flowers are
so large. Floribundas have a different
ancestry from the HT and, because of the
scentless roses in it, few have a
worthwhile fragrance. Arthur Bell,
Chinatown, Dearest, Elizabeth of

*Above right: this low-growing floribunda,
Paddy McGredy, is a good edging variety
Right: Iceberg, a bushy floribunda*

Glamis, Escapade, Harry Edland, Michelle, Orange Sensation and Pineapple Poll do have scent, but breeders are conscious of the lack in most others and are trying, with mixed success, to remedy it.

Advantages of the floribunda

As a race, floribundas are very vigorous and make more new growth in a season than most HT types. They flower more continuously and are very quick to repeat should they rest at all, which gives them an advantage for bedding. And because most have fewer, smaller and tougher petals, they will open better in wet weather. This also means that most floribundas make good cut flowers. The bright vermilion Anne Cocker, with its blooms in tight little rosettes on the truss, will last fully ten days in water – central heating permitting – and many others are almost as good.

Varieties for edging

It is probably best not to mix floribunda and HT in one bed because of the difference in their growth. However, there are a number of low-growing, bushy floribundas coming onto the market that will make excellent edging for a rose bed. Meanwhile, the brilliant scarlet Topsi

(rather prone to black spot in some areas), dark red Marlena, pink Paddy McGredy and the brand new orange-scarlet Stargazer are all suitable for this, or for lining paths or drives. They are excellent, too, for a small bed.

For some years now, both types, HT and floribunda, seem to have been getting taller and taller and, in some cases, even lankier; so this new breeding tendency towards what might be called the rounded, cushion effect is welcome, especially in the smaller garden. It almost constitutes a return to the poly-pom roses from which the floribundas are descended, but the flowers are much better and the plants healthier.

Varieties for hedges and shrubs

The stronger-growing floribunda has a particular advantage over their HT counterparts as hedges and as shrubs. Their growth is more branching and bushy as a rule and the sheer mass of flowers they produce is difficult for anything else to match. Some have tremendous vigour and will reach 1·2–1·5m (4–5 ft) in two seasons, if not overpruned. If you want a tall, narrow hedge, try yellow, disease-free Chinatown, the equally healthy Queen Elizabeth, Southampton or Dorothy Wheatcroft. The Queen Elizabeth can be kept quite bushy and between 1·5–1·8m (5–6 ft) in height if you prune it to about 90cm (3 ft) each year, and this will avoid the 2·2 or 2·7m (8 or 9 ft) specimen that you see so often with all its flowers at the top.

There seems no way to prune the supremely beautiful Fred Loads to curb its reach for the sky. Unlike Queen Elizabeth, it has huge trusses of large flowers in soft vermilion-orange, not all at the top. Although it might be more rightly

Left, and below left: floribundas Topsi, and City of Leeds; below: Peace, the most successful HT cultivar ever grown

classed as a shrub rather than a floribunda, officially it is known as a 'floribunda-shrub'.

The following lists of recommended varieties will serve as a guide but go and see them growing before you decide which ones to buy.

Some varieties to choose

HYBRID TEAS

Alec's Red	cherry red
Alexander	vermilion
Blessings	light pink
Ernest H. Morse	turkey red
Grandpa Dickson	pale yellow
John Waterer	deep red
Just Joey	coppery-orange
Pascali	white
Peace	pale yellow, pink edges
Piccadilly	scarlet, yellow reverse
Troika	apricot-orange
Whisky Mac	orange-yellow

FLORIBUNDAS

Allgold	yellow
Anne Cocker	vermilion
City of Leeds	salmon-pink
Elizabeth of Glamis	salmon-pink
Escapade	lilac-mauve, white reverse
Evelyn Fison	scarlet
Iceberg	white
Lili Marlene	dusky scarlet
Matangi	orange-vermilion, white eye and reverse
Orange Sensation	vermilion
Orangeade	orange-vermilion
Queen Elizabeth	pink
Southampton	apricot-orange
Topsi	orange-scarlet

Roses:
Climbers and ramblers

The important thing to understand straight away is the difference between a rambler and a climber. Their habit of growth is different and, in some cases, their uses are too. They are not always interchangeable and, to make matters a little more complicated, there are two main groups of ramblers.

Ramblers

Most ramblers are either wild or species roses, and their fairly close relatives. By far the greatest number of those grown in the garden are hybrids of *R. wichuraiana*. They produce massed clusters of small flowers, single, semi-double or double, and they bloom in late summer or even early autumn (July or August) and they do not repeat later on. The leaves are attractive and very glossy before mildew claims them as it does with so many ramblers. Like the wild roses of the hedgerows, ramblers send up long, pliable canes from the base of the plant each year. It is on these that the flowers grow so it is best to remove the old canes when blooming is over. Examples of the first rambler group are American Pillar, Crimson Shower, Dorothy Perkins, Excelsa and the very lovely and relatively healthy Sander's White.

Ramblers like the scented Albertine are different. They are also once-flowering, but the blooms are larger and appear much earlier in mid summer (June). While new canes may come from the base, enormously long and vigorous ones will also grow from some way up the main stems; these stems should be shortened back above one of these new growths after flowering. It is much harder to tell this kind of rambler from a climber that flowers only once a year.

Because of the likelihood of mildew, never plant ramblers against a wall or a close-boarded fence, as air circulation there will be poor. Instead, use them for arches or pergolas.

Climbers

Purists maintain that climbing roses are misnamed and that they are not climbers at all. They have no tendrils, certainly, and do not twine round their supports, or cling to the trunk of a tree in the way that ivy does. In nature, they reach aloft by thrusting their way into shrubs, hedges and trees, hooking their often formidable thorns over the twigs and branches. They get up there somehow, even if in the garden they usually have to be tied in to their supports.

Climbing roses, whether incorrectly titled or not, have larger flowers than ramblers as a rule. Once again, they can be single, semi-double or double, but are often as big and shapely as those of a hybrid tea. They may appear in small clusters (though there may be hundreds of these) or they may come out singly, and a large number of climbers are repeat-flowering. This is particularly so with the newer varieties such as Bantry Bay, Casino, Compassion, Danse du Feu, Golden Showers, Grand Hotel, Handel, Pink Perpétue, Schoolgirl and Swan Lake; but old favourites such as Caroline Testout, Gloire de Dijon, Mme Grégoire Staechelin and Mermaid, come into this category, too.

Climbers only occasionally send up new canes from ground level and in some cases virtually never. From this they form a sturdy main framework and concentrate on producing sideshoots and laterals from this. Sometimes a climber can become very bare and gaunt looking at the base but proper training can help to keep it clothed with leaves and flowers low down. With some of the more pig-headed varieties it may be necessary to plant a low-growing bush, preferably an evergreen, in front of it to hide the often rather ugly, gnarled bare stems.

Apart from natural climbers, you should be able to identify the climbing sports of a number of the HT and floribunda races. A 'sport' occurs when a quirk in a bush rose's make-up, probably due to its mixed ancestry, causes one of two things to happen: it will either produce flowers on its stem quite different from those on the rest of the bush (Super

Clematis growing up through a climber adds contrast and extra colour
Above right: glossy-foliaged and large-flowered Chaplin's Pink Climber

Sun, an orange-yellow sport of the red and yellow bi-colour Piccadilly, is an example of this), or else the flowers stay the same but the habit of growth will change. Suddenly the odd bush will develop the long canes of a climber and, as it is possible to propagate from both kinds of sport, a new rose is born. The prefix 'climbing' appears in catalogues before the variety name if the rose is a climbing sport, e.g. Climbing Iceberg.

These climbing sports used to be much more popular than they are today, although they are still sold in large quantities. It has been found that a very large number of them flower with far less freedom than their bush equivalents and some, whether from HT or floribunda, only flower once. So be careful when making your choice and ask your supplier about the variety you are thinking of choosing before you commit yourself. Roses that usually do come up to expectation as climbing sports include Allgold, Crimson Glory, Ena Harkness, Etoile de Hollande, Fashion, Iceberg, Lady Sylvia and Shot Silk. Climbing Peace can grow to an enormous size yet have only one flower in five years; this is typical in Britain though it will flower better in a warmer climate.

Use in the garden

How can you best use climbing roses in the garden? Climbers, as distinct from ramblers, can be trained on walls, but however good the repeat performance of a rose, there will be periods when it is out of flower. Many climbers are described as 'perpetual flowering' but few, if any, really are; at best they are recurrent, so why not grow them up through some other wall shrub that will bloom before they do or when they are resting?

Forsythia suspensa or *Chaenomeles japonica*, for instance, will give colour to

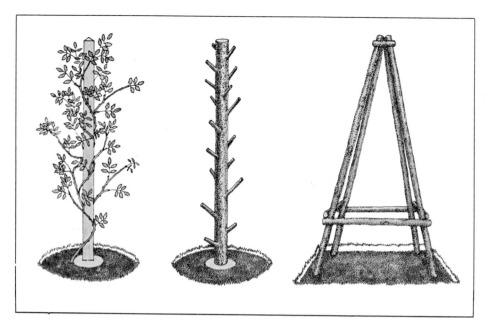

the walls of your house in mid and late spring (March and April). Or you can choose a shrub that flowers when the roses do, but in a contrasting colour. The soft blue of a ceanothus looks wonderful combined with the pale, primrose yellow of the repeat-flowering rose Casino, or with white Swan Lake. Mid summer flowering clematis, grown up through roses, is another way of achieving extra colour in between the first and second flush of rose bloom. Choose kinds that are cut hard back each early spring (February) and do this without fail, or you will end up with the rose struggling pitifully to peer through an impenetrable tangle.

Training the less vigorous climbers and ramblers on pillars is an effective way of using them, provided that the pillar is a substantial one and preferably set in concrete so that its base will not rot. It should be round, or at least have any sharp corners planed away, so that the rose stems are not chafed.

A variant of the straight up-and-down pillar is to use part of the trunk of a small tree, such as a larch, that has branches coming out of it at fairly regular intervals all round. If these branches are sawn off about 30cm (12 in) from the trunk, they are very easy to tie the rose to. For either sort of pillar, train the canes around it in a spiral; this will make it more likely to send out flowering sideshoots low down.

Training techniques

The secret of training climbers and ramblers is, paradoxically, to keep the main growths as horizontal as possible. If they go straight up, the sap flows up them freely, and most of the new growth and flowers will be at the top. If, when used

Above: climbers can be trained up a pillar (left) or larch trunk (centre), but vigorous varieties will prefer a pyramid (right)
Above right: free-flowering rambler R. wichuraiana Excelsa

against a wall or fence, the canes are fanned out to each side and tied in to horizontal wires, the effect of bending the canes will be to restrict the sap flow and to divert it into the side buds along their entire length. These buds develop and form flowering laterals, which in turn are fanned out and tied in, so that the rose moves upwards, gradually, and is covered with flowers and leaves from tip to toe.

The supports should consist of strong, galvanized wire, the strands about 30–45cm (12–18 in) apart, threaded through 15cm (6 in) vine-eyes, so that, allowing for a few centimetres of the eye to go into the wall or fence, the wires will be 13cm (5 in) from the wall surface. This allows some air to circulate between the wall and the rose. You should tie the canes not too tightly (so as to allow for growth) to the outside of the wires with plastic-covered garden wire.

Up pillars Training roses in a spiral on a pillar has something of the same effect as fanning them out, but start the training straight away, as some climbers have very stiff canes that, once developed, are quite difficult to bend.

Up pyramids Probably even better than a pillar is a 2m (7 ft) tall, upright pyramid of either three or four rustic poles, joined at the top and with crosspieces bracing the sides about half-way down. The rose will be much less restricted in its growth on a pyramid than on a pillar, and it is even possible to grow two roses of blending colours at the same time on one support.

As hedges You can form a hedge of almost any height you like with climbers and ramblers. Link upright posts at approximately 1·8m (6 ft) intervals with galvanized iron wires 30cm (12 in) apart, and on these the roses are trained. In time, they will make a fine and very colourful screen, but only in the summer, for in winter the leaves will fall.

As weeping standards Rambling roses make the best weeping standards if you choose them from the first group previously mentioned. Their canes are pliable and hang down all round as they should,

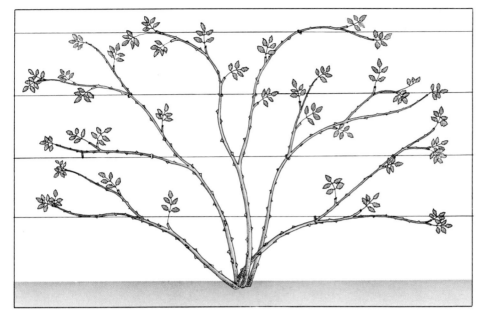

Left: to restrict sap flow and encourage flowering, canes of climber growing against a wall should be trained outwards
Below left: wire umbrella frame on stake will support weeping standard
Below, far left: climber, Alchymist

the old ramblers Rambling Rector, Seagull and Wedding Day. With a little guidance at the beginning, they will ramble quite happily on their own with no tying in, and produce waterfalls of immensely fragrant, small white flowers in mid summer (June). Don't plant them too close to the trunk of the tree, because the rain must be able to reach the roots.

However, a warning is needed about the kind of tree you choose. If your rose is described as reaching 9m (30 ft), it is obvious that you must not pick a tree of 4.5m (15 ft) up which to grow it. An old apple tree can be ideal, but it must not be too old or have rotting branches, for after a year or two the weight and wind resistance of the rose may bring the whole lot down in a gale.

Covering up and ground cover Climbing and rambling roses are invaluable for covering old, unsightly sheds (as well as new, unsightly houses), and ramblers belonging to the *wichuraiana* group can be used for ground cover. *R. wichuraiana* itself will grow quite flat along the ground, spreading out in all directions, rooting as it goes and covered in late summer (July) with star-like, single white flowers. A similar hybrid called Max Graf has pink flowers and in time both roses will grow dense enough to smother weeds. Wandering over a bank that you have been wondering how to cover and that is difficult to keep tidy, they make a really different and attractive feature in the garden.

Some varieties to choose
CLIMBERS

Allen Chandler	bright crimson
Aloha	pink
Altissimo	blood-red
Compassion	apricot
Danse du Feu	orange-scarlet
Golden Showers	daffodil yellow
Handel	cream, edged pink
New Dawn	pale pink
Parkdirektor Riggers	blood-red
Pink Perpétue	pink
Schoolgirl	apricot-orange
Swan Lake	white

RAMBLERS

Albéric Barbier	creamy-white
Albertine	coppery-pink
Excelsa	red
Sander's White	white

laden with blossom, but whatever rose you use, make sure it is supported above the ground by a very strong stake, about 1·8m (6 ft) tall. Wind pressure on a weeping standard can be very great, so something substantial is needed to keep it upright. Nurseries supply suitable wooden stakes, but an old metal gas pipe, painted green, is a good alternative and it will last almost for ever if galvanized as well as painted. The top should go right up into the head of the rose to give it extra support and the rose should be tied to it with plastic ties, one at the top and two equally spaced further down.

Sometimes a wire 'umbrella' frame on the top of the stake is recommended. This should not be needed with ramblers like Excelsa, but with the more rigid canes of Albertine, that is frequently sold as a weeping rambler, you may need an umbrella to persuade its canes to go in the right direction.

Up trees A very lovely way of using the more strong-minded ramblers and climbers is to train them up trees. Many of the old species such as *R. filipes* Kiftsgate and *R. longicuspis* are first-rate for this, as are

Siting and planting roses

Roses like plenty of sun, though there are some climbers that will do quite well on a north-facing wall. They will grow in most types of soil, though are far from their best on chalk. A good, medium loam suits them best of all, so you can help them on light soils by adding as much humus as possible, and peat and other materials on heavy ones, both to lighten them and to improve drainage. The latter is important, for no rose likes being waterlogged. They should have plenty of water if they are to flourish as they should, but they will survive drought far better than they will constant flooding.

Choose, if possible, an open but not a windswept site. Avoid narrow, draughty wind-tunnels such as you find between houses, or shady places under trees, where the roses will grow tall and spindly looking for the light and have to compete with the tree roots for water and food.

How many roses you will need to fill your chosen beds depends not only on how many you can afford, but also on the varieties you select. If you have seen the same varieties growing elsewhere beforehand, you will know just how large they get, and whether they are spreading or upright growers. As a rough guide, it can be said that an average distance between plants of about 45cm (18 in) will suit most hybrid teas and floribundas. This will allow for air circulation, and make spraying and hoeing between them not too difficult a task.

Do not plant new roses in a bed that has grown other roses for some years. The soil will have become what is known as 'rose sick' and the new roses will never do well. You must either replace the soil from another part of the garden, which is a job few people care to tackle if the bed is a big one, or else choose another spot altogether. However, if you are simply replacing a rose that has died in the middle of an established bed, it is not too big a job to dig out a 45cm (18 in) hole, about 30cm (12 in) deep, and put new soil in – still hard work but it should be done.

Preparing the site
Roses will give you twenty years or more of their beauty, so it is only fair and

A fine display of mixed roses resulting from careful siting and planting

sensible to give them the best home possible to live in. The preparation of the site will vary to a greater or lesser extent according to your type of soil. In extreme cases where, for instance, drainage is almost non-existent and the ground waterlogged, it may be necessary to put in land drains, or at the very least put in materials to make it more porous. Light, sandy soils need the opposite approach for, though good drainage is essential, a correct balance must be struck between this and some degree of water retention. Roots need air as well as water to function properly, which is the reason heavy soils need to be broken up so as to make them more friable.

This breaking-up should be done by double digging and keeping the fertile topsoil where it should be, at the top. It is a good idea to put chopped-up turfs, grass side downwards, along the bottom of each trench and, when filling in, add well-rotted compost, leaf mould, granulated peat or stable manure – or a mixture of all of them – whatever organic material you can get hold of, together with a generous dressing of bonemeal.

All this digging and manuring should be done some time in mid autumn (September), about three months before your roses arrive. The ground will have time to settle down and you can recover from a back-breaking job. Heavy work it may be, but you will be more than glad in years to come that you faced up to it, for with good cultivation roses will not only grow and bloom well, but will be much more resistant to diseases.

Finally, a few tips for special conditions. About 1½kg per sq m (3 lb per sq yd) of gypsum (calcium sulphate) added to the bottom of a double-dug trench will help to break up a clay subsoil, though only over quite a long period. On very light, sandy soils, deep digging should not be needed, as both water and roots can penetrate it easily in its natural state. In fact, disturbance of the lower spit will make it even easier for the water to get away, which is the last thing needed on this kind of soil. Plenty of humus in the top spit is the answer here.

If you are gardening on solid chalk, with only a few centimetres of soil over it, it will be necessary to dig out the chalk to a depth of at least 45cm (18 in), and to add plenty of peat to the soil that replaces it. Roses do best in a slightly acid soil, of a pH value between 6·0 and 6·5.

When and how to plant

Your roses will probably arrive from the nursery in early winter (November). This is the best month for planting them, as the soil will still be warm enough for the roots to get established.

If you have to wait a few days before planting, either because you are too busy with something else, or the ground is frost-bound, or soggy from prolonged rain, do not unpack the roses but keep them in a cool, frost-proof shed. If there is likely to be a longer delay, heel them in as soon as weather conditions permit. To do this, unpack the plants and put them along a trench in a spare corner of the garden, burying them so that at least 15cm (6 in) of soil covers the roots. They can remain like this for some weeks if absolutely necessary, but it is always best to get them into their final quarters with the least delay so that they can start to make themselves at home.

Whether you are planting straight away or heeling in, inspect the roses carefully as soon as you have unpacked them. Check the labels to make sure that they are what you ordered, as even the best of nurseries can make mistakes and will always exchange a wrong variety. If the plants are described as being First Grade, they should have a minimum of two firm, healthy canes (stems), at least as thick as a pencil and with smooth, unwrinkled bark. The neck joint between the rootstock and the budding union should be at least 16mm (⅝ in) thick, and there should be a good, fibrous root system. Cut off any leaves remaining on the canes, and cut back any of the latter that are diseased or broken to a point

1 *Dig hole wide enough to spread roots*

2 *Carefully remove wrapping material*
4 *Work planting mixture around roots*

3 *Settle roots in hole and check level*
5 *Fill in and firm down before watering*

just below the damaged portion. Shorten any very long, thick roots by a third; this will encourage the thinner, feeding roots to grow from them. If the roses look dry, put them in a bucket of water for at least an hour.

While they are sucking up the water, you can make up your planting mixture which, while not absolutely essential on good soil, will certainly help to give your roses a good start. You will need about one large shovelful for each rose, consisting of equal parts of soil and moist granulated peat, with a handful of bonemeal or rose fertilizer per plant mixed well in. It is advisable to wear gloves when handling fertilizers.

Dig your first planting hole wide enough for the roots to be spread out as evenly as possible all round, and deep enough so that the budding union comes about 13mm ($\frac{1}{2}$ in) below the soil level. Carry your bucket of roses to the rose bed so that you can lift them straight from it and the roots have no chance to dry out again. Put your first rose in its hole, spread out the roots and check the level by putting a cane across the top of the

hole. Put a shovelful of planting mixture over the roots, tread lightly, and then fill in the hole with soil, treading again rather more firmly. Finally, give each rose at least 8 litres (2 gal) of water. It may be as well to tread the soil once more after a few weeks, especially if there has been a frost that may have loosened the plants.

Climbers
Climbing roses against a house wall, where the soil is certain to be very dry, need slightly different treatment. Plant them at least 45cm (18 in) out from the wall and fan out their roots *away* from it towards the damper ground. If they are long enough, tie in the canes straight away to the lowest support wire to help prevent wind-rock.

Standards and shrubs
Standard roses should have the stake that will support them driven into the hole before planting, so that it will not damage any roots. The stake should be long enough so that it just goes into the head of the bush to give it extra support, but should not show above it. Tie the two together with plastic ties that have a buffer between the plant and stake to prevent chafing, but only fix them loosely at first as the rose may sink a little as the soil settles. After a week or ten days, you can tighten up the ties enough to hold the stem firmly, but not to strangle it.

When planting the larger-growing shrub roses, make sure that you really have left room enough all round for them to achieve their full size.

Container-grown plants
Many people buy container-grown roses from nurseries and garden centres, and these plants should be carefully inspected before buying to make sure that they are up to standard and have genuinely been grown in a container and not just put in one for selling purposes. They have the

Left: a good soaking helps dry plants
Above: standards should be firmly tied

great advantage that they can be planted at any time, even in full flower, provided the rootball is not disturbed too much.

However, don't just dig a hole big enough to take the container, particularly if your soil is heavy. By doing this you might simply be making a sump, that would fill with water after rain and whose sides the roots might find it hard to penetrate. Dig a hole at least 30cm (12 in) across, breaking up the subsoil for drainage. Water your rose well while still in its container, and put it in the hole to check that the depth is right. If it is, slit down each side of the container with a sharp knife, ease it out from under the rootball, fill the hole with planting mixture, tread firm and water well. Should the container be of metal, you will, of course, have to remove the rose before putting it in the planting hole.

Growing under glass
Roses are not hothouse plants, but they can be grown successfully in a greenhouse, at least for part of the year, so that you can have spring blooms long before the garden roses are out.

Use 20 or 25cm (8 or 10 in) pots with 2–3cm (1 in) of broken crocks in the bottom; their size depends on the vigour of the variety. J. I. potting compost, either No 2 or No 3, is a suitable growing medium, with perhaps a small amount of well-rotted garden compost or small pieces of chopped turf immediately on top of the crocks.

Plant the roses in early winter (early November), making sure that the soil level is about 2–3cm (1 in) below the pot rims to allow for watering and liquid fertilizers if you wish to use them. You may well have to cut the stronger roots back quite hard to fit the whole thing into the pot, but they will soon form new, finer ones. Firm planting is important, and all leaves and flower-buds should be removed and long shoots shortened a little.

Leave the pots out of doors until mid winter (early December), and then bring them into the greenhouse.

A cold greenhouse will produce flowers in early summer (May), but some heat will be needed for flowers earlier than that. Good ventilation is important at all times, particularly from above, and some form of shading will be needed if the sun is hot. Prune them at the end of mid winter (December), and do not introduce heat into the house until at least ten days after it has been done.

Prune hard, to the first two or three eyes (buds) or you will get tall, straggly plants. Watering should not be too generous at first, but gradually increased as the plants start into growth. Give a thorough weekly soaking once they are really away, with a liquid feed added to the water two months after pruning.

Pests such as caterpillars and greenfly can be removed by hand if you only have a few roses. Mildew can be largely avoided by good roof ventilation, but if any spraying of the plants has to be done, it is much safer to take them out of the greenhouse so that you do not breathe harmful chemicals.

When the plants finish flowering, towards the end of early summer (May), turn off the heating if this has been used, and open the ventilators to prepare the roses for a move outdoors in two weeks or so. Once outside, sink the pots to their rims in ashes in a sheltered spot, where they can be left until brought indoors again in early winter (December), when re-potting should be done if necessary.

Pruning roses

It is unfortunate that when writing about pruning it tends to sound so complicated. There is no doubt that the best way to learn is to get an experienced rose grower to show you how to do it, provided that he takes the time to explain just why he is doing each operation. If you understand what you are doing and why, pruning all at once loses its mystique and suddenly you wonder what all the fuss was about.

So, first of all, why do we prune? In the wild (and you can see this for yourself in the hedgerows) roses send up new canes each year from the base of the plant or from very near it. The old canes will gradually deteriorate and eventually die off. The best blooms come on the new growth, and all you are doing when you prune is speeding up this natural process of replacement. Also, some of the old canes may very well be diseased, so you are getting rid of these as well.

There are two other things to aim for in pruning. One is to achieve a reasonably balanced bush, though this may not be too important if the roses are growing close together in a bed, and the other to keep the centre of the bush fairly open so that light and air can reach it. A thick tangle of canes in the middle should be thinned out and, if two are crossing so that they will rub together, one of the pair should be removed or at least shortened enough to prevent this happening.

It pays to buy a good pair of secateurs as they will last you for many years. They should always be kept clean and sharp. If they are not, you will bruise the stems of the roses and make rough, ragged cuts, that will encourage the entry of disease spores.

Hybrid teas

The first thing to do is to cut away all weak, twiggy growth – everything, in fact, that is thinner than a pencil. This includes the very small, matchstick-like twigs that often sprout from the main canes, and that will produce no more than a few

The profusely-flowering floribunda Iceberg responds well to good pruning

undersized leaves if left. Cut right out any dead wood, including stumps and snags that may have been left from poor pruning in the past. Some of these may be too tough for secateurs and for them you should use a fine-toothed saw. Dead wood will be brown or greyish, with gnarled and wrinkled bark.

Next, remove any diseased canes, or shorten them back to the first healthy bud below the diseased portion. If you cut through a cane and the centre of it is brown, this is a sign of die-back, so move down, bud by bud, until you reach healthy white wood.

You may find some quite thick and apparently healthy canes that were pruned the previous year, but from which only a few spindly twigs have grown below the old pruning cut. If this is all the canes have produced in a season, they will do no better in the next, so remove them.

All of what might be termed 'rubbish' has now been disposed of, and the remaining green and firm, healthy canes should be shortened to about 15–20cm (6–8 in). The cuts should be made about 6mm ($\frac{1}{4}$ in) above a bud, and at an angle, sloping down away from the bud. If you cannot find a bud where you want one, choose the nearest, preferably an outward-facing one, to encourage the new shoots to grow away from the centre of the plant. But once again, if you cannot find an outward-facing bud, do not think that inward growth will make the rose moody and introspective. In fact, it is not

unusual, even if you do cut to an outward-facing bud, for the one below it, facing inwards, to be the one that starts away first and makes all the running. You try to point the way, but the rose does not always follow.

That is really all there is to the yearly pruning of HT roses for the average gardener. Harder pruning will produce larger flowers, but fewer of them. Rather lighter pruning is probably advisable on poor, dry soils. Unless these have a regular and massive application of fertilizer and humus, there will not be the goodness in them to promote vigorous new growth on the same scale.

Newly-planted roses

Always prune these more severely, to perhaps 8–10cm (3–4 in). This will ensure that top-growth starts later and there is more time for the energy of the plant to go into developing a sound root system early in the year. If you plant your roses in the spring, prune them at the same time.

Everybody argues about the best time to prune. Each expert has his own theory, so who is right? The answer is, of course, everybody. As long as the bushes are dormant, or nearly so, which will probably be from early winter to mid spring (end of November to end of March) in mild areas, and provided that there is no frost about, it does not matter very much when you prune. If there is a severe winter, autumn pruning may mean that you lose a few canes through frost damage; these can be trimmed back later. But this can happen with a bad spring frost, too. In colder districts, it is wiser to leave your pruning until well into mid, or even late, spring (late March or April).

Floribundas

These are grown mainly for their mass effect and continuity of bloom rather than, as with an HT, the beauty of their individual flowers. For this reason, and because they naturally make more new growth than an HT without the encouragement of hard pruning, they can be treated more lightly.

Basically, however, the approach is the same. Weak, dead or diseased wood is removed, and then healthy growths shortened by between one-half and one-third, cutting just above a bud as before.

Below left and right: pruning rules for a standard depend largely on whether it is an HT or floribunda variety; be sure to keep the head a good, even shape
Bottom left: hard pruning will produce larger blooms on HT varieties
Bottom right: cut out old wood at source

Strong laterals or sideshoots should be shortened to the first or second bud.

With very strong and tall-growing varieties, like Iceberg or Chinatown, which may be wanted for specimen planting or for the back of a border, a strong framework of wood can be built up over several years. If the main canes are cut back only moderately, they will produce strong laterals that are shortened in turn the following year, producing yet further branching. Gradually, a very large bush takes shape, from which the main shoots need only be removed as they lose their vigour and are replaced by others.

Ramblers and climbers

As the methods of pruning are different, it is as well to be able to distinguish between the two, but the position is complicated by the fact that there are two types of ramblers, one being much closer to a climber in its habits than the other.

Ramblers With a few exceptions, these only flower once, some varieties doing so as late as late summer or even early autumn (July or August). The first group, that includes varieties like American Pillar, Dorothy Perkins, Excelsa and Sander's White Rambler, have large clusters of small blooms, and throw up new canes 2m (6 ft) or so long from the base of the plant each year. Pruning consists of cutting the old canes to the ground as soon as they have finished flowering and tying the new ones in their place. With a vigorous, thorny rose, this can be a rather fearsome job, and strong, thorn-proof gloves will be needed. It is often easier to remove the old canes by cutting them into short lengths and pulling these out individually.

If new growth is poor one year, a few of the old canes can be shortened by about one-third and left in place. They will produce some flowers but not with the profusion of new ones.

The second type of rambler, that includes varieties like Albertine, has rather larger flowers and tends to produce enormously vigorous new canes, branching out from anywhere along the length of the old ones. Prune after flowering by cutting away the old just above where a new cane has sprouted. Remove unproductive or diseased old wood as and when it occurs.

Climbers As a class, climbers generally have larger flowers than ramblers, some as big and as shapely as HT roses. Many of the newer introductions and a number of the older ones flower twice. Do not prune any of them until the first year after planting. This is especially important with the climbing sports of HT and floribunda, as hard pruning then may cause them to revert to their bush form.

Many climbers do very well with little or no pruning except what is needed to keep them in bounds, but all will do much better if the laterals are shortened by about two-thirds in winter. Some varieties are extremely stubborn about producing new growth low down, and can become very bare at the base. Apart from training the canes as horizontally as possible to encourage new sideshoots to break, strong cutting-back of a main cane may help to produce others from the bottom. If this does not work, there is nothing for it but to plant something else in front of it, though not so close that it will rob the rose of the goodness in the soil.

Standard roses

Usually these are varieties of HT roses or floribundas, and pruning should be done in the same way as for the equivalent bushes. It is always important to bear in mind the balance of the head and to keep it as even as possible, as with a standard you are more likely to be seeing the rose from all sides.

Weeping standards Both of the rambler

Guide to pruning roses

HYBRID TEA **FLORIBUNDA** **STANDARD**	**Hard pruning** Newly-planted, and HT roses for exhibition blooms	**Moderate pruning** Established HT and floribunda	**Light pruning** Roses growing on poor, dry soils

RAMBLER **WEEPING STANDARD**	**Small-flowered** Cut old canes down to ground after flowering Treat head of standard as small-flowered rambler	**Large-flowered** Cut out old flowered wood to base of new lateral

CLIMBER	Don't prune when first planted, but shorten laterals by two-thirds in subsequent years
MINIATURE	Thin out dense, twiggy growth and discard dead wood; trim to shape
SHRUB	Thin out dense growth, discard dead wood, trim to shape; shorten laterals up to two-thirds

groups are used for these standards, though there is no doubt that the first, small-flowered, group are the best as their long, pliable canes weep naturally. Once again the pruning is the same as if they were growing in their natural rambling form. That is, completely remove old canes after flowering for group one; for the second type, cut back old wood above – or, perhaps, below as the canes should be hanging downwards – the point where a strong side-growth has sprouted.

Miniatures

This involves the thinning out when needed of the varieties that produce dense, twiggy growth and the removal of the few shoots that may die back each year. Some of the more vigorous varieties may send up extra-strong shoots oc-

casionally that unbalance the bush, and these should be shortened. Nail-scissors are best to use for pruning miniatures.

Shrub roses

Species roses, except in their formative years when a limited amount of cutting back may be needed in order to produce a reasonably balanced shape, should be left alone apart from the removal of dead wood. This can be taken out at any time. Pruning would destroy the natural habit of growth and this is one of the main charms of a species rose.

Apart from the removal of diseased or dead wood (that applies to all of them), most other shrub roses – damasks, albas, centifolias, moss roses, Bourbons, hybrid musks, hybrid perpetuals and modern shrub roses – need their laterals shortened

by about two-thirds at the most after flowering to encourage new growth, though they will do quite well even without this attention. Occasionally a strong main shoot can be cut hard back to encourage new growth low down.

If used in hedges, both rugosas and gallicas can be clipped over lightly in winter, rather than pruned, but this should be done following in the main their natural outline. If you are using roses you cannot expect (and should not want) the squared-off regularity of a privet or box hedge.

Varieties of shrub roses that bear heps, other than species, can be trimmed in early spring if they need it, and the pruning of tall floribundas that may be used as shrubs has already been described under the floribunda heading.

THE EDIBLE GARDEN
Digging the food plot

The object of single digging (which from here on we shall simply call digging) is to turn over the top 20–30cm (9–12 in) of soil; the lower levels are then exposed and aerated. At the same time annual weeds, such as groundsel and chickweed, are turned in and buried so that they will provide valuable humus. Perennial weeds with long tap-roots (like docks and dandelions) will re-emerge if they are buried, so they should be pulled out, left on the path to die, and then placed in the middle of the compost heap.

Tools for the job

When choosing a digging implement you can opt for a spade or a fork. Both are available with two kinds of handle – T-grip and D-grip. The latter is preferable because all four fingers of the hand are placed inside the D giving a stronger grip and better leverage.

Whichever you choose it is better to pay a little extra and buy a good-quality tool. A good spade or fork is a sound investment.

For spring digging you can use either a spade or a fork. If you have a light or sandy soil, or a good loam, a spade will do a better job; but on a very heavy clay, which has lain undisturbed over the winter a fork will make digging easier.

It is advisable to dig your vegetable plot at least a week or two before you are ready to sow or plant as the soil should have time to settle.

And so to work

First of all dig out a trench one spit deep and about 3–3·5m (10–12 ft) long at one end of the plot. Don't make the trench any longer; it is far better for your morale to finish digging a short strip than to half-finish a longer one. Put the soil from the trench into a wheelbarrow and push it to the other end of the plot (where it will be used to fill in the final trench).

Go back to the start of the row and work your way down the second trench,

turning the soil over into the first one. Continue in this manner until you have finished the strip. A word of advice – don't try to speed the job up by digging great slices out of the soil. It is much easier, and a lot less tiring, to handle chunks no wider than 15cm (6 in) – at least until you have established a relaxed rhythm. Carry on digging down to the end, fill in the last trench, have a rest and then start on the second strip.

The newly-turned earth is now an uneven surface of gleaming clods of soil. Leave it like this until the day you are ready to sow and plant, to give it a chance to dry out and settle. Then all you need do on a dry day is shuffle and tramp all over it to break down the lumps before raking it to a fine tilth.

Fertilizers and manures
If you are to get a good, healthy crop fertilizers are absolutely essential. A top dressing of general fertilizer, such as Growmore or Fish, blood and bone, or one of the proprietary, concentrated animal manures should be spread over the soil at 70–145g per sq m (2–4 oz per sq yd) before you start digging. Digging the plot puts the fertilizer down into the soil where the plant roots will reach and benefit from it in due course.

It is a good idea to keep some of the fertilizer you use and put a little of it, say about 35g per sq m (1 oz per sq yd) over the whole plot just before you start sowing and planting. This will give the germinating seedlings a boost till the roots reach the main feed below.

When and where to lime
Because some plants are lime-haters, lime should be used sparingly in the flower garden. In the vegetable plot, however, lime, used carefully, is extremely beneficial. Being alkaline, lime corrects the over-acidity that repeated doses of fertilizer tend to create and also breaks down heavy clay. But it has other advantages as well. Its main chemical element is calcium which is essential to the healthy growth of many vegetables, especially peas and beans and all members of the cabbage family – the brassicas. Furthermore, its presence in the soil seems to discourage some of the deadly pests and diseases that attack vegetables.

It is often said that the average vegetable garden should be limed once every three years to keep the soil sweet. On the other hand some vegetables react adversely to freshly-limed soil, and unless you keep careful records there is a danger of forgetting whether the three-year period is up.

Potatoes are a prime example of vegetables that do not need lime and, indeed, are adversely affected by it.

The crop rotation system
A good solution to the liming problem is to endeavour to link your liming to a simple crop rotation programme. Under this system, when the vegetable plot is in full production, roughly one-third of the total area will be occupied by brassicas – summer cabbages, brussels sprouts, cauliflowers and so on. The brassicas are grown in their own special section, with a second section devoted to root crops such as carrots, turnips, beetroot and swedes and a third to peas, beans, onions and salad crops.

The crop rotation system entails switching these sections around so that no one group of crops occupies the same ground more than once every three years.

The brassica section is chosen because lime is especially beneficial to cabbages and similar crops. It encourages their growth and discourages slugs from nibbling at the stems of the young plants. It also appears to act as a deterrent to club root disease.

Incidentally, lime should not be mixed with manures or fertilizers, so dig it into the soil at least two months before an application of fertilizer, or alternatively one month later.

Warming the earth
Before leaving the vegetable plot get down a row or two of cloches. Those made of translucent plastic are strong and, of course, unbreakable. Both rows will be placed on the bare, unsown earth and left there for a week or two – depending on the weather. The reason for this is to warm up the soil ready to receive sowings of early peas, lettuce and radish later on in the year.

Potatoes: Planting and tending

Planting times and distances for potatoes vary with variety. Plant first-early and second-early varieties in mid and late spring (March and April) and early-maincrop and late varieties in late spring and early summer (April and May), or even into mid summer (June). Give earlies 25–30cm (10–12 in) between the tubers and 60cm (24 in) between the rows. Early-maincrop and late potatoes should have 38cm (15 in) between the tubers and 68–75cm (27–30 in) between the rows.

If the seed tubers are new Scottish or Irish stock some of them may be rather large. Provided there is at least one good sprout on each half, these can be cut lengthwise down the centre. Don't cut the tubers until you are ready to plant.

Methods of planting
The trench method is one of the most popular ways of planting potatoes. Put a garden line down across the plot and draw it tight. Keeping the back of the spade up against the line, 'chip' out a trench 10–15cm (4–6 in) deep. Plant the tubers in the bottom of the trench, taking care that the sprouts are not knocked off. Then move the line over the required distance (depending on variety) to mark out the next trench. As the second trench is taken out, throw the soil forward to fill in the first trench, and so on.

Another method is to make the planting holes with a trowel. This way you can vary the size of each hole to suit the size of the tuber. In addition you create minimum disturbance of the soil – an important point if manure or greenstuff has recently been dug in.

In the 'lazy bed' method of planting, place the tubers just below soil level so that they stand upright. Then, using a draw hoe, draw the soil over them from either side to form a ridge. This method is of value on heavy soils where the drainage is not too good, as any surplus water that may lie at the bottom of the ridges will then be below the level of the potatoes.

A more modern method is to plant the tubers just inside the soil and cover them with a sheet of black polythene 60cm (24 in) wide. Slit the polythene just above each tuber so that the sprouts can push through. To keep the polythene in place put stones or soil along the edges. The tubers form under the sheet, or just inside the soil. You can pick out the largest tubers for first use by freeing and lifting each side of the sheet in turn.

There is no saving of time by this method but it does cut out hoeing and earthing-up.

Pots and cold frames
If you have a greenhouse with some heat you can grow pots of potatoes on the greenhouse staging. Half-fill some 20cm (8 in) pots with good soil or compost and plant one tuber in each. Add more soil as the plants grow. When a plant has made a good soil ball and is forming tubers, it is quite easy to tap it out of the pot, pick off the largest tubers and then slip the roots back in the pot again.

You can also plant tubers in a cold frame in early or mid spring (February or early March). Ventilate them freely during the day and replace the light at night until the plants have reached the glass.

Protection from frost
Large barn cloches are good for protecting an early row of potatoes. If there is a ventilating pane, take it out so that the plants are not forced too quickly, but replace it at night if there is any danger of frost. The haulms of potatoes are easily damaged by frost. Shoots that are just emerging from the soil can be covered again by drawing soil over them if frost threatens, but this cannot be done once leaves have formed. Sheets of newspaper, kept in place with clods of earth, serve quite well.

If the young plants are blackened by frost, do not assume that they have died; new shoots will soon form. The crop will be later, of course, and in many cases may not be quite so heavy.

Hoeing and earthing-up
Hoe the plants when the rosettes of leaves have formed, but do it as lightly as possible so that the underground stolons (the shoots on which the tubers form) are not cut off.

Earthing-up takes place when the plants are 15–20cm (6–8 in) tall, and consists of drawing soil from between the rows to make a ridge. This prevents the tubers from pushing through into the sunlight. Tubers greened by the sun cannot be eaten.

To earth-up, stand between two rows of potatoes and, with a draw hoe, reach out over the plants and draw the soil up and

Four ways to plant potatoes. Below left: in trenches 10–15cm (4–6 in) deep; below: in individual holes, causing less soil disturbance; below right: by 'lazy bed' method – especially suitable for water-retaining soils; far right: covering with black polythene to save earthing-up

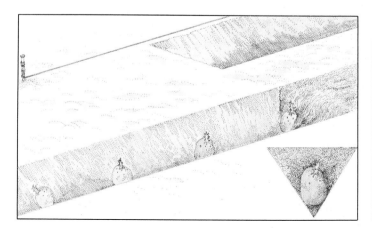

Right: cover plants with newspaper if there is danger of frost

under the lower leaves with a steady hand. Then turn round the end of a row to earth-up the other side. Repeat until all rows have been earthed-up on both sides. It makes for easier earthing if you first loosen the soil between the rows by forking it over.

Pests and diseases

The most frequently-encountered enemies of the potato are potato blight, common scab and potato eelworm.

Potato blight In mid and late summer (late June and early July) spray the plant with a fungicide such as Bordeaux mixture as a safeguard against potato blight. This is a fungus disease that spreads quickly in damp, humid conditions, and its presence is revealed by dark brown blotches on the leaves and the rapid deterioration of the haulms. Any sudden collapse of the foliage should always be viewed with suspicion. If this happens, cut off the haulms about 30cm (12 in) above the soil, remove them from the plot and burn them. This will prevent the blight spores from getting into the soil and infecting the tubers. The tubers may then be left in the soil for a couple of weeks to ripen off.

Common scab Another trouble that may be encountered is common scab; this is caused by a minute soil organism. The trouble is only skin deep and does not affect the eating or keeping qualities of the tubers. It is usually worse in light, hungry soils. Some good compost or grass mowings, placed in the bottom of the trench at planting time, will help to give clean tubers.

Potato eelworm This pest can be a serious problem. The tiny eelworms, too small to be seen by the naked eye, attack the plant stems and roots. Stunted plants with thin stems are an indication of their presence. The only cure is to starve them out by not growing potatoes on infected ground for several seasons. A three- or four-yearly crop rotation is a good deterrent.

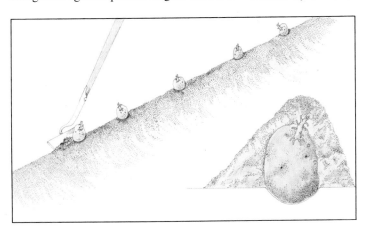

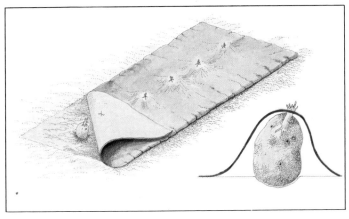

Potatoes: Harvesting and storing

Having described how to plant and tend potatoes, special care should be taken, when the appropriate time comes, to harvest and store them correctly in order to reap fullest advantage of your work.

It is usually the late varieties of potato that are grown for winter use and storage, but if the early ones have not been used up before the haulms have died off there is no reason why these, too, should not be stored. Most earlies, when ripe, will keep until mid winter (late December) at least.

Signs of maturity

The first sign of approaching maturity is a yellow tinge in the lower leaves of the haulms. This is followed by a gradual browning of the leaves and stems, until finally the haulms wither and die.

A change also takes place in the tuber. The skin of a 'new' (that is, immature) potato can be removed easily, whereas that on a ripe tuber is firm; once the skins have 'set', the crop is ready for lifting.

Lifting the tubers

To lift the crop, use either a digging fork (that is, one with square tines) or a potato fork (flat tines). Stand facing the row to be lifted, and thrust the fork in at the *side* of the ridge, not across it, otherwise some of the tubers will be pierced with the tines. Put the fork in at an angle so that when thrust well down, the tines are below the root; then lift the root cleanly and throw it forward. Shake off the dead haulm, and spread the potatoes out so that they are all on the soil surface. Before moving on to the next root, fork carefully through the area to bring up any tubers that remain.

Lift the crop on a dry day, if possible, so that the potatoes can be left out for an hour or two to dry. The soil will then come off them more easily. Rub off as much of it as possible when picking the potatoes up, and sort them into two grades – the eating or 'ware' potatoes, and those too small for use. Never leave the little ones lying about on the soil as they are apt to turn up again later as 'self-sets', producing new potato plants. Any tubers that have been speared by the fork should be placed on one side and used first.

Checking for disease

The ware potatoes can be put into sacks or boxes, or piled up in a heap on the soil.

After lifting, potatoes should be left to dry out for a couple of hours. This makes the removal of soil much easier

If heaped, they must be covered with the dead haulms or some other litter that will exclude light, to prevent them turning green. Leave the tubers for two or three weeks, before sorting through them all over again.

The purpose of this interim period is to give any diseased tubers a chance to show themselves. If the potatoes were stored away immediately after lifting, and not re-examined, any diseased tubers would continue to go bad, and could spread disease through the bag or heap.

Disease shows as a pinky-brownish patch on the skin. It is not difficult to see on white tubers, but may prove more difficult on coloured ones. If in doubt, scratch the skin with a finger-nail to see whether the discoloration goes right into the tuber.

How to store

Sound tubers can now be stored for the winter in a cool, dark, frost-proof place. These three conditions are not always easy to meet indoors. A cool pantry, or an unheated spare bedroom or boxroom, would be suitable, or a brick garage –

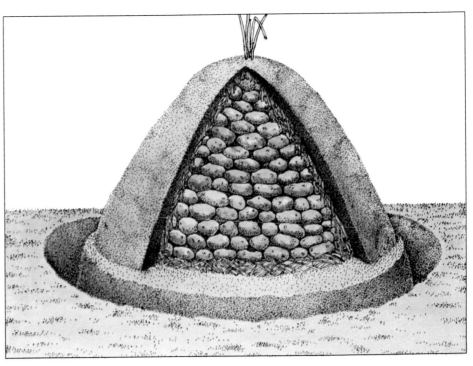

Above: drying off the harvested crop
Right: an outdoor clamp not only saves indoor storage space – the tubers will remain firmer than if in bags
Below right: it is essential to remove any shoots that appear on stored tubers

provided the door is not left open in frosty weather. Wooden sheds are seldom frost-proof, but will serve if extra covering can be put over the tubers during severe frost.

Boxes and sacks If the tubers are stored in boxes, the top of each box must be covered to exclude light. Hessian potato sacks, once so common, are now difficult to obtain and have given way to paper sacks, that can be bought from most large stores. Polythene sacks are not suitable, as a certain amount of light can penetrate and moisture can build up inside.

Outdoor clamp Where the crop consists of more than a couple of sacks, storage space can be saved by making an outdoor clamp (see diagram). This provides ideal conditions, and keeps the potatoes firmer than if they are stored in bags.

To make a clamp, level the soil and tread it firm. Put down a layer of straw to make a bed for the tubers, and pile them up on this. Pack them neatly so that the sides of the clamp are as steep and level as possible. The heap can be round or rectangular, but for average quantities a conical shape is more usual. Then cover the potatoes with a layer of straw (or hay or dried bracken) about 15cm (6 in) in thickness.

The next step is to mark out a circle approximately 25cm (10 in) from the straw. Thrust the spade in all the way round the circle, and dig out the soil beyond it, piling it up on the platform between the mark and the straw. Keep the same depth of soil all the way up. Fill in cracks and hollows with loose soil from the bottom of the trench, and finish by patting the soil smooth with the back of

the spade. Subsoil should not be used, so if necessary extend the trench outwards.

To begin with, leave a wisp of straw sticking out at the top of the clamp. With the onset of colder weather, pull this out and fill in the hole. During spells of severe frost, straw or litter spread over the clamp will give added protection; the most vulnerable parts, of course, are those facing north and east.

Inspect the clamp at intervals to make sure that rats or mice have not found it. If

there are tell-tale holes, fill them in and set traps for the culprits, making sure that these are safe for domestic pets.

If it is necessary to open the clamp during the winter months, make sure that it is adequately sealed up again, and never try to open it while frost is about.

Towards late spring (end of March), get the potatoes out of the clamp and rub off the sprouts. Any tubers that have been stored indoors should also be de-sprouted in the same way.

Onions

Onions do best in a medium to heavy loam; although lighter soils will produce good crops, the bulbs may be smaller.

Prepare the plot early so that winter frost and rain will settle the soil naturally; be sure your digging is completed by mid winter (December). Dig in as much manure and compost as possible, leave the ground rough and finish off with a dusting of lime.

In early or mid spring (February or March) when the soil is dry enough, break down the lumps with a cultivator and a rake. Tread it firmly to a fine tilth. There is a certain artistry and a lot of satisfaction in making a good onion bed.

You can grow onions in the same site year after year – *providing there is no soil-borne disease present.* To do so encourages a rich, fertile soil to build up over succeeding years.

Sowing
Onions will start to form bulbs about late summer (July), irrespective of when the seeds are sown. A late sowing will not mean late bulbing, but smaller bulbs. In general therefore, the earlier the seeds are sown, the larger the bulbs.

Grow onions in rich soil (far right) to produce beautiful golden bulbs like the Rijnsburger Yellow Globe (above)

Outdoor sowings can be made from early to late spring (February to April) whenever the ground is suitable, with a target date of mid spring (March) if possible. Sow the seeds thinly and evenly in drills 13mm ($\frac{1}{2}$ in) deep and 25–30cm (10–12 in) apart.

Sowing in autumn (August to October) gives the plants a longer time of growth and as autumn sowings come to maturity earlier than spring ones, the bulbs can be lifted early in the following autumn (August) while drying-off conditions are still favourable. If you do not time the sowing carefully the plants may get too far advanced by spring and go to seed.

The best sowing date for your area can be determined only by trial and error but, as a rough guide, you should reckon on the beginning of autumn (first week in August) for colder regions; one to two weeks later (mid August) for milder areas; and three to five weeks later (end of August or first week in September) for the more favourable climatic regions. Later sowings will need the protection of cloches throughout winter.

Plant onion sets in shallow drills

Planting onion sets

Growing onions from sets is an especially popular method in less favourable climates. An onion set is a small onion in an arrested state of development; when replanted it grows to full size. Some years ago sets were viewed with suspicion because of their tendency to go to seed, but with today's varieties this is less likely to happen. Some seedsmen are now combating the problem by storing the sets in a high temperature for several weeks. This kills the embryo flower-bud without harming the set.

Experience has shown that only a small percentage of treated sets go to seed, so they are worth the extra cost.

Plant onion sets towards late spring (March–April) in rows 30cm (12 in) apart allowing 10–15cm (4–6 in) between the bulbs (the closer planting will give bulbs large enough for kitchen use). Draw a drill just deep enough to cover the sets. It is sometimes recommended that the tips should show above the soil, but many gardeners prefer to cover them as this stops birds from pulling them out again.

Shuffle along drill to cover with earth

Care of plants

Hoe the soil lightly so that the roots are not disturbed. Keep autumn-sown plants weeded as long as possible or they may be so choked by spring that rescuing them could prove tedious and difficult.

Watering will help in a dry spell, but stop once the bulbs have formed and the tops (leaves) start to topple. The tops fall over when the bulbs begin to ripen as the supply of sap to the leaves is cut off. You can hasten the process by bending the tops with the back of a rake, but do be careful or the leaves may get bruised or broken. You would do better to let the tops go over naturally.

Ease up gently with fork before lifting

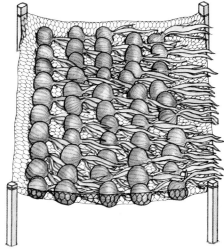

Before storing spread onions out on a bed of wire netting (above) with their roots facing south so that they receive the maximum amount of sun.
Onions are ready for lifting and drying off when their tops fall over (left)

Large onions

If you prefer large onions you will need a greenhouse that can be heated to 10°C (50°F). Make a start in late winter (January), sowing two or three seeds thinly every 4cm (1$\frac{1}{2}$ in) in trays of J. I. No 1 seed compost and thin to the strongest plant.

Harden them off before planting out in late spring (April). The plants must be 20–30cm (8–12 in) apart, with 30–40cm (12–15 in) between each row.

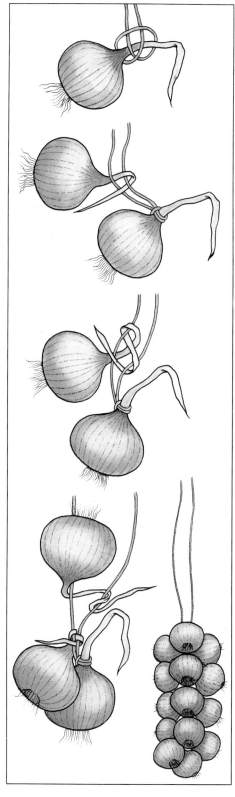

Pickling onions (top) need neither rich soil nor thinning out. For storing choose one of the long-keeping varieties such as Bedfordshire Champion (above)

Harvesting and storing

Beware at this stage of thinking that all the important work is behind you! More onion crops are ruined by poor harvesting and storing than by any other cause. They are ready to harvest when the leaves have turned yellow and the scales of the bulbs are brown. Ease them gently loose with a fork, pull them up and spread them out to dry.

Before storing make sure the bulbs are thoroughly dried off: leave them out in the open, turning them occasionally; place them in an empty frame, or on a path or wire netting suspended above the soil. An excellent drying method is to cover the bulbs with cloches, leaving the ends open to allow the wind to blow right through.

When the tops feel papery and the brown scales on the bulbs can be rubbed off, the onions are ready for storing. Put them in shallow boxes – tomato trays on legs (available from a greengrocer) are ideal as the air can circulate around them. Onions must be stored in a dry, airy place. They will stand some frost, but should be brought indoors during severe weather.

Making an onion string

A space-saving and popular idea is to string the onions together and hang them up instead of storing them away. Take a length of rope or cord and tie a large onion to one end. Using this as an anchor, secure the rest round the rope, building up from the bottom. Hang the completed onion string in a shed, garage or on a sunny wall.

White Lisbon (above) is one of the most popular spring onion varieties. For a constant supply sow 'little and often' throughout the spring and summer

Salad and pickling onions

Salad onions can be sown successionally from mid spring to mid summer (March to June). You can sow the seeds more thickly than for 'keeping' onions, and the rows need be only 15cm (6 in) apart. The plants are pulled while still green, starting when they are about pencil thickness. In dry periods water them well before pulling, and firm any plants that are left to grow on.

Thinnings from autumn and spring sowings of your keeping onions can also be used.

Pickling onions are easy to grow and they don't need rich soil. Sow the seeds thickly in a drill about 15cm (6 in) wide during late spring (April); no thinning is required. Harvest the bulbs in late summer (July).

Other types

There are several other kinds of onion which, although not so popular, are interesting to grow.

Welsh onion Forms a small, brownish, flat base; its stock can be raised from seeds sown in early or mid spring (February or March). Use the stems for salad onions. Keep a few clumps to plant again; split them up and replant in spring or autumn.

Japanese bunching onion Grows from seeds sown in late spring (April) and reaches full size in its second year. Like the Welsh specimen, use its shoots and leaves for salads and replant the clumps.

Everlasting onion Sow in spring or autumn. It is similar in habit to the Welsh and Japanese onions. Unfortunately it isn't widely distributed and might be difficult to obtain other than through catalogues of specialist growers.

Pests and diseases

It is as well to be forewarned of the likely attacks on your cherished plants.

Onion fly is the major hazard. It lays eggs at the base of the plants during early and mid summer (May and June) and the grubs burrow into the soil and attack the immature bulbs. Affected plants turn yellow, then collapse; they must be pulled up and burned. Make sure no larvae are left in the soil. The best safeguard is to apply calomel dust on each side of the rows when the plants are still at the 'crook' stage (before the seedlings have straightened up) and again about ten days later.

The pests are more active in light soils and with spring sowings. Autumn-sown bulbs and onion sets, although not immune, are less vulnerable to an attack.

White rot Fungus disease that causes the leaves of the plant to turn yellow and die. Roots rot and the base of the bulb is covered with a white mould. There is no cure and diseased plants must be burned.

Downy mildew Leaves die from the tips down and are covered with a fine, fluffy growth. It is also incurable, so burn any sick plants.

RECOMMENDED VARIETIES

For early and spring sowings
Ailsa Craig; Bedfordshire Champion; Blood Red.

For autumn sowings
Giant Zittau; Solidity; Reliance; Express Yellow.

Onion sets
Untreated: Stuttgarter Giant; Sturon. Treated: Rijnsburger Wijbo (formerly called Giant Fen Globe).

Salad onions
White Lisbon

Pickling onions
Paris Silverskin; The Queen; Cocktail.

Lettuce

Lettuce are not particularly fussy about their soil requirements – except that the earth must be well drained. They will grow quite happily between rows of slower-maturing plants. Whilst the surrounding soil must never be allowed to dry out, it is equally dangerous for it to become waterlogged. Cold, damp soils are not conducive to rapid growth and should be improved by the addition of sand and peat to lighten them. Light, dry soils can have their water-holding capacity increased by adding peat or other organic materials, such as manure.

Main types
With lettuce, perhaps more than with most vegetables, it is important to sow the right varieties at the right time. An understanding of the three main types is essential in order to have a steady supply over as long a period as possible. The **cabbage head** group can be subdivided into two classes: flat or smooth, that grow over a long period; and crisp or crinkled, that are mainly for summer cropping.

Cos This is a tall, pointed variety of which there are two kinds – large and intermediate. The cos is generally a summer crop that can be overwintered. While they are not nearly so popular as the cabbage lettuce, cos deserve to be more widely grown, and the intermediate ones are certainly gaining in popularity.

Loose-leaved This type does not make a heart, but produces a succession of tender leaves which can be picked as required. It has the advantage of standing well in hot weather.

Successional sowing
The aim of every salad-lover growing his own lettuce is to have a steady succession for as many months of the year as possible. This is easy to achieve on paper but much more difficult to accomplish in practise. Successional sowings, however carefully planned, have a habit of taking different times to mature according to different weather conditions – and these, unfortunately, are outside your control.

There are two ways of planning for succession. One is to make successional sowings of the *same* variety; the other is to sow two *different* varieties at the same time. Sometimes a combination of both methods will give the best results. If, for example, a flat lettuce is sown at the same time as a crisp variety, a succession

Row upon row of the beautiful pale-leaved Suzan, a smooth cabbage variety. Sow them under glass in autumn for transplanting early in the winter. The first of the crop will be ready for the table by late spring

is almost assured because, on average, the crisp varieties take longer to mature.

Transplanting is another aid to succession: transplanted plants, however carefully moved, are bound to be checked (slowed up) and so will take longer to mature than those left undisturbed.

In order to avoid having too many lettuces ready at once, the golden rule is to make small sowings at frequent intervals from mid to late spring (March to April), and transplant from these until mid summer (June). These sowings will be under glass. In summer months it is better to sow *in situ* (directly into the soil) and thin out, throwing away unwanted seedlings. This is because plants that are transplanted during this period are more liable to go to seed.

Growing under glass

The use of glass will help to extend the season at both ends. Few people will want to heat a greenhouse specially for growing lettuce, but where heat is needed for other plants, a few can be grown in deep boxes or in 13cm or 15cm (5 or 6 in) pots on the staging. Lack of daylight in winter is the main obstacle, and only the specially-bred varieties should be grown.

Heated frames Where heat is provided through a soil-warming cable buried a few centimetres below the surface, a frame is much more economical than a heated greenhouse, and can be used for growing lettuce – at a minimum temperature of 10–13°C (50–55°F) – during the winter. (A transformer will be needed to reduce the voltage, for safety reasons, and it cannot be too strongly emphasized that the equipment must be installed by a qualified electrician.)

Cold greenhouses These, and especially the glass-to-ground type (which traps all the available winter light and heat), are a boon to lettuce-growers as seeds sown in late summer can be planted out inside the greenhouse from late autumn to early winter (October to November).

Alternatively you can sow *outdoors* and bring the seedlings under glass at planting time. The lettuce will be ready for cutting from mid spring to early summer (March to May). Any plants that may be in the way if you have tomatoes ready for transplanting can be pulled up and used first.

Cold frames These are useful for providing an early crop, especially the metal types with glass all round. Seedlings that have been started under glass during the winter as already described, can be planted in the soil bed and the frames then put over them.

The older type of frame with sliding

Three crisp, sweet lettuce that are sown outdoors for summer and autumn salads. Webb's Wonderful (above) and Lobjoit's Green Cos (below right) last well in hot, dry weather. Little Gem (right) is also known as Sugar Cos

lights (glass lids) generally requires a soil bed to be made up inside it, so that the soil level is raised and the plants are reasonably close to the glass.

Growing under cloches

The simplest method of growing lettuce under glass is to use cloches. The tent-shaped (inverted 'V') cloches will cover a single row (or two of a small variety) while barn cloches (shaped like miniature greenhouses), cover three rows. Glass is preferable, but there are various plastic and polythene cloches available that are satisfactory provided they can be securely anchored and are not in too exposed a position.

Sow the seeds directly into the soil – which will have warmed up a little if you place the cloches in position a week or two before sowing. Sow as thinly as possible, in drills about 12mm ($\frac{1}{2}$ in) deep. Thin out or transplant the young plants as soon as they are about 10cm (3–4 in) high. Subsequent cultivation consists simply of keeping the surrounding soil clear by weeding and hoeing, but you must take care not to damage the roots which lie just below the surface. It is also a good idea to give a liquid feed every

ten days while they are actively growing.

Lettuce do best in an open, sunny position, but some shade is an advantage for those maturing during the hottest months, so put them in the lea of a row of runner beans or other tall plants.

General pests

The main pests to guard against are slugs, birds and aphides. Slug bait will help to keep them down and spraying with a good insecticide will control the greenfly. It is wise to spray occasionally before the hearts have formed, even if no greenfly can be seen, as it is impossible to get at them once the lettuce begin to 'heart up'.

Watch out for birds as they can soon ruin a promising crop, sparrows being especially notorious for this. The old method of using black cotton (not thread) is still effective. Simply push in sticks at intervals and then run the cotton from stick to stick, just clear of the plants. A

Unrivalled (left) and Tom Thumb (above left) can be sown 'little and often' for cutting from spring to autumn

touch of the cotton on a bird's wings is enough to send it winging away. Or you can try proprietary bird repellents.

Main diseases

The two main diseases are mosaic disease and grey mould (*Botrytis cinerea*). Mosaic shows up as stunted growth and a yellow mottling of the leaves. It is a virus spread by aphides and once plants are attacked there is no cure, which is another good reason for early spraying against aphides.

Grey mould is much more widespread and serious. Affected plants wilt and then collapse. If a collapsed plant is pulled up you will find that the stem has turned brown and rotted at soil level. Although there is no cure at this stage, some measure of control is possible by spraying the fungicide Benlate at the first sign of trouble.

Grey mould is generally a disease of plants grown under glass or cloches and is rarely encountered outdoors. This gives us a valuable clue to its prevention – adequate ventilation. Where plants under

RECOMMENDED VARIETIES

Type	Variety	When to sow	When to transplant	When to cut	How to grow
smooth cabbage	Kwiek	early autumn	late autumn	mid winter to early spring	heated greenhouse or frame
	Premier Suzan	mid autumn	early winter	late spring to mid summer	cold frames, cold greenhouses or cloches
	Imperial	early autumn	thin out instead	early summer to mid summer	outdoors
	Tom Thumb	early spring and early autumn	thin out instead	early summer, and late autumn to early winter	outdoors; good under cloches
crisp cabbage	Unrivalled All The Year Round	mid spring to early summer	late spring to mid summer	mid summer to early autumn	outdoors
large cos	Webb's Wonderful Avoncrisp	mid spring to early summer	late spring to mid summer	late summer to mid autumn	outdoors
intermediate cos	Lobjoits Green Paris White	mid spring to late summer	late spring to mid summer	late summer to mid autumn	outdoors
	Little Gem (also listed as Sugar Cos)	mid spring to late summer	late spring to mid summer	mid summer to mid autumn	outdoors; good under cloches
	Winter Density	mid autumn	early winter, or thin out instead	late spring to mid summer	under cloches
loose-leaved	Salad Bowl	mid spring to early summer	thin out instead	mid summer to mid autumn	pick leaves as required

Key to seasons

early spring (February)	early summer (May)	early autumn (August)	early winter (November)
mid spring (March)	mid summer (June)	mid autumn (September)	mid winter (December)
late spring (April)	late summer (July)	late autumn (October)	late winter (January)

glass are given plenty of ventilation, grey mould should not be a problem. Open up frames in all but the severest weather; leave a slight gap between cloches, and where there is a ventilating pane, close it only in hard weather. Lettuce are much tougher than is generally supposed.

Another safeguard against grey mould is good hygiene. Yellow leaves, or any lying flat on the soil, should be removed, and any affected plants disposed of at once. Keep the plants free from weeds, with a good circulation of air round them.

Care of plants

When it is necessary to water lettuce in frames or greenhouses, do so early in the morning so that the soil has time to dry out before nightfall. Water the soil *between* the plants and keep it off the leaves as much as possible. There should be no need to water those under cloches during the winter, as enough water will seep in from the soil at the sides.

Outdoor varieties Most of these need about 30cm sq (12 in sq) in which to mature, but under glass this can be reduced to 23cm sq (9 in sq) so that the optimum use is made of the glass. The variety Tom Thumb is small, quick-maturing and needs only 15cm sq (6 in sq). It makes a useful crop for both early and late sowings.

Imperial is one of several varieties which can winter outdoors in a sheltered spot for maturing in early spring. These varieties will survive an average winter, though they may not come through a severe one. The increasing use of cloches, however, means that these 'winter' varieties are of less importance now, and they are being replaced by more tender ones.

Cutting time

Cabbage lettuce should be firm when pressed gently at the top of the heart; test a cos by pressing at the tip – never squeezing from the sides. With your early spring crop, it is a good plan to plant at 13–15cm (5–6 in) intervals and then to cut every other lettuce when the row begins to look crowded. These surplus plants, although not properly hearted, will be welcome, and mean an earlier start to the season.

One final point: nothing equals home-grown lettuce for freshness and flavour, but do cut them when they are at their best. Avoid the heat of the day, when they are limp and flaccid, and cut them in the early morning or late evening.

The loose curly leaves of Salad Bowl are picked individually as required

Spinach and spinach substitutes

Spinach is an excellent 'food value' vegetable, rich in vitamins A, B1, B2, and C. It also contains useful quantities of calcium, protein and iron. For spinach lovers there are also several other leaf vegetables – perpetual spinach, New Zealand spinach and Good King Henry – that have a similar flavour.

SUMMER SPINACH

The round-seeded or summer spinach can be sown from mid spring through mid summer (March to the end of June) and is 'in pick' 8–10 weeks after sowing. It needs a fertile soil with good, moisture-retaining properties. On light or hungry soils the danger is that the plants will soon go to seed.

If the ground is being prepared especially for this crop, dig in some manure or good compost during the winter months. Some well-dampened peat may also be incorporated and will help to keep the soil moist. In many cases, however, spinach can be used as an intercrop; for example, it can be grown between rows of peas or dwarf beans.

Sowings maturing during the summer will benefit from a little shade for part of the day. Good sites for these sowings are between rows of tall peas or in the lee of a row of runner beans.

Sow the seeds thinly in drills 2–3cm (1 in) deep and 30cm (12 in) apart. As soon as the seedlings are big enough to handle, thin them to stand 15cm (6 in) apart. When the plants have grown until they touch each other, take out every other plant and use them in the kitchen.

Regular hoeing will keep the weeds down by creating a loose, dry, layer of earth that acts as a mulch. Water during dry spells; do not allow the plants to dry out or they will go to seed.

Picking can begin as soon as the leaves are large enough. Cut the leaves off close to the stem, taking a few from each plant.

Even well-grown plants of summer spinach will not crop for long, and to keep up a regular supply it is necessary to make successional sowings every two or three weeks.

WINTER SPINACH

The prickly, or winter, spinach – 'prickly' applies to the seeds, not the plants – is sown in early to mid autumn (August to September) for use during the winter

months. It makes a good follow-on crop to some of the earlier sowings. Before sowing, rake in a general fertilizer at 70g per sq m (2 oz per sq yd). An open site with some shelter from cold winds is preferable. Sow the seeds in drills 2–3cm (1 in) deep and 30cm (12 in) apart. Thin the seedlings to stand 23cm (9 in) apart. If the soil is dry at the time of sowing, water the drills well beforehand. Once established there should be no watering problem as the normal rainfall of an average autumn and winter will be enough for their needs.

Although the plants are hardy they give a better and cleaner crop if some protection can be given, ideally with cloches, during the winter months. Straw or short litter tucked around the plants is one way of doing this.

Picking is the same as for summer spinach, the largest leaves being taken first; but pick rather more sparingly as leaf production in the winter months is slower. In early spring a dressing of nitro-chalk at 35g per sq m (1 oz per sq yd) will help the plants along, by increasing production of leafy growth which in turn will help to give you earlier spinach pickings.

SPINACH SUBSTITUTES

In addition to 'true' spinach there are several spinach-type vegetables that have a similar flavour. All are very little troubled by pests and diseases.

Perpetual spinach This is another name for spinach beet (which was included in the leaf beets described in Week 23). The leaves of spinach beet are thicker and fleshier than those of the true spinach and are preferred by many people for this reason.

Sow in drills 2–3cm (1 in) deep and 38–45cm (15–18 in) apart, and thin the plants to stand 23cm (9 in) apart. Sow in late spring (April) for summer use and in early autumn (August) for winter use. If the winter row can be cloched, a heavier and cleaner crop will result. Pick the leaves as they become large enough and never let any leaves grow on until they become tough, or the production of new leaves will be hindered.

New Zealand spinach This half-hardy annual thrives best in a light to medium soil and in a sunny position. Unlike summer spinach it will tolerate hot, dry conditions without running to seed. It has a low, spreading habit and needs plenty of room. Allow 90cm (3 ft) between the plants.

For an early crop, sow in mid spring (March) under glass and prick the seedlings off into 9cm (3½ in) pots, ready for planting out towards mid summer

Above left: Viking, a comparatively new summer spinach variety
Below left: low-growing New Zealand spinach thrives in hot, dry conditions
Below: versatile Good King Henry, another spinach substitute, that can also replace broccoli on the menu

(late May). Alternatively, sow *in situ* in late spring (April) and cover with cloches until the risk of frost has gone. If protection cannot be given, delay sowing until early summer (mid May). The seeds are hard and should be soaked overnight before sowing.

Keep the plants watered in dry spells, and pinch back the shoots to encourage the production of more leaf-bearing sideshoots. The dark green, triangular leaves are smaller than those of summer spinach but picking is done in the same way (by taking individual leaves). Plants bear freely until cut down by frost.

Good King Henry This is a hardy, perennial plant, not widely known outside its native English county of Lincolnshire. It is a useful, dual-purpose plant; in the spring shoots are produced from the leaf axils and these can be cut and cooked like spring broccoli. Later the large triangular leaves can be used as a substitute for spinach.

The plants can be propagated by division or from seeds sown in late spring or early summer (April or May) in drills 30cm (12 in) apart. Soak the seeds overnight before sowing. When the seedlings are large enough, thin them to stand 30cm (12 in) apart.

Because the plant is a perennial and needs to build up its reserves for the following season, shoots should not be taken later than mid summer (June), but leaves can be removed until early autumn (August).

Radishes

Radishes prefer a light-to-medium, fertile loam; they do not like cold, wet soils. The best radishes are those that are grown quickly. The summer radishes are better known, and if it takes them more than six weeks to reach the pulling stage they will usually be 'woody' (tough and stringy) rather than 'hot'.

A soil that was manured for the previous crop is the best choice. If there is some good, well-rotted compost available it can be pricked into the top few centimetres of soil. It is a good plan to mix this with equal parts of a good brand of moistened peat, to keep the soil damp.

SUMMER RADISHES

The summer varieties may be round, oval or long. For early forcing and growing under cloches the round varieties are to be preferred. Where successional sowings are to be made it is not economical to buy the seed in small packets. Buy in larger packets or by the 28g (1 oz). Nowadays, several seedsmen offer packets of mixed radish seeds. These are a good buy for the main sowings as they prolong the period of pulling.

How to sow

Make small, successional sowings to avoid having too many come ready at

Three recommended varieties for summer: quick-growing Scarlet Globe (above left) has crisp, delicately-flavoured flesh; sweet-tasting Icicle (right) – seen with globe-shaped Sparkler – is also quick growing and crisp; and king-sized Red Prince (above) is a juicy, tasty newcomer

once, for the roots should be pulled when they are at their best. Radishes are the ideal intercrop and should never need to have ground reserved especially for them. They can be grown between rows of peas or beans, on the sides of celery trenches, or in the spaces reserved for brassicas; anywhere, in fact, where there is a patch of ground that will not be needed for the next six to eight weeks.

Radishes are also useful as 'markers'. If a few seeds are trickled along the drill when slow-growing crops such as parsnips, onions or parsley are sown, the radishes will come through first, thus enabling you to identify the rows and hoe between them before the other seedlings are through.

Sowings can begin in early spring (February) in frames or under cloches, or in mid spring (March) outdoors. Where lettuces have been sown under cloches, a single line of radishes may be sown

between the rows of lettuce. These will be cleared before the lettuce need all the room available.

Successional sowings outdoors can be made at 10–14 day intervals. From late summer until mid autumn (late June until early September) make the sowings, if possible, in the lee of taller subjects such as peas or beans so that the radishes will have some shade for part of the day.

Except for single rows under cloches, do not sow the seeds in a V-shaped drill; instead sow thinly in a broad band about 15cm (6 in) wide. Make the sowing on the soil surface and then rake thoroughly with a rake or cultivator. This will put

Flea beetle This pest eats holes in the leaves and can decimate a crop if not checked. Prevention is better than cure, so as soon as seedlings are through the soil, dust them with derris. Renew the application if rain washes it off. When the plants are past the seedling stage, the danger is over.

Birds Sparrows particularly may attack the seedlings, but a few strands of black cotton criss-crossed over the rows will be enough to drive them away.

WINTER RADISHES

The winter radishes are not nearly so well known as the summer ones, but they are not difficult to grow and seed is easy enough to obtain as most seedsmen stock the main varieties. There are both round and long types. They are much larger than summer radishes, with roots weighing up to 500g (1 lb) each. They can be used as a vegetable but are generally sliced thinly for use in winter salads.

The seeds should not be sown until late summer (July). This makes them useful as a follow-on crop to some of the earlier sowings. Sow the seeds thinly in drills 13mm ($\frac{1}{2}$ in) deep and 25cm (10 in) apart, and when the plants are large enough to handle, thin them to stand 20cm (8 in) apart. Keep the plants clean by hoeing and weeding and see that they do not lack water during dry periods.

The roots will be ready for use from late autumn (October) onwards. They will store well in boxes of dry sand or soil in a little clamp, but in light-to-medium loams they can be left in the ground to be dug as required. In severe weather cover the roots with a little straw or litter, to prevent them deteriorating.

most of the seeds just beneath the soil surface, which is deep enough.

Thinning and tending

If any thinning is necessary, do it as soon as the plants are big enough to handle. Ideally one plant to every 6 sq cm (1 sq in) is enough. It is not customary to weed radishes as the crop is on the ground for such a short time. Generally speaking, each radish patch can be pulled over three or four times. Any plants that are left after this will have failed to develop properly or will be too tough, so hoe them up with the weeds and put them on the compost heap.

Two recommended varieties for winter: Black Spanish, available in both round (above left) and long (above) forms, and China Rose (top). Like all winter radishes, they are much larger than summer varieties and can be used as vegetable or salad

Radishes should never be allowed to dry out, especially on light soils; in dry periods give them plenty of water to keep them moving.

Pests and diseases

Flea beetle and birds are the main enemies of the radish grower.

RECOMMENDED VARIETIES

SUMMER RADISHES

Cherry Belle Globe-shaped and scarlet; good for forcing under cloches.
French Breakfast Red with white tips; a long radish and one of the best known.
Icicle Long, all-white radish.
Scarlet Globe Early and crisp.
Red Prince Recent introduction, two or three times the usual size.
Yellow Gold Egg-shaped, yellow radish with white flesh.

WINTER RADISHES

China Rose Oval root, about 15cm (6 in) in length; rose-coloured with white flesh.
Black Spanish Black skin and white flesh; available in both round and long forms.
Mino Early Japanese introduction with white flesh and a mild flavour.

Beetroot and leaf beets

The first tender, succulent young roots of beetroot are one of the joys of the vegetable gardener's year. Furthermore it is a root which most people can grow without difficulty.

There are three types of beetroot – the globe beet (which is the most popular), the intermediate or cylindrical beet and the long beet. Although the long beet is still grown commercially and for exhibition, it has been superseded to a great extent by the other two kinds. For early sowings always use the globe beet. The intermediate beet is bigger but it grows more slowly, so it is more suitable for maincrop use.

Sowing the seed clusters
Beetroot is unusual in that each 'seed' is really a capsule containing several seeds. Extra care should be taken, therefore, to sow thinly. You can sow early crops in a continuous row, but where the maincrop and late sowings are concerned, it is better to sow one or two seed clusters at 10cm (4 in) intervals and then thin to the strongest plant. The drills should be 2–3cm (1 in) deep and 30cm (12 in) apart.

Sow seed capsules thinly at intervals

Early sowings
For an early crop, sow in early spring (February) in a cold frame or under cloches. A barn cloche will take three rows, 23cm (9 in) apart. Outdoor sowings can begin after the middle of spring (after mid March). Although the beetroot is a biennial plant, forming a root in its first year and seed in the second, it can telescope this process if sown early, and throw up seed stalks in the first year. Gardeners describe this as 'bolting'. For these early sowings, therefore, choose a variety which is known to have some resistance to bolting.

Maincrop sowings
Do not sow maincrop beetroot too early – towards the end of early summer (mid May to early June) is a good time. If you

are sowing in late summer (July), go back to using the small, globe beet as these are the quickest to mature, providing the summer is not too hot and the autumn mild. They will give tender young roots for use in late autumn and early winter (October and November).

Long beetroot need a deep, fertile soil, free from stones. They should be thinned to 23cm (9 in) apart with 38–45cm (15–18 in) between the rows.

Tending beetroot
In periods of drought give the beetroot a good soaking of water to keep them

growing. Dry weather tends to affect the eating quality of the roots; it is also one cause of the plants 'bolting'.

Be very careful when hoeing beetroot; once the leaves have begun to hide the roots do not hoe too close to the rows. A tiny nick at this stage will turn into an ugly crack later on; so if need be, hand weed around the plants.

Harvesting and storing
Beetroot are ready for pulling as soon as they are big enough to use, and some thinning of the earliest sowings can be done in this way. However, it always pays

to do a little preliminary thinning as soon as the plants are big enough to handle. beetroot is relatively hardy but can be injured by severe frost, and it is wise to lift the roots by about the end of autumn (end of October). The foliage shows the approach of maturity by beginning to lose its bright, fresh colour.

Ease the roots up with a fork and rub off any soil adhering to them. Take great care, when digging up long beet, so that the roots are not damaged. Twist off the tops about 5cm (2 in) from the crown. Long beetroot have a much greater tendency to 'bleed' when cut than the other kinds; to prevent this always twist off their tops.

Sort the roots through, putting on one side any that are cracked or damaged for immediate use, and store the remainder in boxes of peat, sand or soil – a thin layer of roots followed by a layer of the medium, until the box is full. The medium should be just damp enough to stop the roots from shrivelling. An alternative method is to make a little clamp (as you do for carrots) in the garden.

Other types of beetroot

In addition to the ordinary beetroot there are several leaf beets that make excellent vegetables. Here the process is reversed, for it is the leaves which are used and not the roots. All the leaf beets throw up flowering stems in their second year. Let these run up (but not to seeding point), then chop them up and put them on the compost heap.

Above: twist off tops to prevent 'bleeding'
Right: pull spinach beet leaves as needed
Above left: beetroot in a straw-lined storage clamp
Left: a popular globe beet, Avonearly, and right, Detroit variety

Spinach beet Probably the best known of the spinach beets and a substitute for spinach. It also appears in the catalogues as Perpetual Spinach. The roots, when at their peak, produce lots of thick, fleshy leaves which you can boil like spinach, but without boiling them down nearly so much. To harvest, take a few leaves from each plant; fresh leaves will grow in their place.

Sow spinach beet in mid or late spring (March or April) in rows 2–3cm (1 in) deep and 38–45cm (15–18 in) apart. Thin the plants to 23cm (9 in). They require no other attention, except for hoeing and watering in dry weather. A good row of spinach beet will give pickings for a year; but if you make a sowing in early autumn (August), this will give plenty of young leaves for picking in the spring. The advantage of an early autumn (August) sowing, where space is at a premium, is that you can use it as a follow-on crop to some of the earlier vegetables.

Seakale beet or Swiss chard The plant produces large fleshy leaves with a broad white mid-rib. This is a dual-purpose vegetable, for in addition to using the leaves as spinach, the broad mid-ribs can be cut out, chopped in pieces and used as a substitute for seakale *Crambe maritima*, which is grown for its tender shoots that must be forced.

Sowing times and distances, and cultivation are the same as for spinach beet, and the early autumn sowing is particularly useful where space is a problem. The seed is usually listed as seakale beet or Swiss chard, but there is now an F.1 hybrid called Vintage Green, which is said to be more vigorous and prolific. Spinach beet and seakale beet (Swiss chard) are both forms of *Beta vulgaris cicla*, but the latter provides leaves as well as mid-rib shoots for eating.

Ruby chard An ornamental form of Swiss chard with long, bright red stalks and crumpled leaves and can be cooked in the same way as seakale beet. Sowing and cultivation are as for seakale beet.

Below: Boltardy, a magnificent example of a globe beetroot
Bottom: two forms of Swiss chard, seakale beet (left) and ruby chard (right)

Pests and diseases
Blackfly and boron deficiency can be a problem when growing beetroot.
Blackfly Keep a close watch for this insect and spray with derris at the first sign of trouble.
Boron deficiency Causes the heart leaves to turn black, and black spots appear inside the roots. If you have encountered this trouble before, take preventive action by watering the plants with a foliar feed containing trace elements.

RECOMMENDED VARIETIES

GLOBE BEETROOT
Boltardy (resistant to bolting)
Avonearly (resistant to bolting)
Early Bunch (resistant to bolting)
Crimson Globe
Burpee's Golden (for leaves and roots)
Snowhite
Detroit Little Ball (late sowings)

INTERMEDIATE BEETROOT
Cylindra
Housewives' Choice

LONG BEETROOT
Cheltenham Green Top
Long Blood Red

SEAKALE BEET/SWISS CHARD
Vintage Green (F.1 hybrid)

Carrots

In length carrots may be short, intermediate or long. In shape they may be round, cylindrical with a blunt end (known as stump-rooted or short-horn), or tapering. From a harvesting point of view they fall roughly into four groups: early round; early stump-rooted (picked young in bunches); intermediate and long. The intermediate and long carrots are grown for storing and using during the winter months; they may either be stump-rooted or tapering.

If space in the garden is at a premium it may be necessary to drop intermediate and long (maincrop) varieties from the cropping programme and concentrate on 'bunching' carrots—young carrots from the early stump-rooted varieties.

Soil requirements
The ideal carrot soil is a light but deep loam which does not dry out too quickly. Such soils are found naturally in various parts of the country, although they are not widespread. Fortunately, carrots will do reasonably well in most soils, with the exception of sticky clays and very light soils. In heavy loams they may split in wet weather, and in shallow soils only the stump-rooted varieties are suitable. In stony soil they may become misshapen or the roots may fork.

Fresh manure is not suitable for carrots as it may also cause forking roots, but you can use well-rotted manure or compost if it is dug or forked in a week or two before sowing. The tap root (main root) of a carrot should be able to go straight down into a soil where the food values are evenly distributed; a site previously well-manured and cultivated for a crop like potatoes is ideal. Before sowing rake in a balanced fertilizer, such as Growmore, at 70g per sq m (2 oz per sq yd).

Sowing under glass
If a heated frame is available, sow round or stump-rooted carrots in late winter (January). It is better to delay sowing in a cold frame or under cloches until early spring (mid-February). Make up a bed, about 23cm (9 in) deep, of prepared soil in the frame and sow the seeds thinly in rows 15cm (6 in) apart. The soil should be a good, riddled loam with some coarse garden sand and peat added. (The John Innes formula of 7 parts loam, 3 parts peat and 2 parts sand is a good guide.)

If using one of the modern glass-to-ground frames, fork over the bed, removing any large stones, and add some well-moistened peat and the balanced fertilizer. For sowing under cloches, prepare the soil strip in the same way. A large barn cloche 58cm (23 in) wide will take four rows of carrots sown 15cm (6 in) apart or five rows sown at 10cm (4 in) apart. Prepare the soil in good time so that you can put down the cloches three or four weeks before sowing. This will warm up the soil and give the crop a better start.

Below: easing up carrots with fork before lifting. Below left: prime examples of stump-rooted Chantenay Red Cored

Outdoor sowings

Sow (thinly) outdoors from mid spring (mid March) until late summer (mid July). Make the intermediate maincrop sowings in early summer (May or early June). It used to be recommended to sow considerably earlier than these times, but it has been found that later sowings are more likely to escape the carrot fly.

Long carrots should be sown by early summer (mid May); so limit late spring (April) sowings to small sowings of the early stump-rooted varieties which can be harvested quickly before the long varieties go in. Stump-rooted varieties can be used again in late summer (July) to give tender young roots for pulling in autumn. For outdoor sowings, allow 20–23cm (8–9 in) between rows for early short-horn varieties and 25–30cm (10–12 in) for maincrops.

Block method Another way of growing carrots is to sow a block of six rows only 8–10cm (3–4 in) apart. If sowing more than one block put a 60cm (2 ft) wide path between blocks. Plants kept in rows are easier to weed. The seeds in the blocks can be sown broadcast but this means more hand-weeding. Eventually the foliage takes over and stops further weeds from growing. An old table knife, heated and then bent over at the end, makes a useful tool for hoeing such narrow rows. The block method is space-saving and gives a heavier crop over a given area, but the individual roots may be a little smaller.

Thinning the seedlings

Theoretically you should sow carrots so thinly that no thinning out is necessary. But as this is hardly practical, just aim to sow as thinly as possible.

While some thinning can be left until the pulled roots are big enough to use, always make a preliminary thinning to 2–5cm (1–2 in). Thin maincrops to stand 8–10cm (3–4 in) apart, and the late summer (July) sowings to 5–8cm (2–3 in). Do this as soon as the plants are big enough to handle. With the late summer (July) sowings it is essential to thin the plants as early as possible or they will not have time to make usable roots.

In dry weather water the rows well before thinning. Afterwards, always firm the soil back with your feet and water again. Never leave thinnings lying around as they may attract the carrot fly. Drop them into a bucket as they are pulled out and put them on the compost heap. Do

Top: round carrots are particularly good on shallow soils. Left: cylindrical Early Nantes is excellent for the first spring sowings in frames or under cloches

not make early pullings from the maincrop rows as this also helps the carrot fly by leaving uncovered soil in which eggs can be laid; leave the roots in until harvest time comes round.

Lifting and storing

Lift and store maincrop carrots for the winter months. Although in theory carrots are hardy enough to spend the winter outdoors, in practice it is better to dig them up. Slug damage may occur during mild periods and heavy rains can cause cracking if they are left in the ground too long.

Lift the roots in late autumn or early winter (the end of October). By that time the foliage will have lost its rich green and turned a dull colour. Carefully ease up the roots with a fork before pulling them out, and rub off any soil. Cut the tops off

Cover them with a layer of hay, straw, dried bracken or any dry litter which will not rot, and cover this, in turn, with about 10–15cm (4–6 in) of soil, leaving a wisp of the covering material sticking out of the top as an air vent to prevent the carrots going off. A heavier soil covering is not necessary. Although slight frost will not harm the carrots if it penetrates into the clamp, it is wise to leave them undisturbed until the frost has gone. In mid spring (March) push off the soil covering or the roots will rapidly make new growth. Rub off any new shoots that may have formed, and transfer the carrots to a box for use.

Pests and ailments

The foliage of healthy, growing carrots should be a rich, lustrous green. If it loses this richness, suspect either greenfly or carrot fly.

of spraying. Weathered soot (soot from house chimneys which has been stored under cover for about six months) is also a help in keeping the fly away and has a slight nitrogenous value. Although later sowings often escape the flies, they are not immune.

Bright sunlight Sometimes causes greening of the roots at the shoulders (just below the leaf stems). Although this is not a serious ailment, it does detract from their appearance. Prevent this problem by drawing a little soil up over the tops of the roots if they are exposed. Where carrots are grown close together the leaves will give adequate protection.

Below: for indoor storage, pack carrots head to tail between layers of dry sand
Bottom: carrots can be stored outdoors in a clamp made of straw and soil

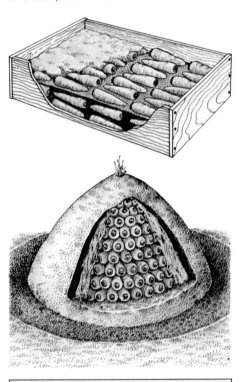

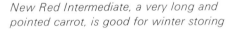

New Red Intermediate, a very long and pointed carrot, is good for winter storing

about 13mm ($\frac{1}{2}$ in) from the crown. Put aside for first use any carrots which are split or damaged.

The sound roots can be stored in one of two ways. For storage in a garage or shed, take a wooden box and put a layer of sand, peat or reasonably dry soil in the bottom. Follow this with a layer of carrots packed head to tail. Alternate layers of covering and carrots until the box is full. The covering medium prevents the roots from shrivelling.

To store carrots outdoors, keep them in a little clamp. Pack the carrots in a conical heap with the roots pointing inward.

Greenfly The delicate, ferny foliage is liable to be attacked by these pests (aphides), but they can be prevented if the crop is sprayed with derris.

Carrot fly Appears any time from late spring to mid summer (April to June) and lays eggs in the soil close to the roots. As the maggots hatch and attack the roots, the foliage first takes on a reddish tinge and then turns yellow. The little cracks and tunnels made in the roots are often enlarged by slugs and wireworms until the vegetables are of little value. Prevent carrot fly by dusting the seed-drills with an insecticide such as BHC before the seeds are sown, or by spraying the young plants with a trichlorphon-based insecticide. Do not eat the vegetables within three weeks

RECOMMENDED VARIETIES

EARLY ROUND
Parisian Rondo

EARLY STUMP-ROOTED (SHORT-HORN)
Amsterdam Forcing
Early Horn
Early Nantes

MAINCROP SHORT
James' Intermediate
Chantenay Red Cored
Autumn King

MAINCROP LONG
St Valery
New Red Intermediate

Parsnips

Parsnips do best in deep, loamy soil (shallow, stony ground is suitable only for the stump-rooted varieties). Grow them on ground that was well-manured for a previous crop; fresh manure can cause the roots to fork. If your soil is not already limed, rake in a dressing of garden lime at 70g sq m (2 oz per sq yd).

When to sow

Start sowing in early to mid spring (February to March), when the soil is easily worked to a fine tilth. You can sow as late as mid to late spring (mid April) and still get good-sized roots.

Make shallow drills (furrows) with a hoe or side of a rake, 2·5cm (1 in) deep and 40cm (15 in) apart, and sow a few seeds at 15cm (6 in) intervals.

Parsnip seeds are very light, so choose a calm day for sowing. (Alternatively you can use pelleted seeds.) They are slow to germinate, and the best way to keep weeds under control is to sow a few fast-germinating radish seeds between each parsnip station (cluster of seeds). When the radishes are large enough for eating, pull them up and hoe the soil.

Parsnip seeds soon lose their viability (ability to germinate), and any left over from a packet should be thrown away.

Tending and harvesting

Once the seeds are sown all you have to do is keep the plants free from weeds until their foliage meets. Autumn frost cuts down the foliage but does not harm the roots: in fact, unlike some crops, parsnips taste even better when they have been frosted.

Leave the roots in the ground in winter and dig them up as required. If severe weather threatens, lift a few roots and keep them in a box of sand or dry soil in a shed or garage, so that you have a supply if the ground becomes frozen.

The end of the harvesting season is mid spring (March), when new growth is seen. Dig up all remaining roots at this time before they become woody.

Parsnips are generally free from pests, but there is an incurable disease known as parsnip canker, which is encouraged by cold, damp soil. The symptoms are cracks on the shoulder of the root, followed by brown patches and, in severe cases, rotting of the crown. A wet autumn after a dry spell encourages canker to develop in the root.

Later-sown crops are not so liable to suffer an attack, and once the trouble has been encountered, the next year's seeds should not be sown before late spring (April): use a canker-resistant variety.

Smooth, long-rooted Tender and True parsnips (right), show a marked resistance to canker. Equally smooth is the stump-rooted variety (below)

RECOMMENDED VARIETIES

Improved Hollow Crown Long, well-shaped roots.
Tender and True Long, smooth roots.
Offenham Stump-rooted, with broad shoulders.
The Student Intermediate roots of good quality.
Avonresister Small, conical roots. This variety has some resistance to parsnip canker.

Brussels sprouts

You can choose from tall, half-tall and dwarf varieties of sprouts. The dwarf and half-tall types are especially useful for small gardens and exposed sites. There are now a number of F.1 hybrids that give uniform sprouts of medium size and these varieties are specially recommended for freezing.

Plants are readily available from market stalls or garden centres; choose plants that are a healthy green colour and not too large.

Preparing the site

Choose an open site where the soil is 'in good heart'. Sprouts need plenty of nourishment and will not do well in poor soils. A medium to heavy loam is the best choice, but they will do quite well in lighter soils providing the site has been prepared several months in advance.

This early preparation is all-important. Dig in as much manure or compost as you can spare. Farmyard manure is still the best, but is often difficult to come by.

Useful alternatives are spent mushroom compost, deep litter from poultry houses, or garden compost. It does not matter if the compost is not fully rotted as the process of decomposition will be continued in the soil. Try to complete the manuring and digging by the end of the year and leave the soil rough.

If garden lime has not been used recently, apply it during early or mid spring (February or March) at about 135g per sq m (4 oz per sq yd); but do not apply it within 3–4 months of manuring. In mid spring (March) break down the soil with a cultivator.

One of the disadvantages of growing sprouts is that ground must be reserved for them; unlike cabbages or cauliflowers they cannot be used for double cropping as the planting period is too early. Planting should be completed before late summer (the end of June) and preferably a couple of weeks earlier.

However, by careful planning, the ground can be cropped until the sprouts are quite well grown. Lettuce, radishes, spring onions and summer spinach, or turnips, beetroot and carrots for pulling young, may be sown in rows 60–75cm (2–2½ ft) apart. It is then a simple matter to plant out the sprouts between the rows of the earlier crops. These will be cleared by the time the sprouts need the space.

When and how to sow

When you sow depends on when you want to harvest. For a very early crop – in

Left: good, even-sized sprouts. Below: recommended variety Irish Elegance

mid autumn (September) – sow in an unheated greenhouse in late winter (January). When the seedlings are big enough to handle, prick them off, 5–8cm (2–3 in) apart, into trays about 15cm (6 in) deep. Alternatively, sow outdoors in early or mid autumn (August or September) and then cover the young plants with cloches later. Four rows, 10cm (4 in) apart, can be accommodated under a barn cloche.

There is, however, little point in having brussels sprouts while there is still a selection of autumn vegetables available. Many gardeners consider that sprouts taste much better after the first frost. For a mid season picking from late autumn to mid winter (October through December), sow outdoors in early to mid spring (late February or March). Where this early sowing is likely to present problems (as in cold areas or on heavy soils), place cloches in position a few weeks in advance of sowing to warm up the soil.

For a late picking from the middle of winter (late December) onwards, sow in mid to late spring (March or the first week or two in April). Plants from these sowings should be ready for moving in early or mid summer (May or June). Sow the seeds thinly in short rows 13mm ($\frac{1}{2}$ in) deep, and when the seedlings are big

enough to handle, thin them to 5cm (2 in) apart. This gives straighter and stronger plants. Dust the seedlings with derris to protect them from flea beetle.

How to transplant

When the plants are about 20cm (8 in) high they are ready for transplanting. Ease them out with a fork, then separate them carefully and move them with as much soil as possible. A showery period is the best time for transplanting but this cannot always be arranged! In dry periods water the seedbed well a few hours before transplanting.

To protect the young plants from cabbage-root fly, either dip the roots of each plant in a paste made from calomel dust or sprinkle a small teaspoonful of the dust around each plant.

It is important to plant firmly, with the lower leaves just clear of the soil. A dibber or trowel is needed for this work; a trowel is better as it makes a bigger hole and avoids cramping the roots. A simple test for firmness is to pull gently at the topmost leaf of a plant. If the plant 'gives' it is not firm enough; if the end of the leaf tears, all is well.

The planting distances for sprouts are 68–75cm ($2\frac{1}{4}$–$2\frac{1}{2}$ ft), all ways, for taller

varieties and 60cm (2 ft) for the dwarf varieties. These should be regarded as minimum distances, for sprouts need room in which to mature.

Tending growing plants

Unless your site is a sheltered one, you may need to stake taller plants. Where the plants are grown in a block it will be the corner plants that are most at risk, particularly those facing the prevailing wind. With the approach of autumn, draw a little soil up to the plants to give them better anchorage. Feeding should not be necessary if you prepared the ground well in the first place, but sprouts do respond to foliar feeding, and this is an extra boost that can be given at about fortnightly intervals during the peak growing period of late summer and early autumn (July and August).

Snap off any lower leaves that go yellow during the late summer and put them on the compost heap. If you leave them on the plants they may cause the lower sprouts to go mouldy or rotten.

'Blown' sprouts are those which remain open and refuse to button up into solid sprouts. Loose soil is often the cause and this is one reason why you should prepare the site early, particularly on light soils.

Above: early-maturing crops like lettuce can be grown between rows of sprouts
Below: transplant when sprouts have 4 leaves; test for firmness by pulling a leaf

Above: bend buttons sharply down to pick
Below: stake corner plants to avoid damage

Overfeeding with nitrogenous fertilizer is another cause of 'blown' sprouts.

One method of building up the sprouts is to pinch out the growing point of the plant when its optimum size has been reached – usually in late autumn (October). This practice is known as 'cocking'. Remove only a small piece, about as big as a walnut, but don't confuse this with the practice of removing the whole top of the plants.

Below: red sprouts taste like red cabbage
Below right: recommended variety Peer Gynt is a half-tall early cropper
Bottom: a fine crop ready for picking

These cabbage-like heads do make an excellent vegetable and are preferred by some people to the sprouts – but do not remove them too early. The outer leaves of the plant, and its head, are there to protect the sprouts from the winter weather. If you remove them too soon this protection will be lost. It is better to leave them in place until mid spring (March), when the worst of the winter is over, and then make use of them. The topmost sprouts will then fill out.

One of the advantages of sprouts is that they yield their crop over a period. You can remove a few sprouts from each plant as they become ready, and leave those

higher up the stem to grow up to size.

To gather the sprouts, hold the plant with one hand, take off the leaves as far up the plant as you intend to remove the sprouts, and then snap the buttons off with a downward pressure of the thumb. If, as sometimes happens, the buttons are so tight and close together that removal is difficult, use a sharp knife. Whatever method you use, take the sprouts off cleanly so that no portion is left to go mouldy or rotten. In late spring (April) any sprouts or tops that have not been used will burst open and throw up seed stems. Do not allow these to flower, for it is at this stage that the plants are taking most nourishment from the soil. Chop off all the green leaves and stems and dig them in. The roots should be forked out and burnt on your next bonfire. The greenstuff will eventually rot down into humus and will, in the meantime, help to keep the soil open. Late spring (April) is the time for planting potatoes, which like a loose soil, and there is no better crop than potatoes to follow brussels sprouts.

Pests and diseases
Brussels sprouts are vulnerable to the pests and diseases that commonly attack the brassica family.

Cabbage-root fly The transplanting period is the time when precautions should be taken against this pest that lays its eggs against the stems of the plants. The maggots that hatch from the eggs burrow into the soil and attack the stems below soil level. Affected plants wilt in sunshine and will eventually collapse. Sprinkle a small teaspoonful of calomel dust around each plant or dip the roots and stems of the seedlings in a paste made from the dust prior to planting out.

Club root A fungus disease that causes swollen and deformed roots. There is (as yet) no cure, but it can be controlled if lime is used as recommended in the section on preparing the site. Calomel dust will also give some control.

RECOMMENDED VARIETIES

Early Half Tall Produces a very early crop of large, good-quality sprouts.
Bedford Filbasket Mid season variety with large, tightly-packed sprouts.
Irish Elegance Tall, mid season variety.
Cambridge No. 5 Tall, late variety.
Peer Gynt (F.1 hybrid) Early, half-tall variety with medium-sized sprouts; recommended for freezing.
Citadel (F.1 hybrid) Mid season variety, recommended for freezing.
Red Produces sprouts that look and taste like miniature red cabbages.

Cabbage

The cabbage, despite its rather un-glamourous reputation, is a useful vegetable which no garden should be without. Not only is it a valuable food source, containing calcium and vitamins A and C, but it is available all year round and is easier to grow than most brassicas.

Cabbages can be divided into five main groups: spring, summer, winter, savoy and red. There is also Chinese cabbage.

Preparing the soil

Like all brassicas, cabbage does best in a firm and preferably alkaline soil. A light to medium soil is ideal, but it will grow quite happily in all soils, providing they are well drained.

In many cases cabbages will be planted as a follow-on crop to other vegetables. If the ground was manured for the previous crop a further manuring is not necessary, but you could usefully apply a general fertilizer at 70g per sq m (2 oz per sq yd).

Sowing and transplanting

Cabbages are easily raised from seeds sown in a seedbed. Most of the summer varieties can be sown for succession and it is better to make several small sowings rather than one large one. It is important at this stage to sprinkle calomel dust along each seed drill as a precaution against club root, and where cabbage-root fly is a problem, use either a bromophos or diazinon insecticide, according to the maker's instructions.

When the seedlings are large enough to handle, thin to 5cm (2 in) apart. This gives them room to make good, sturdy plants.

The move into their final quarters should take place when the plants are about 15cm (6 in) high. Ease the plants up with a fork and separate them carefully. Leave as much soil on the roots as possible and plant them at once. A dibber can be used but a trowel makes a bigger hole and gives the roots more room. Plant so that the lower leaves are just clear of the soil, firm around the roots and water the plants well in. Then keep the plants free from weeds and see they do not lack water during dry periods.

Spring cabbage

Spring cabbage have a distinct 'nutty' flavour of their own, as well as having much else to commend them. They mature in spring when vegetables are scarce; there is usually no caterpillar

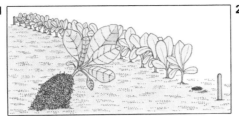

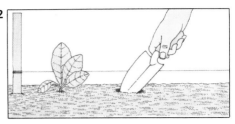

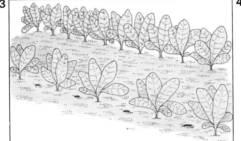

1 *Cabbage seedling ready to transplant*
2 *Transplanting to final growing position*
3 *Thinning out for use as spring greens*
4 *Earthing-up with a swan-necked hoe*

Left and above: summer cabbage Golden Acre Baseball and winter Avon Coronet

problem; being late they often miss the cabbage-root fly and they are seldom attacked by club root, which is not active during the winter months.

Sow in late summer or early autumn (July or August) and transplant during mid or late autumn (September or October). It is as well to make two sowings, about three weeks apart, and take the best plants from each. If the weather is dry at sowing time, water the seed drills well a few hours beforehand.

Spring cabbage usually follow one of the summer crops. They are ideal for following potatoes, and in this case the soil will only need lightly forking over before the plants are put out. Do not give them any manure, and use no fertilizers until the spring. The aim is to grow a strong plant to withstand the winter.

One mistake often made with spring cabbage is to give them too much room. Planted closer together they protect one another. For the smaller varieties, allow 38cm (15 in) between the rows and for the larger ones 50cm (20 in). Small cabbages can go as close as 30cm (12 in) between plants, but the larger ones will need 45cm (18 in). If enough plants are available it is a good plan to halve the distance between the plants and then take out every other plant in mid or late spring (March or April) for use as 'spring greens'.

In mid spring (March) a top dressing of a high nitrogen fertilizer will give the plants a useful boost. Hoe it into the soil and let the rain wash it in.

The main enemy of spring cabbage is not the weather but wood pigeon. In severe weather they will be desperate enough to attack plants in home gardens. Cover them with cloches – large barn cloches will cover two rows – to protect them from attack and produce an earlier crop. The thin, plastic strawberry netting also gives good protection. Make sure, though, that it hangs well clear of the plants.

Summer cabbage

The season for summer cabbage is late summer to late autumn (July to October). You can make a first sowing of an early variety in early spring (February) if you have a frame or cloches. During mid and

Winter cabbage

Sow winter cabbage in late spring or early summer (April or May) for harvesting from late autumn to early spring (October to February). Winter cabbage comprise the Dutch-type white cabbages like Winter White, the Christmas Drumheads selection and one outstanding variety known as January King. They are noted for their ability to stand several weeks without cracking open. Use them to bridge the gap between the summer cabbages and the savoys, and as a follow-on crop if planted out in late summer (July). If the variety Winter White is dug up by the roots and hung head downwards in a shed or cellar it will keep well for weeks.

Savoy cabbage

The leaves of the savoy cabbage are dark green and heavily crimped, and they will survive even a severe winter. Sow in late

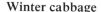

RECOMMENDED VARIETIES		
Type	**Variety** (P) pointed hearts (others are round)	**Size**
Spring cabbage	April (P)	sma
	Durham Early (P)	med
	First Early market (P)	larg
Summer cabbage	Greyhound (P)	sma
	Golden Acre	med
	Winnigstadt (P)	large
	Vienna Baby Head	sma
Winter cabbage	Winter White	large
	Christmas Drumhead	medi
	January King	medi
Savoy cabbage	Savoy King	medi
	Ormskirk Rearguard	medi
Red cabbage	Large Blood Red	large
	Niggerhead	medi
Chinese cabbage	Pe-tsai	
	Nagaoka (F.1 hybrid)	

Key to seasons

early spring (February)	early summer (May)
mid spring (March)	mid summer (June)
late spring (April)	late summer (July)

late spring (late March or April) make successional outdoor sowings, with a final sowing (again of an early variety) in early summer (May).

They will be ready for planting out from early to late summer (May to July). Those that you leave till later in the summer (late June or July) can make use of ground vacated by the first potatoes, peas or broad beans. You may also be able to do some intercropping by planting early summer cabbage between rows of peas or dwarf beans. In the first instance the peas will be cleared by the time the cabbages need more room, and in the second the cabbages will have been cut by the time the beans are at their peak.

Above: hardy savoy cabbage Lincoln Late
Right: hardy, slow-growing red cabbage

spring or early summer (April or May) to harvest from mid winter to late spring (December to April). There are early and late varieties. You can even plant out the late varieties in early autumn (August), making a useful follow-on crop.

Red cabbage

Although red cabbage is mostly used for pickling, it also makes quite a good table vegetable. As it needs a long period of growth, sow not later than mid spring (March). An early spring (February) sowing under cloches is better. The finest red cabbage of all comes from a sowing

anting distance rows	plants	When to sow	When to transplant	When to harvest
cm (15 in)	30cm (12 in)	mid to late summer	mid to late autumn	late spring to mid summer
cm (18 in)	38cm (15 in)	mid to late summer	mid to late autumn	late spring to mid summer
cm (21 in)	45cm (18 in)	mid to late summer	mid to late autumn	late spring to mid summer
cm (15 in)	30cm (12 in)	early spring to early summer	early to late summer	late summer to mid autumn
cm (18 in)	45cm (18 in)	late spring	mid to late summer	mid to late autumn
cm (21 in)	45cm (18 in)	late spring to early summer	mid to late summer	mid to late autumn
cm (15 in)	30cm (12 in)	mid spring to early summer	early to late summer	late summer to mid autumn
cm (21 in)	53cm (21 in)	late spring	late summer	early to mid winter
cm (21 in)	45cm (18 in)	late spring	late summer	early to mid winter
cm (21 in)	53cm (21 in)	late spring	late summer	mid winter to early spring
cm (24 in)	53cm (21 in)	late spring to early summer	late summer	mid winter to early spring
cm (24 in)	53cm (21 in)	late spring to early summer	late summer to early autumn	late winter to late spring
cm (24 in)	60cm (24 in)	early to mid spring or late summer to early autumn	early to mid summer	mid to late autumn
cm (21 in)	53cm (21 in)	early to mid spring or late summer to early autumn	mid to late spring	mid to late autumn
cm (30 in)	20cm (8 in)	late summer	do not transplant	mid to late autumn
cm (30 in)	20cm (8 in)	late summer	do not transplant	mid to late autumn

ly autumn (August)	early winter (November)
autumn (September)	mid winter (December)
autumn (October)	late winter (January)

attacks the root system and causes swellings which deform the roots. This, in turn, causes the plant to wilt and look stunted. There is, as yet, no cure – but the disease can be prevented. Club root is always worst on acid soils, so if your soil is acid, give it a dressing of garden lime at 100–135g per sq m (3–4 oz per sq yd) prior to planting, and sprinkle calomel dust along the seed drills. When transplanting, make a paste from calomel dust and dip the roots in it.

Cabbage-root fly This insect lays its eggs against the plant stems. From the eggs little white grubs hatch out and burrow down into the soil where they attack the roots. It is always advisable to give the ground a routine dressing of bromophos or diazinon to prevent this pest.

Cabbage whitefly This pest is particularly

Below: lettuce-like Chinese cabbage

bad on all members of the cabbage family and renders many vegetables almost unusable. Spray at the first sign of attack with a pesticide based on resmethrin.

Cabbage white butterfly During the summer and autumn, keep a close watch for the cabbage white butterfly. The caterpillars which hatch out from the eggs have voracious appetites and, if they are not dealt with quickly, the plants will soon look like lace curtains. Do not wait for this stage, but as soon as a butterfly is seen spray the plants with derris or trichlorphon or malathion and repeat the spray whenever necessary.

Flea beetle This pest can be a problem when the seedlings have germinated. Spray or dust with a BHC compound.

made at the same time as spring cabbage in late summer or early autumn (July or August). The plants grow more slowly than spring cabbage and, as they are perfectly hardy, can be left in the seedbed until mid or late spring (March or April).

Chinese cabbage

Although described as a cabbage, this vegetable closely resembles a large cos lettuce. Its crisp, delicately-flavoured head can be boiled like cabbage or used in salads.

The plants are easily grown from seed but should not be transplanted. A good, medium-to-heavy loam suits them best; on poor, light, hungry soils they tend to go to seed quickly.

Because of this tendency towards seeding, it is better to delay sowing until late summer (July), and this means that they are useful for following earlier vegetables. A good site is in the lee of a taller crop that will give the plants some shade for part of the day. Sow the seeds in drills 6mm ($\frac{1}{4}$ in) deep and 75cm ($2\frac{1}{2}$ ft) apart. The easiest and most economical way is to sow a few seeds every 30–38cm (12–15 in) and then thin to the strongest.

Beyond keeping them free from weeds, the plants need no special attention, but see that they never lack water.

Pests and diseases

Some pests and diseases affect cabbages badly. Watch out for signs of trouble.

Club root (known as 'finger and toe')

Cauliflowers

Cauliflower seeds are expensive (but not, of course, as expensive as cauliflowers themselves) and you may not wish to buy several new packets every year. But fortunately the seeds remain viable for several years and there is no reason why a packet should not be spread over two seasons. A better method is to buy new seeds each year and share them – and the expense – with another gardener.

Preparing the ground
Cauliflowers are gross feeders and like a rich, deep loam. They will not thrive on heavy, badly-drained clays, on very light loams which dry out in the summer, or on poor, hungry soils. If you plant them in these conditions they tend to retaliate by forming only small heads (a process known as 'buttoning') which open quickly and shoot up to form seed.

Choose, if possible, a site in full sun and with some shelter from cold winds. Dig this over during the autumn, working in as much compost or manure as can be spared. If you have not limed the ground recently spread a dressing over the soil surface at 135g per sq m (4oz per sq yd) and let the rain wash it in.

Sowing for all seasons
There are different varieties for different periods, so you can plan for a succession of harvests.

Cauliflowers for cutting in mid and late summer (June and July) should be sown in mid autumn (September) and over-wintered under glass. Those for heading in early and mid autumn (August and September) are sown in mid or late spring (March or April), and those for maturing in late autumn and early winter (October and November) should not be sown until early summer (May).

There are several ways of raising plants of the early varieties. You can, for instance, sow the seeds outdoors in mid autumn (September) and then prick off the plants into trays of potting compost as soon as they are big enough to handle. Keep the plants in a cold frame or a cold greenhouse throughout the winter. Or you can thin the plants where they stand and cover them with cloches. In either case leave about 8cm (3 in) between the

plants; this will give them room to make strong, healthy growth. Transplant them, with a good soil ball, in the spring.

If you miss the mid autumn (September) sowing you can sow in a warm greenhouse in late winter (January) or in a cold one in early spring (February). Sow two or three seeds at 8cm (3 in) intervals in one of the soilless composts, as these encourage the formation of a good rootball. Thin to the strongest plant. Although the plants need protection during the winter you should ventilate them during the daylight hours whenever possible. Begin to harden them off in mid spring (March) so that they can be put out into their final positions during late spring (the second half of April).

Maincrop sowings are made outdoors in late spring (April). Thin the plants, as soon as you can handle them, to stand 4–8cm (2–3 in) apart. Don't leave the rows overcrowded; bent, spindly plants will be the result.

One of the drawbacks to growing cauliflowers in the past has been the fact that so many of them mature together, giving a glut one week and none the next. You can offset this to some extent by making two sowings – with a fortnight between – instead of one. If you have a deep-freeze the problem of coping with a surplus becomes less important as the summer varieties can be frozen for future use at your convenience.

Buying plants
Although plants can be bought from market stalls and garden centres you would do far better to raise your own. Some of the soil is bound to be knocked off the roots of bought plants in transit and very few of them are named. If, for any reason, it becomes necessary to buy plants, choose those with a good colour and straight stems. Avoid plants that are too big; one of about 15cm (6 in) will tolerate the move better and establish itself more quickly than a larger plant.

How to transplant
The importance of transplanting healthy plants with a good rootball cannot be stressed too much. Any check to the growth of cauliflowers is liable to cause

buttoning, and transplanting is one of the danger periods. The best method is to ease up the plants with a fork, then lift them out with as much soil as possible and put them straight into their final positions. Plant firmly, with the lower leaves just clear of the soil, and water them well in.

Plants of the early varieties should be spaced 45cm (18 in) apart all ways. The summer varieties will need 55cm (22 in) and the later ones 60cm (24 in).

As the later varieties are not ready for transplanting until late summer (July) you can use them as a follow-on crop to peas or early potatoes. There is no need to dig the plot over; simply prick over the top few centimetres with a fork, apply a general fertilizer at 70g per sq m (2 oz per sq yd) and rake level.

Tending and harvesting

In periods of drought give the plants as much water as possible in order to keep them growing, for drought can check growth and cause premature heading, ruining your crop.

When the plants are growing strongly they will appreciate doses of liquid manure at weekly or fortnightly intervals. Use either a proprietary liquid manure or a home-made solution, made by suspending an old sack containing several fork-loads of manure in a tub or tank and leaving it for a few days. Dilute the manure water until it has the appearance of weak tea. Young children should be kept well away from it.

Keep a close watch on the crop once the curds (florets) begin to form as they come quite quickly, especially during the summer months. Bright sunlight turns the curds yellow; to prevent this, snap the stems of a few of the outer leaves and fold them down over the developing curd to shut out the light. The same protection can be given to the late varieties if frost threatens. However, the modern strains of late cauliflowers are mostly 'self-protecting' – the inner leaves fold over the curd naturally and therefore give good protection.

Fresh cauliflowers will keep in good condition for about a week if you dig them up by the roots and hang them, head downwards, in a cool, dark place. If the soil is at all dry, water them well an hour or two before lifting.

This firm-headed cauliflower with crisp white curd has been carefully tended in rich, well-prepared soil, given plenty of water in the growing season, shielded from frost and bright sunlight and protected from pests and diseases

Pests and diseases

Cauliflowers, unfortunately, are subject to quite a variety of pests and diseases.

Birds The tender young leaves of newly-transplanted plants may be attacked by birds. Use black cotton, or flashing strips of foil to keep them off.

Rabbits On open allotments, and sometimes even in home gardens, rabbits can be terribly destructive. The only really effective remedy is to surround the whole brassica plot with 90cm (3 ft) high chicken-wire. Although this is expensive initially, you can use it over and over again. You can also try spraying or dusting with an animal repellent – quite harmless to pets.

Cabbage-root fly A more subtle, but no less dangerous, enemy that lays its eggs at the base of the plant. When the maggots hatch they burrow into the soil and attack the stem below ground. The first sign of trouble is when the leaves begin to flag. Later, the leaves turn yellow and the whole plant collapses. At this stage the maggots can often be found in the stem. You must then dig up and burn affected plants.

If the fly can be deterred from laying, or killed, there will be no eggs and no maggots. So as soon as the leaves have straightened up after transplanting sprinkle calomel dust around the plants – a small teaspoonful to each plant. As an alternative method, mix some of the powder in water to form a paste, and then

Above: Flora Blanca type cauliflowers with large, solid, very white curds

Right: club root disease turns the fine roots into thick, swollen 'fingers'

Below: protect from sun or frost by snapping leaves over the curd

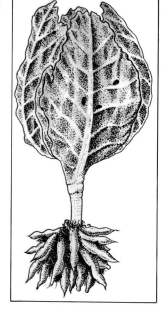

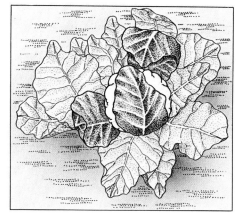

dip the roots and stems in the paste as you are transplanting.

If, in spite of this treatment (or due to lack of it), you find that cabbage-root fly has taken hold do not write the crop off. If the attack is not too severe you can encourage the plants to overcome it by forming new roots. They will do this if earth is drawn up under the lower leaves so that the stems are covered. Providing that you never allow them to dry out, these new roots will be enough to carry the crop through.

Caterpillars Summer varieties are especially vulnerable to the caterpillars of cabbage-white butterflies. The best remedy is to pick them off by hand, but this is time-consuming and not for the squeamish. A spray or dust with derris is effective, but you may need several applications. Derris has the advantage of being safe to use right up to the time of heading. Do not wait for trouble – at the first sign of any cabbage-white butterflies spray at once.

Club root (known in some areas as 'finger and toe'). This is the disease that you have most to fear from when growing any of the brassicas. Affected plants are stunted and sickly and the roots are swollen and deformed.

There is, as yet, no cure for club root but it can be controlled. Adequate liming of the soil helps to discourage it. Calomel dust is another good method of control; sprinkle in the drills before sowing and use it again (as described above) at transplanting time. You can 'starve out' the disease by ceasing to grow brassicas on the diseased soil but this takes a long time. Where incidence is severe it is wise to omit brassicas from the cropping plan for a few years. Remember that turnips and swedes are also members of the brassica family and are liable to be attacked.

RECOMMENDED VARIETIES

EARLY SOWINGS under glass for summer cutting:
Snowball; Mechelse Delta; Dominant.

MAINCROP SOWINGS – late spring (April) for summer cutting:
All the Year Round; Flora Blanca; Kangaroo.

MAINCROP SOWINGS for late autumn to early winter (October to December) cutting:
South Pacific; Flora Blanca No 2 (formerly Veitch's Autumn Giant); **Igea** (also known as Snow White).

SUCCESSIONAL SOWINGS
All the Year Round

Broccoli

Above: shoot of white sprouting broccoli

Nowadays it is customary to find the heading varieties of broccoli listed in the catalogues as 'winter cauliflower'. This is reasonable enough, but it should be noted that there are differences between the cauliflower and the heading broccoli. The broccoli is not quite so white and often a little coarser in texture than the true cauliflower, and it is ready for harvest at a different time of year.

Of the two, broccoli is easier to grow. It is much hardier and less demanding in its soil requirements, and will do well in most soils if they are in a good, fertile condition. It does not need freshly-manured soil – in fact it does better without it. With broccoli, as with spring cabbage, the aim is to produce a plant that is large enough and hardy enough to stand through the winter. Lush, sappy growth should be avoided.

Preparing the soil

As the plants do not need to be planted out until mid or late summer (June or July) they make a good follow-on crop to the first broad beans, peas or potatoes. If the ground was manured for the previous crop, simply prick over the top few centimetres of soil with a fork. A top dressing of superphosphate of lime, at 70g per sq m (2 oz per sq yd), is a beneficial addition. Remember, also, that broccoli, like all the brassicas, likes firm ground.

Sowing times

Seeds can be sown from mid spring to early summer (March to May) according to variety. The harvest season (except for calabrese) extends roughly from late winter to mid summer (January to early June). Those that mature in late winter and early spring (January and February) will be mainly confined to the milder, frost-free districts. In colder areas choose varieties to harvest from mid spring (March) onwards.

If you are growing more than one row, then use several varieties; that way you will have a succession of curds.

Sow the early varieties of both heading and sprouting broccoli in mid or late spring (March or April), and the later varieties in late spring (April) except for those which do not mature until early or mid summer (May or June): these need not be sown until early summer (May). Sow the seeds thinly in a seedbed, in drills 13mm ($\frac{1}{2}$ in) deep and 25cm (9 in) apart. Make sure that each variety is labelled before the rows are raked in. Sprinkle calomel dust along each seed drill as a precaution against club root and where cabbage-root fly is a problem, use either a bromophos or diazinon insecticide according to maker's instructions.

Thinning and transplanting

As soon as the plants are large enough to handle, thin them to 5cm (2 in) apart. This thinning (which is too often neglected) makes for good, straight plants.

The move into their final quarters can be made when the plants are about 15cm (6 in) high. Dull, showery weather is the best time to move the plants, but it is not always possible to wait for these conditions. If the ground is dry and hard, water the plants well a few hours before moving them.

To transplant, first ease the plants with a fork and lift them carefully. Keep as much soil on the roots as possible and plant them in their new quarters straight away. Allow 60cm (24 in) between plants and rows; if space is a problem you can reduce this to 50cm (20 in). Plant firmly so that the lower leaves of each plant are just clear of the soil, and then water them in. If your plants are strong and well-grown, and if you move as much soil with them as possible, the check from transplanting will be minimal.

Buying ready-grown plants
If you were unable to sow seeds, plants are usually available from garden centres and market stalls. Always find out the variety and when it is likely to mature. Do not choose plants which are weak and spindly. Ensure the plants are sturdy and about 13–15cm (5–6 in) high. Providing the rootball is not too badly damaged they should settle down quickly in their new positions.

Perennial broccoli and calabrese
An unusual member of the broccoli family is the perennial broccoli, usually listed as Nine Star Perennial. This plant produces from six to nine heads instead of the usual one. They are smaller than the normal heading types, but much larger than the heads of sprouting broccoli. The plant will continue to produce heads for several years providing you do not allow it to seed. The plants need extra room in which to develop, so allow 90cm (3 ft) between plants. They are best put out alongside a path or fence where they can be left undisturbed. After their first flowering, top-dress the plants each spring with some well-rotted manure or compost.

The green Italian sprouting broccoli, more commonly known as calabrese, deserves a special mention. Large quantities of this are now grown commercially and used in the frozen vegetable trade. It is becoming increasingly popular with housewives and is as easy to grow as the sprouting broccoli. Some varieties have a large, central green head which is followed by a limited number of sideshoots; other varieties have a smaller head and more spears. The shoots are tender and of first-rate flavour.

Sowing and cultivation are the same as for sprouting broccoli, but the plants mature in autumn and early winter, not in the spring. Their main season is mid to late autumn (September to October) but in an open autumn they will continue to produce their shoots into early or mid winter (November or December).

Above right: purple sprouting broccoli
Right: white sprouting broccoli

RECOMMENDED VARIETIES

Type	Variety	When to sow	When to transplant	When to cut
	*St Agnes	mid to late spring	mid to late summer	early to mid spring
	*Snow-white	mid to late spring	mid to late summer	mid spring
	Veitch's Self-protecting	mid spring	mid summer	mid winter
	St George	late spring	mid to late summer	late spring
	Walcheren Winter	mid spring	mid summer	late spring to early summer
	Late Queen	early summer	late summer	early to mid summer
	Mirado	early summer	late summer	mid summer
	*Not completely hardy – for mild areas only			
Sprouting broccoli	Early White	mid spring	mid to late summer	early to mid spring
	Early Purple	mid spring	mid to late summer	early to mid spring
	Late White	late spring	late summer	mid to late spring
	Late Purple	late spring	late summer	mid to late spring
Perennial broccoli	Nine Star Perennial	late spring	mid summer	mid spring
Calabrese	Express Corona (F.1 hybrid)	mid to late spring	mid summer	early to mid autumn
	Autumn Spear	late spring	late summer	late autumn to early winter

Key to seasons

early spring (February)	early summer (May)	early autumn (August)	early winter (November)
mid spring (March)	mid summer (June)	mid autumn (September)	mid winter (December)
late spring (April)	late summer (July)	late autumn (October)	late winter (January)

Harvesting broccoli

Like cauliflowers, heading broccoli tend to mature quickly if the weather conditions are suitable. Cut them as soon as they are at their best, when the edges of the curd are just beginning to open; the head is then usually 15–20cm (6–8 in) in diameter.

The sprouting broccoli are ready for picking when they look like miniature cauliflowers about 15cm (6 in) in length. It is not necessary to wait until the curds can be seen. The plants will produce further small curds over several weeks.

Pests and diseases

Although this is a relatively easy crop to grow, there are a few pests and diseases which you may encounter.

Club root Often known as 'finger and toe', this attacks the root system and causes swellings which deform the roots. This, in turn, causes the plant to wilt and look stunted. There is, as yet, no cure but the disease can be prevented. Club root is always worst on acid soils, so if your soil is acid give a dressing of 100–135g per sq m (3–4 oz per sq yd) of garden lime prior to planting and sprinkle calomel dust along the seed drills. When transplanting, make a paste from calomel dust and dip the roots in it.

Below: picking off shoots of broccoli

Cabbage-root fly This insect lays its eggs against the plant stems. From the eggs little white grubs hatch out and burrow down into the soil where they attack the roots. It is always advisable to give the ground a routine dressing of bromophos or diazinon to prevent this pest.

Cabbage whitefly This pest is particularly bad on all members of the cabbage family and can make many vegetables almost unusable. Spray at the first sign of an attack with a pesticide based on resmethrin.

Cabbage white butterfly During the summer and autumn, keep a close watch for the cabbage white butterfly. The caterpillars which hatch out from the eggs have a voracious appetite and, if they are not dealt with quickly, the plants will soon look like lace curtains. Do not wait for this stage, but as soon as a butterfly is seen spray the plants with derris or trichlorphon or malathion and repeat the spray whenever necessary.

Flea beetle This pest can be a problem after germination. Spray or dust with a BHC compound as a precaution.

Turnips, swedes and kohl rabi

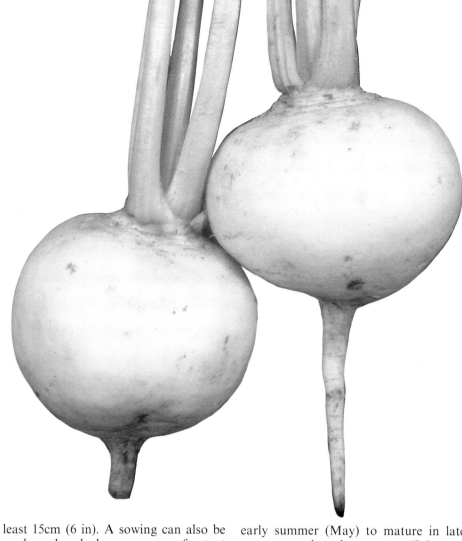

Turnips are not difficult to grow, have a long season of use and will thrive in any good garden soil which does not dry out too quickly. Swedes are larger and sweeter than turnips; they are also hardier and store well. Kohl rabi is often thought of as just a substitute for the turnip; it is, however, an excellent vegetable in its own right and in addition stands well in hot, dry conditions where turnips are likely to fail.

Turnips, swedes and kohl rabi all belong to the cabbage (brassica) family and their treatment is very similar.

Turnips are grouped according to whether they are ready for harvesting in spring and summer, or in autumn and winter. The autumn and winter varieties can be stored, but spring and summer varieties (which take about 10 weeks to mature) do not store well.

Spring and summer turnips
If you have a cold frame you can make a sowing of turnips in early spring (February). You will need a soil depth of at

Below: Purple Top swede, one of the most popular varieties. Above: Green-top White turnip

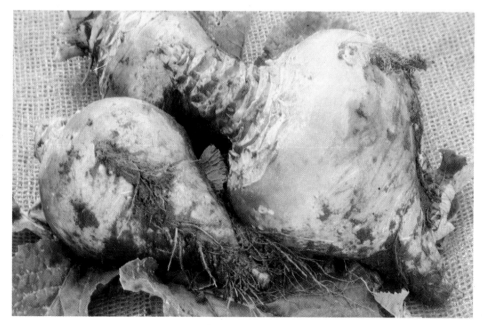

least 15cm (6 in). A sowing can also be made under cloches – one row for tent cloches and three rows, 25cm (9 in) apart, under barn cloches.

Start outdoor sowings from mid to late spring (mid March) in rows 13mm ($\frac{1}{2}$ in) deep and 30cm (12 in) apart. Sow the seeds thinly along the drill, or else in clusters 15cm (6 in) apart. In either case, thin the plants to some 15cm (6 in) apart. Make successional sowings throughout

early summer (May) to mature in late summer and early autumn (July and August). These sowing may suffer if the weather is hot and dry as turnips dislike such conditions. It is, therefore, a good plan to site these sowings in the lee of a taller crop; this will give turnips some shade for at least part of the day. Water well in a dry spell. The summer turnips, especially, need to be 'kept moving'; if they take too long to mature they tend to become stringy or woody.

Autumn and winter turnips
Sow autumn and winter varieties in mid summer (June) in drills 13mm ($\frac{1}{2}$ in) deep and 38cm (15 in) apart. These can be grown as a follow-on crop in the ground vacated by the first peas or potatoes. Thin the plants to 20cm (8 in) apart. These varieties take a little longer to mature and will be ready from mid autumn (September) onwards. About the end of autumn (late October) lift any roots that are left and store them in boxes of sand or soil, or in a little clamp in the garden. Leave about 2–3cm (1 in) of stalk on top of the turnip and shorten the roots a little – but do not trim them right back.

Turnip greens
Late varieties of turnip can also be sown in early or mid autumn (August or

September) to provide turnip tops for use in the early spring. These turnip greens are rich in iron. For the production of tops, sow the seeds thinly in a continuous row and do not thin them. Allow 30cm (12 in) between the rows.

Pests and diseases

Flea beetle and a condition resulting from boron deficiency are the main enemies of turnips.

Flea beetle This attacks the seedlings as soon as they have formed their first leaves. It is often referred to, rather vaguely, as 'the fly'. A severe attack can cause a row of seedlings to disappear overnight. Do not wait for trouble; as soon as seedlings appear, dust the rows with derris and repeat the application if rain washes the dust off. The danger is over once the plants are through the seedling stage.

Boron deficiency Occasionally turnips may suffer from boron deficiency, a condition which shows itself in a brown rot when the roots are cut open. The remedy is to apply borax; only a tiny quantity is needed – about 2g per sq m (1 oz per 20 sq yd). To obtain an even distribution, mix it with sand.

SWEDES

Swedes are milder and hardier than turnips. Sow the seeds thinly in early or mid summer (May or June), in drills 13mm ($\frac{1}{2}$ in) deep and 40cm (15 in) apart. Thin out to 20cm (8 in) apart.

They are hardy enough to remain outdoors all winter and can be lifted as required. Any remaining in the ground by spring will also produce edible tops.

Pests and diseases

Swedes occasionally suffer from boron deficiency (see under Turnips).

KOHL RABI

There are two kinds of kohl rabi – white and purple; the white is generally considered to have a better flavour. You can either boil the swollen stems or grate them raw in salads. It has a distinctive 'nutty' flavour.

Sow from mid spring to early autumn (March to August) in drills 13mm ($\frac{1}{2}$ in) deep and 45cm (18 in) apart. Thin the plants to stand 20cm (8 in) apart. Any soil 'in good heart' will grow kohl rabi, and no special cultivation is required. Keep the plants free from weeds and water them during dry spells.

As the plants grow, the stems begin to swell just above soil level. This swollen stem is the edible part of the plant. Use it when it is about the size of a cricket ball; if it gets too large it tends to become coarse and stringy. The plants are hardy and late sowings can be left outdoors all winter. After thinning, any surplus plants can be transplanted.

Pests and diseases

Kohl rabi may be attacked by the flea beetle (see under Turnips).

Above: Two fine examples of the Laurentian variety of swede
Below: Roggli's Blue, a popular and easily-grown variety of kohl rabi

Peas

There are tall, medium and dwarf varieties of peas. The choice will to some extent depend on what time and staking materials are available, and whether the site is sheltered or exposed.

A row of tall peas generally gives the best return but, on the other hand, rows of dwarfs can be grown closer together.

Peas prefer a deep, moisture-retentive soil in which their tap roots can thrust well down. They do not thrive on cold, sticky clay soils; nor do they like light, gravelly ones. Fresh manure, while not harmful, is not recommended because peas do not occupy a site long enough to make use of it; a strip that was manured for a previous crop is more suitable.

Sowing time

A sowing can be made in early winter (November) for picking in early summer (May). In favoured districts on a sunny, sheltered border the crop could come through winter without protection; in other areas it is wise to use cloches.

Round-seeded varieties are hardier than the wrinkled-seeded and should be used for an autumn sowing. For summer picking, seeds can be sown from early spring to early summer (February to May). Use round-seeded peas for an early spring (February) sowing, then move on to a wrinkled-seeded variety.

Tall peas are also sown in late spring and early summer (April and May) and take about 14 weeks to mature (about two weeks longer than dwarf types).

For sowing from mid to late summer (June to July) turn to the wrinkled-seeded varieties.

How to sow

Peas can be sown in a broad drill 15cm (6 in) wide and 5cm (2 in) deep, containing three rows of seeds, or in a narrow drill of only one row. A broad drill is better for tall peas. Space the seeds about 5 cm (2 in) apart. The distance between each row is the same as the height of the plants.

To save space tall peas can be sown alongside a path. Trenching will get the best results from here, but it needs to be done well in advance of sowing. Dig out a trench 60cm (2 ft) wide and a

Fat, ripe pea pods ready for harvesting, the result of careful cultivation

spade's depth. Shovel out the loose soil and break up the subsoil with a fork. Add good compost or well-rotted manure before returning the soil.

Other types of peas

There are several less common types that are well worth growing.

Sugar pea (mangetout) When the peas can be felt in the pods, but before they have filled out, is the time to cook them whole for eating pod and all. Sow in late spring to early summer (April to May).

Petits pois These are smaller than the ordinary pea but many consider them to be of better flavour. Sow from mid spring to mid summer (March to June). Staking is advisable.

Asparagus pea (winged pea) This type has reddish flowers that are followed by small three-sided pods. The flavour is supposed to resemble that of asparagus, hence the name. It is not as hardy as an ordinary pea and should not be sown before late spring or early summer (April or May).

Sow the seeds 10cm (4 in) apart in drills 2–3cm (1 in) deep and 60cm (2 ft) apart. The plants grow up to 60cm (2 ft) and some twiggy support is advisable. Gather the pods when they are about 4cm (1½ in) long.

Care of growing plants

Peas must be hand-weeded, especially when they are in a broad row, and it is best to do it when the plants are 15–23cm (6–9 in) high. If left too long, the weeds cannot be pulled out without disturbing the peas. Keep the hoe going between the

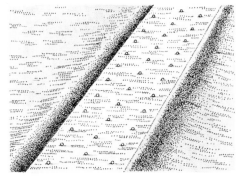

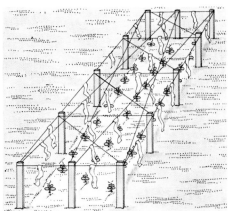

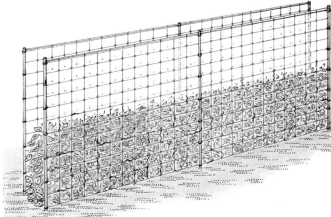

Sow peas in staggered rows (above left); protect seedlings from birds with black cotton (left); two rows of netting give maximum support (below left); hold bine as well as pod when picking (below)

rows for as long as possible.

When peas are about 15cm (6 in) high they can be sprinkled with super-phosphate of lime at about 30g per metre run (1 oz per yard), along each side of the rows. Keep it an inch or two away from the plants and hoe it in.

Peas have root nodules which contain a nitrifying bacteria so they require little, if any, additional nitrogenous fertilizer.

Watering can pose a problem because peas are deep-rooting. During a drought this is an asset, providing you water them thoroughly. A mere sprinkling from a watering can, however, will do more harm than good.

Mulching with compost, lawn-mowings, old mushroom-manure or peat, will help to conserve moisture. Spread the mulch along each side of the rows, but not touching the plants; leave about

5cm (2 in) of bare soil either side so that rain can get through. The mulch should be 5cm (2 in) deep and put on when the soil is moist – *never* when it is dry.

Methods of support

Tall peas need staking and, although dwarfs are not supposed to need it, you will find that anything more than 45cm (18 in) tall will do better if staked. Twiggy sticks are ideal, though often difficult to come by. If you grow raspberries, you can use the prunings from the raspberry canes. Trim them and then push them into the soil on each side of the peas, leaning them inwards, so that they come together at the top.

Cord or plastic netting is used for tall-growing crops. You will find the thin 15cm (6 in) plastic-mesh type satisfactory, but it must be firmly erected and kept taut. The weight of a row of tall peas at peak harvesting time is considerable and once blown down it cannot be put back. A strong stake should be driven in at each end of the row and tall canes inserted at 2m (6 ft) intervals.

It is best to put netting up each side of a row and let the peas grow in between. Modern varieties do not climb as readily as the old kinds and are easily blown away from a single row of netting.

How to harvest

A good row should give at least three pickings, starting with the lower pods which fill out first. When picking hold the pea bine (haulm or stem) in one hand and pull off the pod with the other. This prevents damage to the bine; if it gets bent or bruised the top pods will not fill.

When the crop is finished cut off the bines at soil level and leave the roots in the ground so that the nitrogen from the root nodules can be released into the soil. This will benefit any plants that may follow.

Pests and diseases

Mice Always guard against mice, especially with autumn sowings; it is advisable to set one or two traps after sowing.

Sparrows These birds have a liking for the first tender leaves and can create havoc with a crop. Pea-guards, made from wire netting fixed over a wooden frame, helps keep the birds at bay, but when the leaves eventually grow through the netting the guards have to be removed.

An alternative precaution is to thread black cotton in and out of the staking material and add further layers of thread as the peas grow. Strips of tinfoil that flash and crackle in the sun and wind are also effective; buy them at seed shops or

Asparagus pea pods are eaten whole. Pick the pods young, before they get stringy

Feltham First, a very early garden pea, does well in the open or under cloches

111

garden centres. A bird and animal repellent will ward off the enemy, but apply according to the manufacturer's instructions. Cloches give excellent protection in the early stages.

Dwarf peas grown in an open allotment may also be troubled by crows and jackdaws, which are adept at slitting the pods. The birds will be scared off if you encircle the rows and criss-cross over the tops with string and tie torn sheets of newspaper to it, forming a cage.

Pea weevil This tiny, beetle-like creature eats holes in the leaves of young plants and inhibits their growth. As soon as the seedlings are through, dust with derris and re-apply if rain washes it off. When the plants are 10–15cm (4–6 in) high, the danger period is over.

Grubs The pea moth makes its appearance when flowering begins and the grubs may be found inside the pods. Spray the flowers with a reliable insecticide as they open, and again 10 days later. Peas that mature in autumn (August or September) are seldom attacked.

Thrips (thunder flies) Sometimes appearing in large numbers, thrips make silvery streaks on the leaves and flowering may be affected. Control these pests by

RECOMMENDED VARIETIES

Dwarf (round-seeded)
Feltham First, 60cm (2 ft) early winter sowing.

Dwarf (wrinkled-seeded)
Kelvedon Wonder, 60cm (2 ft) and Early Onward, 75cm (2½ ft), mid and late spring sowings; Onward, 75cm (2½ ft) and Hurst Green Shaft 75cm (2½ ft), late spring and early summer sowings (the latter has mildew resistance); Little Marvel, 45cm (18 in), mid to late summer sowing.

Tall-growing
Alderman, 1·50m (5 ft), Lord Chancellor, 1m (3½ ft) and Miracle 1·20m (4 ft), late spring and summer sowings.

Other types of peas
Sugar pea (mangetout) – tall-growing
Carouby de Maussane, 1·50m (5 ft);
dwarf Sweetgreen, 45cm (18 in) and Grace, 75cm (2½ ft).
Petits pois – tall-growing Gullivert, 1–1·5m (3–3½ ft).
Asparagus pea (winged pea) – dwarf, 45cm (1½ ft).

A good row of peas gives at least three pickings (below); start with lowest pods

Kelvedon Wonder (above) is wilt-resistant and excellent for successional sowings

Onward, a first-class early maincrop variety, has large, blunt-nosed pods

spraying with an insecticide such as BHC or liquid malathion.

Mildew A common disease among peas, the powdery form of mildew covers leaves and stems with a white dust. It can be kept in check by spraying with dinocap. Unlike downy mildew, which appears as a grey fungus on the undersides of young leaves, it is more prevalent during a dry season. Late sowings suffer most from it and the best safeguard is to ensure that the peas have an open, sunny position with a good circulation of air.

Broad beans

Choose Aquadulce Claudia for an early-season crop. It has white flowers (above) and fine, long pods (below)

A medium to heavy loam gives the heaviest crops, but broad beans can be grown in any well-drained soil. They are lime-lovers and if their patch hasn't been recently limed, give it a dressing at 70g per sq m (2 oz per sq yd), before sowing.

When to sow
The two sowing periods are early to mid winter (November to December) for an early crop; early to late spring (February to April) for a maincrop harvest.

An early winter sowing is debatable, for though reasonably hardy, broad beans are not immune to frost. Fortunately cloches give the plants adequate protection. Outdoor crops may succeed in warmer areas, but cloches are probably necessary until late spring (end of March) in colder northern regions.

Don't sow cloche crops until early winter (mid November), or the plants may reach the glass roof before it is safe to de-cloche.

Broad beans are usually grown in a double row 25cm (10 in) apart and 20cm (8 in) between the seeds, which are spaced out in a drill 5cm (2 in) deep. Sow the seeds in staggered positions along the rows. If you intend growing more than one double row allow 60cm (24 in) between each pair. Single rows should also be set 60cm (24 in) apart.

First unprotected sowings can be made from early spring to early summer (late February to May), with the heaviest crops coming from the earlier sowings. If outdoor conditions are unfavourable, begin sowing in early spring (February) in a cold greenhouse. Fill a 10cm (4 in) seed tray with compost and put the seeds in 2·5cm (1 in) deep and 8cm (3 in) apart. Transplant in late spring (April).

Care of growing plants
Tall varieties can grow to about 1·2m (4 ft) high and staking is usually necessary. Insert bamboo poles on each side of the rows and firmly wind garden wire or tough string from cane to cane.

Blackfly is the greatest pest menace to the broad bean, particularly later sowings; a severe infestation can cripple a whole crop. They attack the soft-growing points of the plant; once the first flowers have set, cut out the damaged tips.

In early summer (May) spray the plants with derris or a reliable aphicide and continue spraying until the pests have been eliminated.

Mice are broad bean nibblers and can quickly cause havoc to your crop. Set traps or spray a strong repellent around the base of the plants.

Chocolate spot disease is prevalent in heavy rainfall areas. It appears as dark brown blotches on leaves, stems and pods, and a severe attack can drastically reduce your crop. Check it in the early stages by spraying with Bordeaux mixture fungicide.

RECOMMENDED VARIETIES

The two main types are the Longpod and the Windsor. The latter is less hardy but is considered by many to be the better flavoured.

A lesser-known broad bean is the Dwarf type. This breaks (makes side shoots) to form several stems. The seeds are sown 30cm (12 in) apart with 40cm (15 in) between each row. They crop heavily over several weeks and have a good flavour.

Longpod: **Aquadulce Claudia** (autumn sowing); **Dreadnought** (winter sowing); **Bunyard's Exhibition** (winter sowing); **Imperial White** (winter sowing); **Imperial Green** (winter sowing).

Windsor: **Giant Green** (spring sowing); **Giant White** (spring sowing).

Dwarf: **The Sutton** (successional sowing).

Runner beans

Runner beans will grow in most soils. On heavy soils which warm up slowly do not sow too early, and on very light soils you may find it difficult to keep the plants sufficiently well watered. These are the extremes, however, and in between them the runner bean requires no special consideration. If lime has not been given recently, apply it at about 135g per sq m (4 oz per sq yd) when the site is prepared.

Preparing a trench

For best results dig out a trench 90cm (3 ft) wide and a spade's depth. Shovel out the loose soil and then break up the subsoil with a fork. As the soil is put back, mix in some compost or well-rotted manure. Leave a shallow depression at the top of the trench to help with watering later on. The trench should be prepared well in advance of sowing time – mid spring (March) is a good period.

Some gardeners line the bottom of the trench with thick layers of newspaper which are then thoroughly soaked with water. The newspapers hold some of the moisture and give it up when the plant roots need it.

If manure or compost cannot be spared for the runners, open up the trench in the autumn. Keep every scrap of kitchen waste in an old bucket, well covered. When the bucket is full, empty it into the trench and cover the waste with an inch or two of soil. Continue this process, with an occasional sprinkling of lime, until the trench is full. Although in good, fertile soil the beans will grow without any special preparation, better results can be achieved by trenching, and it is worth the extra trouble involved.

Sowing the seeds

Make an early start by sowing seeds in a cold greenhouse or frame in late spring (April) and transplanting them later. Plant one seed in a 9cm (3½ in) pot, or put the seeds 8cm (3 in) apart in a tray 10–15cm (4–6 in) deep. J.I. No 1 or one of the soilless composts makes a good medium. When the seedlings are through, give them as much light as possible with good ventilation during the day, and then harden them off before planting out.

An alternative to this is to sow the seeds directly into the soil where they are to mature and cover them with cloches. Do not sow until late on in spring (mid April) or the plants may grow too big before it is safe to decloche them. Barn cloches will cover two rows 45cm (18 in) apart. The plants must be staked as soon as the cloches are removed.

The conventional way of growing runner beans is to sow two rows of seeds 5cm (2 in) deep with 30 cm (12 in) between the seeds and 60cm (2 ft) between the two rows. The sowing can be made at the beginning of summer (first half of May in the warmer areas and about two weeks later in cooler districts). If the plants have been raised under glass, put them out in two rows early in mid summer (the first two weeks of June). The seeds, or plants, should be directly opposite each other in the rows.

Staking the plants

Bean poles are usually made of larch wood and can be bought from garden centres, but poles cut out from other brushwood will do just as well. They should be about 2–2·5m (7–8 ft) long. Wooden laths 2–3cm (1 in) square are sometimes used instead, or heavy-grade bamboo canes.

Place the butts of the poles a few centimetres into the soil. Draw together the tops of two opposing poles and cross them about 20cm (8 in) from the top. Do this all down the row. Then lay other poles horizontally above where the upright poles cross, and fasten securely at each junction.

A row of runners in full leaf and crop presents a large area to the wind, so be sure to build the supporting palisade carefully. If the plants are blown down in a summer gale it is a very difficult job to get them up again.

It cloches are not being used, it is easier to put the poles up first and then put one plant, or two seeds, against each pole. If both seeds grow, pull one out.

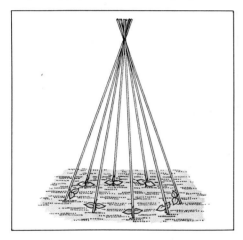

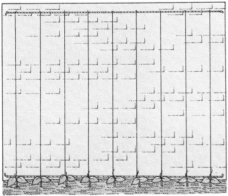

Top: staking runner beans by a wigwam of poles drawn together and fastened at the top. Above: beans can be grown up a wall by erecting a 'fence' of strings for them to cling to. Right: the most common way of staking is to use bean poles made of larch wood or heavy-grade bamboo

Harvesting Streamline runner beans. This variety produces vigorous plants and crops over a long period. The long, fine-flavoured pods are borne in clusters

Making a wigwam
Another method of growing runner beans is to grow the plants in circles or 'wigwams'. Mark out a rough circle 1·2–1·8m (4–6 ft) in diameter, and put the poles in round the circumference. Draw all the poles inwards towards the centre and fasten them at the top. Then put the plants or seeds in against the poles in the usual way. The circles take up less room than a straight row and can often be fitted into odd corners, and as they do not present a straight surface to the wind they are far less likely to blow down.

Growing along a fence
A third method of growing is to sow or plant a single row at the foot of a fence and let them climb up it. A temporary fence can be made with a few stakes, horizontal strands of garden wire at the top and bottom, and lengths of string stretched vertically between the two wires. The plants will climb the strings without difficulty.

Once the runners have twined round the poles they will soon begin to climb. When they have reached the top, pinch out the growing points to keep the row uniform and make the plants bush out. Where they are climbing up a fence they can be left to fall over and cover the other side. Keep the rows free from weeds and in dry weather give them plenty of water.

Growing without stakes
It is also possible to grow runners without stakes. In this method the seeds are sown 20cm (8 in) apart in single rows 90cm (3 ft) apart. The plants run along the ground and form a continuous row. If the runners reach out too far and threaten to become entangled in the next row, pinch out the growing points. To pick, lift up the foliage on each side of the row in turn.

The obvious advantage of this method is that it is easy because no stakes are required. In hot weather the pods, being mostly under the leaves, do not become old so quickly. The disadvantages are that in wet weather some slug damage is likely, and that where the pods touch the ground they no longer grow straight. But for the gardener who has little time to spare and is not short of space in his vegetable plot, this method has its points.

Dwarf varieties reaching a height of only about 75cm (18 in) need little or no staking. A few twiggy sticks pushed in amongst the plants keeps them upright.

Ailments and pests
There are a few problems that may affect your growing plants, so take precautions.
Bud-dropping The flowers do not open properly and fall off without being fertilized. This can be caused by cold winds, rapid changes of temperature, or dryness of the root system. Spraying with clear water night and morning may be of some benefit, but it does not take the place of a good watering around the roots. During a very hot summer, it shows clearly that beans which are watered regularly bear far more pods than plants left to fend for themselves.

Blackfly (aphides) can sometimes be a nuisance, especially if they have already infested broad beans in the vicinity. These aphides will gather round the tender tips of the shoots, inhibit flowering and make the plants unpleasant to handle. Do not let them reach this stage. Keep an eye open for them and at the first sign of trouble spray with derris or malathion.

If the attack comes late, when pods have already formed, use only derris as malathion is poisonous for a few days after application. Repeat the spraying until the plants are clear.

Frost warning
The runner bean is not a hardy plant and cannot be put out while the danger of frost is present. If a late frost threatens after the plants are through the soil, or just after they have been transplanted, cover them with newspaper, plant-pots, straw, leaves or anything else that will protect them. Plants which are only touched but not killed by frost will shoot again, but the crop will be later.

Picking the beans
When cropping begins, look over the plants every few days. Pick the pods while still young, before the beans have started to form in them, as old pods will be 'stringy'. If pods are missed and have become too old at the next picking never leave them on the plants. Pull them off and put them on the compost heap. Do not be tempted to leave them for seed, for as soon as the plants are permitted to form seed the production of young beans rapidly falls off.

If it is intended to save seed, leave one or two plants at the end of a row and do not pick any pods from them. When the pods have become dry and papery pull them off, shell out the beans, and store them in a dry, cool place.

RECOMMENDED VARIETIES

DWARF
Hammond's Dwarf Scarlet and **Hammond's Dwarf White** (both good under cloches).

TALL
Streamline, Enorma, Crusader, Achievement, Kelvedon Marvel, and **Fry** (F.1 hybrid).

French beans and haricots

FRENCH BEANS

Some varieties of French bean are flat-podded; others are round. The round varieties are sometimes called 'snap' beans – the test for quality and freshness being that the pods break cleanly when they are snapped in half.

Most varieties of French bean are dwarf, the plants forming a little bush 30–38cm (12–15 in) tall, but there are also climbing varieties that will grow to a height of 1·5–1·8m (5 or 6 ft). These give a heavier crop and are especially useful where you have a trellis or boundary fence to support them.

French beans will grow in most soils provided the drainage is good. Light to medium soils are preferable as they warm up more quickly than cold, heavy soils in which the seeds tend to rot. A soil that was manured for the previous crop will suit them, and if lime has not been applied recently, work in a dressing at 100g per sq m (3 oz per sq yd) a few weeks before you start sowing.

Sowing under glass

Unfortunately, French beans are tender subjects and cannot be planted outside while frosts are expected. But you can get an early crop by sowing the seeds in a cool greenhouse in mid spring (mid March), using 9cm (3½ in) pots. When the plants have made their first pair of true leaves they can be planted in the greenhouse border, or under cloches outside.

An alternative, where staging is used, is to grow the plants in 25cm (10 in) pots and keep them on the staging. Sow six or eight seeds in a 25cm (10 in) pot and then select three of the best for growing on. When the flowers begin to appear, syringe the plants night and morning with clear water to ensure good fertilization.

Sowing outdoors

For outdoor crops a sowing can be made *in situ* under cloches in late spring (April) or without protection from early summer (mid May). A late sowing in mid to late summer (the second half of June) will give pickings until the first frosts, and if this sowing is cloched in mid autumn (September) the period of cropping will be extended for a few more weeks.

Sow the seeds in drills 5cm (2 in) deep, spacing them 15cm (6 in) apart. Sow two seeds at each spacing and if both germinate pull one seedling out. Put in a few extra seeds at the end of each row for filling up any gaps that may occur. If the plants are to be grown in single rows, allow 53–60cm (21–24 in) between the rows. Another method is to grow the plants in double rows. If it is necessary to move any plants to fill up gaps, do this with a trowel, taking as much soil as possible with each plant.

Tending, staking and picking

The French bean stands drought better than the runner, but if watering becomes necessary give the plants a good soaking and then mulch them with good compost, lawn mowings (not too thickly) or moist peat.

Some kind of support is essential for the climbing varieties. If a trellis or wire fence is not available then tall brushwood, as used for tall peas, is ideal. Large-mesh netting is a good alternative.

Above: bamboo canes and string provide ample support for dwarf types
Right: climbing French bean in flower with (below) Romano, a good variety

For the dwarf varieties all that is needed is something to keep them upright. If they keel over, the lower pods will touch the ground and slug damage may result. Twiggy sticks, pushed in among the plants, is one way of supporting them. Another good method is to push in bamboo canes at intervals down each side of the row, and then run string from cane to cane about 15cm (6 in) above ground.

Begin picking as soon as the pods are large enough to use. It is better to pick on the young side than to let the pods go past their best and get tough. Pick several times a week, and take off all the pods that are ready whether they are needed or not. Any surplus can be frozen or salted.

Pests and diseases

The two pests most likely to be encountered are slugs and blackfly.

Blackfly Keep a close watch for these insects and spray with derris or malathion at the first sign of trouble.

Slugs In addition to eating any pods that touch the soil, slugs may also attack seedling plants. It is always a good plan to scatter a few slug pellets along the rows when the seedlings are pushing through.

HARICOTS

Apart from being dried for winter use, the seeds of haricot varieties can also be eaten in the green state – when they are known as flageolets.

Haricot varieties are grown in the same way as the other dwarf beans, but the plants are allowed to form seeds from the beginning. As the seeds ripen, the pods turn yellow and then brown and papery. At this stage they can be detached from the plant and the beans shelled out.

In a warm, dry autumn the ripening process may be completed on the plants, but in cooler, showery weather some help may be needed. If the pods have not dried off by late autumn (October), pull the plants up, tie them in bundles and hang them on a sunny wall to dry. Alternatively, pull the plants up and cover them with cloches. The ends of the cloches must be left open so that air can blow through.

When you have shelled the beans, spread them out on paper in a warm room to finish drying. They can then be stored, preferably in jars, though paper bags will do. Leave the jars open and give them an occasional shake; this prevents any mould forming.

RECOMMENDED VARIETIES

FRENCH BEANS – dwarf
The Prince Popular variety with long, slender pods.
Tendergreen Early variety with round, fleshy pods.
Remus Bears its pods above the foliage, making picking much easier.
Kinghorn Waxpod Round, slightly curved, yellow pods.

FRENCH BEANS – climbing
Earliest of All Heavy cropper with white seeds that can be used as haricots.
Largo Round pods and white seeds.
Romano More recent variety with fleshy, stringless pods.

HARICOTS
Comtesse de Chambord Popular, white-seeded haricot variety.
Granda Slightly larger than Comtesse de Chambord.
Dutch Brown Excellent 'meaty' bean, larger than most.

Garlic and leeks

There is a widespread belief that garlic is difficult to grow. This may come from its association with warmer climates, and the fact that the standard variety is listed as Best Italian. Whatever the cause, the belief is a mistaken one, as garlic is quite hardy and easy to cultivate. Leeks are also very easy to grow, and few vegetables are more accommodating. The leek can be used as a follow-on crop to early vegetables; it is not much troubled by pests or diseases; it is perfectly hardy; and it matures during winter and early spring when a change of vegetable is welcome.

GARLIC

The best soil for garlic is a light to medium loam, well supplied with humus. Prepare the site, which must be in full sun, in mid autumn (September) by digging in some well-rotted manure or compost. The bulbs can be planted as early as late autumn (October), but early to mid spring (February to March) is preferable as they make little growth in the winter.

Planting the bulbs

Each bulb of garlic is made up of a number of segments or cloves. Bulbs can be planted whole to give larger bulbs, but it is more economical to plant the best cloves separately. Insert them 2–3cm (1 in) deep and 25cm (9 in) apart, in rows 30cm (12 in) apart. Buy bulbs from a leading seedsman; you can, however, use those bought for the kitchen. After the first year select some of the best quality bulbs for the next planting.

Garlic requires no special cultivation beyond keeping the weeds at bay. The

Left: garlic bulbs hanging up to dry
Below: when dry, remove loose skin and dead foliage from bulbs, and store

plants are usually free from pests and diseases. Watering is not necessary, except in very dry seasons. Pinch out flower-heads if they appear.

Lifting, drying and storing

In late summer or early autumn (July or August), according to the time of planting, the foliage begins to yellow, starting at the leaf tips. This is the signal to lift the bulbs and spread them out to dry. Put the bulbs in an empty frame with the lid raised to admit air, or in a cloche or two with the ends left open, or simply tie them in bunches and hang them on a sunny wall. When the bulbs are thoroughly dry, rub off any loose skin and dead foliage, and store them in a dry, light and frost-proof place.

LEEKS

Leeks will grow in most soils, but they do best where the soil's pH is 6–6·5. If it is lower than this, apply hydrated lime according to maker's instructions. As the plants are not put out until late summer or early autumn (July or August), they usually follow an earlier crop, and if manure was used for this crop the soil will be in good condition. If the site was not manured earlier, dig in some good compost if available. As leeks are deep rooting, the compost must be put down where it will retain moisture and the roots can take hold of it.

Sowing from seed

The plants are easily raised from seeds, which should be sown in mid to late spring (March or early April) in shallow drills 6mm ($\frac{1}{4}$ in) deep. If onions are being grown from seed, sow leeks at the same time alongside the onions. If the seeds are sown thinly, no further thinning out will be necessary. Gardeners who miss this sowing can obtain plants from markets or garden centres during the transplanting period.

Planting out

Where only a few leeks are required, an excellent way of obtaining the best results is to dig out a trench 60cm (24 in) wide and a spade's depth. Shovel out the loose soil, break up the subsoil with a fork, and then put in a layer of well-rotted manure or compost. Return about half the topsoil and mark the site of the trench with sticks. Do this a few weeks before planting so that the soil has time to settle. The trench will take two rows of plants 38cm (15 in) apart. Allow 20cm (8 in) between the leeks, and stagger the two rows.

Right: mid-season leek, Musselburgh

Top: composition of trench suitable for planting out a few leek seedlings
Above: before planting leek seedlings, cut back roots and trim leaves as shown

For harvesting in midwinter, plants will need to go out in late summer (July). An early autumn (August) planting will give leeks from late winter (January) onward. As there is usually no shortage of other vegetables before this time, there is little point in planting out too early.

To transplant from the seed row, first ease the plants with a fork, then pull them up and separate them carefully. Throw out any plants that are bent or very short in the stem – these will never make good leeks – and take off any loose skin. Cut back the roots to about 4cm (1½ in) from the stem, and shorten the tops by about half. This does not harm the plants, which soon form fresh roots, but it does make transplanting much easier. The plants are ready for moving when they are about 15–20cm (6–8 in) long, usually about 10–15 weeks old.

A dibber is the best tool for planting but a trowel can be used. Make a hole deep enough to take the plant up to its lowest leaves, drop it in, trickle a little soil over the roots and pour some water into the hole. It is unnecessary to fill the hole in, as this will be done during subsequent cultivation.

When the plants are put out in the open ground, allow 20cm (8 in) between them and a minimum of 30cm (12 in) between the rows; 38cm (15 in) is better, and if you are intending to earth the plants up a little, 45cm (18 in) will be required.

Care of growing plants
Take care when hoeing that the stems of the leeks are not nicked with the hoe, as any wound is an entry point for pests and diseases. Being deep-rooting, the plants do not suffer too quickly from drought, but if it becomes very dry they will appreciate a good soaking of water. An occasional application of liquid manure or soot water will also be beneficial.

The edible part of the leek is the blanched stem, and this area can be increased if a little soil is drawn up the stems. Do this only when the soil is dry and friable and will run through the hoe; to plaster wet soil against the plants will do more harm than good. A dry day in late autumn or early winter (late October or November) is the time to choose. With a draw hoe, carefully pull up the soil to each plant and take care that soil does not fall into the heart of the plant. Where the plants are being grown in a trench the remainder of the dug-out soil is returned to the trench as the plants grow.

Pot leeks
The pot leek differs from the ordinary leek in having a shorter but much thicker

To transplant leeks: **1** draw drill with hoe; **2** make planting holes with a dibber; **3** drop plantlets into holes; **4** trickle soil over roots, and pour in water, but don't fill in hole

stem. Its culture is the same as that of ordinary leeks, but its popularity is limited and mainly confined to certain northern areas of Britain.

Pests and diseases
As a rule leeks are trouble-free, but they may be attacked by onion fly or white rot.
Onion fly This pest can become a menace around the time when the seedlings are transplanted. If there is a history of onion fly in the garden, sprinkle calomel dust up each side of the row while the plants are still in the seedling stage, or dust with BHC.
White rot Calomel dust will also protect against white rot, a white fungal growth at the base of the plant. If this occurs, destroy infected plants and do not grow leeks there again for several years.

Harvesting and storing
Leeks are dug as required and present no storage problem. If severe frost threatens it pays to dig up a few leeks and keep them in the garden shed with the stems covered. An alternative method is to surround a few plants with peat or short litter (composted manure). This will absorb most of the frost and make it possible to dig up the leeks even when the surrounding ground is frozen.

Leeks will continue to grow from the time of planting to the onset of winter. The rate slows down with the arrival of colder weather, although some growth may still be made in mild periods. In mid to late spring (March to April) there is a surge of new growth that culminates in the formation of seed heads. Any plants still left in the ground at the end of spring (late April) should be lifted. These can be stored for a few weeks in a shady corner of the garden, with a little soil over the roots and the blanched stems covered to exclude light.

When digging, make sure that the spade is thrust well down, or the bottom of the leek may be chopped off. The leek makes a mass of fibrous roots, and these help to break up heavy soil.

RECOMMENDED VARIETIES

GARLIC
Best Italian Standard variety, readily available, prolific and easy to grow.
Jumbo Recent variety that can be grown from seed to maturity in about 18 months.

LEEKS
The Lyon (also known as Prizetaker) Popular early variety with long stems and mild flavour.
Marble Pillar Early variety with long white stems.
Musselburgh Mid-season variety, has long, thick stems and broad leaves.
Winter Crop One of the hardiest of the late-cropping leeks.

Tomatoes: Sowing and planting

When growing tomatoes under glass, beware of starting off your tomato seeds too early. Plants which suffer a check from too low a temperature take a long time to recover. It is the *night* temperature of the greenhouse that is most important. A constant 18–21°C (65–70°F) is necessary to start the seeds off, with a follow-on minimum night temperature of about 12°C (54°F).

From late mid spring (the second half of March) or, with insufficient heating facilities, a few weeks later, you can sow seeds in a box of John Innes Potting Compost No 1 (J.I. No 1) or one of the soilless composts. Space the seeds 4cm (1½ in) apart, and cover them with a light sprinkling of compost. Water gently with a fine rose on the watering can, and keep the compost moist but not over-wet.

When the seedlings have made their first pair of true leaves (after the little seed leaves) pot them up into 9 cm (3½ in) pots containing J.I. No 2 or a similar mixture.

Ripe, heavy trusses of delicious tomatoes reward you for your weeks of loving care

Transplanting the young plants

The plants will be ready for transplanting into their final quarters when they are about 20–25cm (8–10 in) high, probably from early summer (early to mid May) onwards. If they are to be grown on staging they will need to be put into 25cm (10 in) pots.

The best results are generally obtained from plants in a 'glass-to-ground' greenhouse. Here the tomatoes can be planted directly into the soil bed, which should be enriched with good compost or well-rotted manure. It is important to dig in the compost or manure in good time, so that the soil can settle before the tomatoes have to be planted.

If you have no heating at all, it is better to buy the plants from a good nurseryman. Look for plants that are short-jointed, well-grown and a rich dark colour.

Transplant the young shoots carefully into the prepared bed, so that the soil ball is just below the soil level, and water them well, using a fine rose on the watering can. They should be spaced some 40–45cm (15–18 in) apart.

Giving support

Instead of an individual cane for each plant, a good alternative method of supporting them is to run a wire from end to end of the greenhouse above the plants and just below the roof. Strong, galvanized wire hooks are pushed into the soil close to each plant and a length of stout garden string is fastened to the hook at one end and the wire at the other. It is then a simple matter, as the plant grows, to give the string an occasional twist round the stem.

Support tomato plants by tying to canes (below), or by twisting string from wire hooks to a horizontal line (below right)

Growing by ring-culture

The drawback to planting directly into the greenhouse soil bed is that the soil soon becomes 'sick' (unhealthy in gardening terms), with the resultant risk of

Lining for ring-culture bed and cross-section of plants in bottomless pots, one plant in earlier stage of growth

disease affecting your tomatoes. To avoid this, the soil bed should be dug out to a spade's depth every couple of years and then filled up with new soil.

However, a less arduous way round the problem is to grow your tomatoes by the ring-culture method. Remove the soil to a depth of 15cm (6 in) and replace with pea-gravel, weathered ashes, or peat: gravel is the longest lasting. If a strong polythene sheet is laid across the bottom and up the sides of the trench before the aggregate is put in, moisture will be retained and less watering will be required.

Bottomless pots (usually sold as ring-culture pots), which can be bought from any good seedsman, are placed on the aggregate and filled with J.I. No 3, or a similar mixture; the tomato plants are then planted out into them. The object in ring-culture is to encourage the plants to form two sets of roots—one in the pot for feeding and the other in the aggregate below the pot for supplying water.

Once the plants are growing strongly

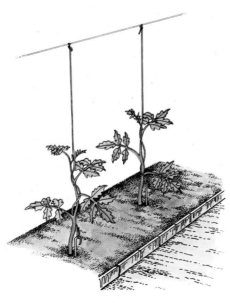

and have sent out roots into the aggregate, watering in the pots should cease, except when feeds are given. If the aggregate is kept moist the plants will take up all their water from below. By using this method, contact with soil-borne diseases is eliminated.

Using 'Gro-bags'

A third method is to grow your tomatoes in the new 'Gro-bags'. These are bags of specially-prepared growing medium which are simply laid on the greenhouse soil or staging. The tomatoes are planted directly into the bags through pre-marked openings, and the only chore then is to keep the medium in the bags watered.

The cordon method

Practically all greenhouse tomatoes are grown by this artificial method that restricts all the growth to one main stem. All tomatoes, if left to themselves, will produce sideshoots that will grow on to make additional stems on which fruit can be borne. These sideshoots come from the leaf axils where the leaves join the stem. By adopting the cordon method the plant is kept from sprawling, and produces earlier and better fruits. Pinch out the sideshoots between finger and thumb as soon as they appear.

GROWING OUTDOORS

Here you have three methods of growing and three different types of plant: the *cordon* type (already described), the *dwarf* and the *bush* tomato. The dwarf tomato is a distinct type which breaks (forms sideshoots) naturally to form several stems. In the bush tomato the stems are more numerous and more pliable and the low-growing plants form a small bush. Neither dwarf nor bush tomato is suitable for greenhouse culture.

In the cold frame

If you have the old type of cold frame, with a sliding light (glass lid), it can be used to start off a few plants. Allow about 30cm (12 in) between the plants when putting them in. Provide a good enriched soil, as for the greenhouse soil bed, and cover with the light until the plants are touching the glass. Plant them in early summer (mid May) and if the nights are cold, or frost is expected, be prepared to cover the glass with old sacks, matting, or anything else that will prevent heat loss—but remember to remove the covering in the morning.

You must also be sure to ventilate the frame on sunny days; even early summer sun can 'toast' the plants badly when it is shining through glass. Remember, however, to close it again in the evening.

When the tops start touching the glass, remove the light and support the plants. You have given them a good start and every week saved is of vital importance when growing outdoor tomatoes.

For the newer types of garden frame, which have more headroom, the dwarf or bush varieties are better, and it may be possible to keep them covered throughout their growth, although adequate ventilation must still be provided if weather conditions demand it.

Under cloches

The bush and dwarf tomatoes are also ideal for growing under barn-shaped cloches. Decide on the strip of soil to be covered and prepare it well in advance. It should be 'in good heart' (that is, a good fertile soil) but not too enriched or the plants will produce plenty of foliage at the

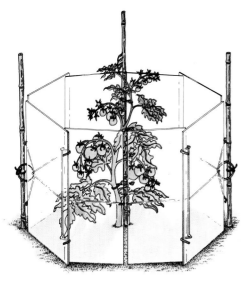

Barn cloches standing on end, anchored by canes tied to the handles, protect young tomato plants growing outdoors

RECOMMENDED VARIETIES

FOR THE GREENHOUSE

Moneymaker   Probably the best-known variety for the greenhouse. Can also be grown outdoors.
Ailsa Craig   Another old favourite of first rate quality.
Alicante   A more recent introduction of fine flavour.
Big Boy   Very large fruits, fleshy and meaty; needs extra support. Not suitable for outdoors.
Golden Sunrise   A fine yellow variety. The yellow tomatoes deserve to be more widely grown. A little sugar sprinkled over them helps to bring out the flavour.

FOR OUTDOORS

Outdoor Girl   Cordon type. Sometimes produces a few misshapen fruits but is a heavy cropper. Outdoors only.
Pixie   Dwarf type. Specially suitable for frames with headroom of 60–90cm (2–3 ft). Attractive fruits of good quality.
French Cross   Dwarf. A heavy cropper of first-class fruits. For frames or cloches.
The Amateur   Bush type. Perhaps the best-known bush variety. Fine for cloches.
Yellow Amateur is the yellow counterpart.
Sleaford Abundance   Bush type. Quality fruits and a good cropper but rather later than Amateur.

expense of fruits. Old bonfire ash makes an excellent dressing for outdoor tomatoes and should be worked into the soil as the strip is prepared. If no ash is available, sulphate of potash at about 35g per sq m (1 oz per sq yd) will help to promote strong flower and fruit production. Incidentally, if the strip has been really well prepared, additional feeding during the growing period should not be necessary. Put the plants out in early summer (the second half of May), allowing about 30–45cm (12–18 in) between plants, according to the vigour of the variety, and cover with the cloches.

If the plants outgrow the available headroom, remove the cloches carefully and stand them *on end* round the plants. Secure a cane to the handle of each cloche and into the soil so that it cannot be blown over. Later, when the weight of fruit pulls the plants down, the cloches can be put over them again to assist ripening. At the same time, cover the ground under the fruit trusses with straw or polythene to prevent any contact with the soil.

Growing without glass

While many thousands of tomato plants are sold each year for planting outdoors, they are nearly all cordon varieties. Very few nurserymen offer dwarf or bush varieties as young plants. This means that if you want to grow them, you must raise them from seed. If you have neither greenhouse nor frame, you can still get results by sowing the seeds in a pot or seed tray placed in the window of a warm kitchen and then following the method already outlined. When the seedlings are ready, set out the number you require into 9cm ($3\frac{1}{2}$ in) pots and keep them in the window, turning the pots each day so that growth is even. Gradually harden them off by moving them to an unheated room and then to a sheltered sunny position outdoors during the day (but bring them in each evening), before planting them out into their final positions.

For plants which have to grow and fruit without any glass protection at all, choose the sunniest and most sheltered spot available. A border facing south, backed by a house wall or close-woven fence, is ideal. Another good site, often overlooked, is the corner of a sunny patio which will accommodate a few plants in large pots or tubs. If the plants have to be grown right out in the open, some shelter can be given by putting in short stakes on the north side and fastening old sacking or sheets of plastic to them. Make sure, however, that this barrier is quite firm and that there is no danger of it blowing down onto the plants.

While all three types can be grown outdoors, the cordon varieties are usually preferred. Because the growing season for outdoor tomatoes is relatively short, it is usually accepted that a plant cannot be expected to set more than five trusses of fruit with any hope of ripening them. So when the stem has reached two leaves beyond the fifth truss, pinch out the growing point with your finger and thumb. You can also use the ring-culture method for growing tomatoes outdoors.

Having explained the various methods of growing tomatoes either in or out of doors, we shall now look at some of the problems likely to be encountered as they ripen and become ready for harvesting.

Tomatoes: Growing and ripening

When your tomato plants are growing strongly, your main tasks are weeding, training and watering. The little onion hoe is the best weeding tool to use for the soil of the greenhouse border (and in frames and under cloches), but hoe only lightly or you may damage the roots.

Training and supporting
Keep cordon plants to one stem by nipping out the sideshoots which form in the axils of the leaves (where the leaf joins the stem). Do remember that sideshoots come from the *axils* of the leaves and fruiting trusses from the stem *between* the leaves.

Nip out the sideshoots as soon as they appear; this lessens the danger of damage to the plants. If you are a smoker with nicotine-stained fingers, wash your hands thoroughly before doing this job or else use a pocket knife. Tomatoes are highly susceptible to nicotine virus, and this can be transmitted from your fingers.

As the plants grow, continue to tie them to their stakes at regular intervals to keep them upright, or twist the supporting string gently round them.

Dwarf tomatoes need little or no training. They produce sideshoots naturally, on which the fruit is borne. An easy way of supporting the plants is to fasten each one to a short stake with a single tie; then run a string, in and out of the plants, from stake to stake.

Bush tomato stems also divide naturally, but their sideshoots are more numerous and more pliable. Stakes are not needed, but when the fruits are swelling their weight will pull the sideshoots to soil level. So put down some slug bait and then slide straw, hay, peat or black polythene under the fruits to keep them clear of the soil.

Some bush plants tend to produce more foliage than is required, particularly if they are on good soil. About early autumn (the middle of August) go through them and cut out stems which are just flowering as they will not give sizeable fruits before the end of the season. By removing these surplus stems you give the plants more light and air.

Plenty of water
Watering always poses something of a problem. There are no hard and fast rules, but for greenhouse tomatoes there are

broad guidelines. When you transplant, give the plants a good watering; after that water only sparingly until new roots begin to form and new growth is seen. From then on increase the supply as the plants grow. When they are mature it is almost impossible to overwater, and in hot weather it may be necessary to water them twice a day.

With plants in frames or under cloches let nature help. Push down the frame lights, or remove the ventilating panes of the cloches when rain is imminent. Plants under cloches will draw much of the water they need from the sides of the cloches where rain has run down into the soil.

Avoid too dry an atmosphere in the greenhouse. Damp down the path and staging and spray the plants with clear water night and morning to keep the air moist. See that ventilation is adequate; in hot weather leave a ventilator a little way open all through the night.

Heat is more important than sunshine to tomatoes once the fruits start ripening

Setting and feeding
When the plants are flowering, encourage the fruits to set by gently tapping the supporting canes or strings about the middle of the day to help distribute the pollen. With dwarf or bush plants this treatment is not necessary.

Don't start feeding until the first fruits have begun to swell. Use a good, proprietary liquid fertilizer and follow the manufacturer's instructions exactly. If you prepared the tomato bed well, then dwarf and bush tomatoes should not need feeding; bush plants in particular will tend to produce lush foliage at the expense of fruit if given too rich a diet.

Ripening the fruit
As the sun begins to lose strength and the nights turn colder, ripening inevitably

slows down. If you have a cool greenhouse, and you have any form of heating, turn it on at night towards mid autumn (late August and September) so that the remaining fruits will ripen. Where you started off the plants in a frame and then grew them on as cordons, cut the strings holding the plants to their supports, remove the canes and then lay the plants down gently onto clean straw or black polythene. Follow the same procedure with plants that outgrew their cloches. Put the frame lights or the cloches back in place, and the fruits will continue to ripen throughout late autumn (October).

Pick all the fruits which have no protection at all by the end of mid autumn (September) and ripen them indoors. Putting the fruit in a sunny window is not the best way of ripening them; neither is it

Below: give fruiting bush plants more light and air by trimming surplus stems

Below: fruits may split if you allow the soil to dry out and then water it heavily

necessary to denude the plants of their leaves in order to expose the fruits to the sun. Leaves should not be taken off unless they have yellowed naturally or are diseased. Both practices spring from the mistaken belief that sunshine is essential for ripening tomatoes; it is not. Providing the temperature is high enough tomatoes will ripen without sunshine. It is quite a common occurrence to find ripe fruit hidden beneath the leafy foliage of a bush tomato plant.

To ripen tomatoes indoors, put them in a basket, cover them with a piece of cloth and keep them in a warm kitchen. Another good way, particularly with the greener fruits, is to put them on layers of cotton wool in a drawer in a warm living room. Any fruits from greenhouse, frames or cloches which have not ripened by the end of autumn (late October) can also be brought in and treated this way.

Pests and diseases

The modern tomato is a highly-developed plant and as such is subject to various diseases – most of them occurring in the fruiting stage. However, if you raise and tend your plants carefully, you should be able to harvest a healthy crop without difficulty. The list which follows are the more common troubles that can occur.

Potato blight (so called because it commonly affects potatoes). Affected plants show brownish-black patches on the fruits which quickly go rotten. There is no cure but the disease may be contained if you pick off the leaves and fruits as soon as you see signs appearing. You can help prevent it by spraying with a suitable fungicide towards the end of mid summer

To finish ripening outdoor cordons, lay the plants down on a bed of clean straw

(end of June), with a second spraying a fortnight later. Keep potatoes and tomatoes as far apart as possible to avoid contamination. Blight is generally confined to outdoor plants but may appear in frames or under cloches.

Leaf mould This is a serious disease of greenhouse tomatoes. The symptoms are a greyish mould on the underside of the leaves with yellow patches on the upper surface. Remove and burn affected leaves and spray with a systemic fungicide. A stagnant atmosphere, especially at night, is the cause and adequate ventilation is the best safeguard. The disease is more prevalent in some areas than in others; if you know it to be troublesome in your district, spray with the fungicide in mid summer and again in late summer (June and July) as a precautionary measure. The variety Supercross (F.1 hybrid) and some strains of Eurocross are immune to this disease.

Blossom-end rot Generally a greenhouse disease in which the end of the tomato opposite the stalk becomes blackish-brown and shrunken and finally rots. There is no cure. The cause is irregular and faulty watering.

Greenback This is not a disease but a condition. Affected fruits have a hard, yellow patch which refuses to ripen. It may be caused by too much sun, or lack of potash. Eurocross and Alicante are among several modern varieties which are resistant to greenback.

Split fruits Caused by letting the plants get dry and then watering heavily. The fruits cannot absorb the water fast enough and the skin ruptures. It ought not to occur in a greenhouse where watering can be controlled, but it is sometimes difficult to prevent outdoors when periods of drought are followed by heavy rains unless you water regularly during dry spells.

Leaf curl When the leaves curl upwards this is generally a sign that the plants are receiving too much nitrogen. Occasionally it may be caused by minute quantities of spray from a selective weedkiller. Tomatoes are especially vulnerable to these and the greatest care must be taken when using them anywhere near tomato plants.

Red spider mite This tiny creature can be a nuisance under glass, though it is not usually a problem outdoors. It is encouraged by a dry atmosphere. The mites feed on the underside of the leaves which become mottled and may turn yellow. Spray or dust with malathion to control them. The mites dislike water, so regular spraying will discourage them from taking up residence.

Apples

Many of the apple varieties bred over the past few decades do not grow well on their own roots. This means that cuttings rooted may not grow at the required pace or strength. To solve these difficulties, apples are budded (grafted) onto specially developed rootstocks. The rootstocks resemble the original species of *Malus* from which most apple trees are derived. They are usually denoted by numbers and letters which refer to the research stations where they were developed. All apple trees bought from a nursery will be grafted on a selected rootstock.

Always plant bushes and cordons with the graft unions between the rootstock and the chosen variety clear of the soil, and never allow soil to cover them in later years. The union is the swelling at about 15cm (6 in) above the stem base. If the trees are planted to the soil mark on the stem, the unions will be at the correct height above soil level.

Bush trees

The ultimate size of a bush tree depends primarily on the rootstock. Determine the choice of rootstock by the general nature of the soil. The stocks which give dwarf and semi-dwarf trees are M9 and M26 respectively. There is also MM106, which gives trees somewhat bigger than true semi-dwarfs and produces bigger crops, but which is still easily managed from ground level.

Planting and staking

Dwarfs grow well in rich soil, but are often too weak for light, sandy ones. On these soils plant either semi-dwarfs or trees on MM106 stock. On rich soil, dwarfs reach a final overall height of about 1·4m (4½ ft), and at maturity will produce an average annual yield of about 11kg (25 lb) of fruit.

Semi-dwarfs on lighter land will reach about 1·8m (6 ft) at maturity, to give an average of 14kg (30 lb), and trees on MM106 on light land will reach 2·5–3m (8–10 ft) with a cropping range averaging 16–18kg (35–40 lb). Trees grafted on M26 and MM106 can grow on rich land, when final tree heights will be above those for light soil, and crops therefore bigger.

Bush trees are free-growing. Plant them at minimum distances of 2·5m (8 ft) on M9, 3m (10 ft) on M26 and 3·7m (12 ft) on MM106.

Permanent stakes are needed for dwarfs; semi-dwarfs will need initial staking, but stakes can sometimes be

RECOMMENDED VARIETIES

DESSERT APPLES	WHEN TO EAT
George Cave	early to mid autumn (August–September)
James Grieve	mid autumn (September)
Merton Worcester	mid to late autumn (September–October)
Lord Lambourne	late autumn to early winter (October–November)
Sunset	late autumn to mid winter (October–December)
Chivers Delight	late autumn to late winter (October–January)
Merton Russet	late winter to mid spring (January–March)
Sturmer Pippin	mid spring to early summer (March–May)

CULINARY APPLES	
Arthur Turner	late summer to late autumn (July–October)
Grenadier	mid autumn (September)
George Neal	mid to late autumn (September–October)

All these apples are of excellent quality and are comparatively easy to grow. Although the culinary varieties overlap they are worth planting as a trio, because each has its distinct flavour.
Cox's Orange Pippin is a universal favourite but can be difficult for beginners, so choose Sunset instead.
Some of the listed varieties may be difficult to obtain. Other varieties which are quite good and reasonably easy to grow as dessert apples are:

Discovery	early to mid autumn (August–September)
Ellison's Orange	mid to late autumn (September–October)
Golden Delicious	early to late winter (November–January)
Egremont Russet	late autumn to mid winter (October–December)

removed later. Trees on MM106 usually do not require stakes.

Shaping bush trees
Except for simple formative pruning, you can leave bush trees for the most part to grow at will. There are some detailed systems of pruning but simple methods give good results, bring the trees into crop at the earliest possible time, and keep them in crop thereafter.

The principle is to have an open, cup-shaped arrangement of four or five main branches (main leaders), each with at least one fork (sub-main leader), to give a final complement of at least eight or ten branches. These provide a more or less permanent basic structure, and should receive little pruning to keep them in shape once the structure has been established. They support the many side shoots (laterals) which carry the fruit.

If you buy a two- or three-year-old tree it should have had the basis of this arrangement already formed in the nursery. However, in the first winter you must tip back each leader to just short of an outward-facing bud, removing 15–25cm (6–9 in) of wood. This will stimulate the growth necessary to build up a rigid framework. You may have to repeat this tipping for the following two or three winters (according to whether the trees were planted as three- or two-year-old specimens). Be sure, also, to cut out any strong inward growths that would cause congestion or compete with leaders. Never allow laterals to rub against leaders. Some young trees may be without sub-main leaders, but these will grow later. When they appear treat them exactly as for the main leaders.

Carry out routine annual pruning of the formed tree in winter. Remove congesting laterals and keep the tree's centre open to air and sunlight. If you do this every year you will find there is not much wood to remove each time.

Top left: James Grieve has an excellent flavour and is frost-resistant. Far left: Merton Russet crops heavily and is crisp and tart. Left: Sturmer Pippin is an excellent early-fruiting variety

Cordons

Cordons are single 'rods' between 1·8m (6 ft) and 2·5m (8 ft) long, clothed throughout most of their length with short fruiting spurs. They are planted 60–90cm (2–3 ft) apart and inclined at 45 degrees, being trained along 2·5m (8 ft) bamboo poles which are fixed to three wires at about 60cm (2 ft), 1·2m (4 ft) and 1·8m (6 ft) from ground level, tightly stretched between strong end posts. These posts should be 2·5m (8 ft) long, buried 60cm (2 ft) and with extra support from wood

Below: first pruning of dwarf bush. Inset shows graft union 8cm (3 in) above soil

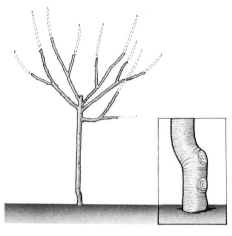

Below: cordon supports. Insets show knot for tying cordon to poles, and graft union

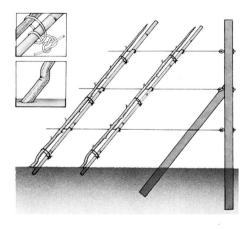

Below: summer pruning of laterals and sub-laterals on cordon apple trees

inside strainers. Long rows need intermediate posts at 4·5m (15 ft) intervals. A typical garden row of cordons takes up no more room than a row of runner beans. Make alleyways 1·8m (6 ft) wide between the rows to allow easy access.

Pruning cordons

On newly-planted trees cut back all laterals longer than 10cm (4 in) to three buds. Good strong rods seldom need cutting, but tip weaker ones back by 15–25cm (6–9 in). Thereafter lateral pruning is done in summer, but any further rod tip stimulation needed is done only in winter.

Above: an apple bough in blossom. Below: Lord Lambourne flowers early and is a regular and heavy cropper. Below right: Sunset, a good tree for garden cultivation, bearing fine-flavoured apples

Lateral pruning aims at fruit spur formation, and a good rule of thumb is: 'laterals to three leaves, sub-laterals to one leaf'. So cut all laterals growing directly from the rods to the third good leaf from the base, and cut all other shoots (sub-laterals) to one good leaf from the base. Cut only when the shoots are mature along the base portion – that is, when the base is woody, the shoot sturdy, and the leaves fully-formed and a dark green colour. As they do not all mature at once, the cutting process goes on over a period from late summer until early autumn (mid July to mid August) according to the area in which you live.

It is absolutely imperative that you don't cut the shoots until they have reached the correct stage of ripeness. Cutting immature wood leads to masses of secondary growth and ruins all attempts to get fruit spurs to form. Even with perfectly-timed pruning some secondary growths may occur from time to time, and these must be removed at their points of origin in mid autumn (September).

Choosing an apple tree

The choice of apple varieties is very wide and it is essential to ensure that the ones you choose will cross-pollinate. Most apples will only produce fully and regularly if their flowers are pollinated by pollen from another variety that blossoms at the same time. There are a few self-pollinating varieties, but even these crop better if cross-pollinated.

If you only have room for one tree, check to see whether any of your neighbours own an apple tree and choose a variety to complement it.

Consider only top quality trees. They cost more than inferior ones, but they will pay over and over again. Cheap trees usually end up on the bonfire. Find a first-class nurseryman, order your trees in good time and take the advice offered in the catalogue.

Pears

To grow well, pears need a soil that is warm, fairly rich, moisture retentive and well drained. Use a good-quality compost, dug in to a spade's depth when planting and also as a spring mulch. Give new trees a good start by picking off any flowers appearing in the first spring after planting, but leave on all the surrounding leaves. Do this at white bud stage when the blossoms are easily handled.

There are several tree forms you can grow. Pears are ideally suited to the trained systems, which are very attractive, and the normal forms of these are fans, cordons and espaliers.

Pruning bush trees

Bush trees, the easiest form to grow, are planted 3–3·5m (10–12 ft) apart. Their shape is virtually the same as that of the bush apple. They have an open centre and a cup-shaped arrangement of main and sub-main leaders.

The formative pruning work is the same as for apples: cut back the leaders of the newly-planted tree by about 15–25cm (6–9 in) to stimulate further extension growth and repeat the process in subsequent winters until the tree has made a sturdy framework.

Most pears are free flowering. This means that the laterals growing from the main and sub-main leaders (the branches and their forks) will form many fruit-bearing spurs – the fat-looking buds that are seen in winter. On some varieties multiple spurs (or spur clusters) develop from the original buds. The pears will hang from these in bunches. If you cut the laterals too much they will not make fruit spurs, but will make growth instead. So keep lateral pruning on bush trees to the essential minimum to ensure good crops.

You must, however, remove congesting laterals; cut back fruited ones that are past their prime (and are producing poorly or not at all) to growth buds near the base, so that fresh laterals will grow out for future cropping.

One of the signs of a neglected tree is a vast conglomeration of old, unproductive fruit spurs, with few or no young laterals. This condition need never arise if you cut back laterals in winter when they begin to show symptoms of decline.

Some varieties (such as Doyenné du Comice) droop noticeably. This is a natural habit, and it would be wrong to try to prevent it by excessive cutting. Nevertheless, some corrective work may

be needed. Where a badly drooping leader has a strong shoot growing near the bend, cut off the drooping part flush with the point of origin of the upright shoot. The latter will then become a replacement leader. If there is no shoot present, cut back the drooping part to a fruit spur just behind the bend.

It cannot be emphasized too strongly that you must not prune bush pear trees hard or haphazardly. Prune lightly, with a definite purpose for every cut. If you are in doubt, wait until the summer before doing any corrective pruning.

Pruning trained pears

With trained forms the pruning system is entirely different. Whether you are growing fans, cordons or espaliers, comparatively hard summer pruning is essential. The underlying reason is that trained forms are kept to the right shape and size, and encouraged to bear heavy crops by a combination of root and top restriction. This can be achieved only by summer pruning, since this automatically checks growth and stimulates fruit bud formation. Winter pruning has the completely opposite effect.

Prune as for cordon apples, by cutting

Far left: blossom on recommended variety Conference; below far left: fruit of Beurré Superfin; below left: Conference pears; right: fruit of the drooping-branched Doyenné du Comice

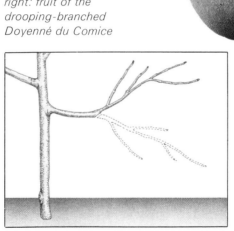

Above: cut back a drooping leader to an upper shoot, which then becomes the replacement leader.
Below: upright cordon showing graft

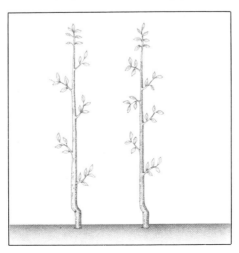

all laterals growing directly from the cordon rods (or from the main branches of fans and espaliers) to the third good leaf from the base; cut all other sideshoots to the first good leaf from the base.

As with apple trees, do not prune pear shoots until they are ripe along their basal portion – that is, when they are clothed in dark green leaves along that portion and resistant to bending. This stage is reached earlier than with apples, occurring throughout early to mid summer (mid June to mid July). In autumn remove any secondary shoots arising from the cuts at their points of origin.

Training cordons

You can grow cordon pears either at an angle or vertically. The latter way is excellent for training up pergolas or arches. Plant the trees 75cm (2½ ft) apart and train them up the two sides of the pergola. Then lead the trees over the top so that each tree meets its opposite number to form a covered arch.

Upright pear cordons are ideal for a sunny wall, especially if it is high and narrow. Bear in mind the balance between the size and shape of your wall and the dimensions of the tree you wish to grow. A wide wall is suited to fans and espaliers, a narrow one to vertical cordons. Do not make the mistake of cramming a fan or espalier onto a short wall as you would need to chop the trees hard in order to make them fit the space.

Training espaliers
Espaliers are horizontal cordons arranged in parallel tiers left and right of a central stem. Several nurseries supply partly-formed specimens, usually of three tiers, that are just right for small or medium-sized gardens. Tip back the branches or 'arms' of the newly-planted espalier by 15–25cm (6–9 in) to encourage further extensions. When they have grown to the length you require, remove the tip growths in early spring (February) to form lateral buds; in due course, these will become the fruiting spurs. Continue winter tipping for two to three seasons.

Espaliers can be grown against walls or fences, either as path edgings or as divisions between different parts of the garden. The overall length at maturity varies somewhat according to type, but on average is about 3·6m (12 ft), that is 1·8m (6 ft) on both sides of the stem. Thus you should estimate 3·6m (12 ft) as the minimum planting distance where more than one tree is wanted. Initially, you will need a supporting system of posts and wires. Train the branches along the wires – the supports can often be removed later once the tree has established its shape. Do not train the trees directly against the wall, as free air circulation behind the trees is imperative; instead, use a temporary structure of light posts.

Training fan trees
Fan pear trees are best bought partly formed, with foundation branches growing out left and right from a short stem. Tip back the leaders or 'ribs' in winter for extension growth; the fruit is carried on short spurs along these. All trained pear trees are, in effect, multiple cordons until they reach their desired length.

Picking and storing
The seasons given under Recommended Varieties are for edibility and not necessarily for picking. It is extremely important to pick at the right time and store properly. Skin colour is not a guide to picking and pears must never be left to ripen on the tree. Instead, use the 'lifting' test; it is not infallible, but it is the safest guide to follow. Lift each pear to a horizontal position; if it parts readily from the spur, then it is ready for picking. If they fall into the hand at a touch, then this usually means they have been left too long; if they fall off untouched then they are definitely past the picking stage, and may go mealy or 'sleepy' in store. If they leave the spur with a snap, then you are probably picking too early, and the pears will shrivel up in storage.

Right: the variety William's Bon Chrétien will cross-pollinate with both Buerré Superfin and Conference
Below: three-tiered espalier, showing the branches trained along the wires

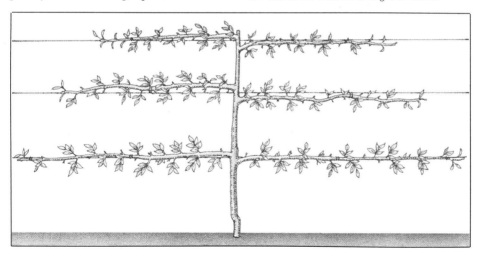

RECOMMENDED VARIETIES

TYPE	WHEN TO EAT
Doyenné du Comice	early winter (November)
William's Bon Chrétien	mid autumn (September)
Conference	late autumn to early winter (October–November)
Buerré Superfin	mid autumn (October)
Marie Louise	late autumn to early winter (October–November)
Winter Nelis	early to late winter (November–January)

Of course, they will not all reach picking stage together, so you can pick them over a period and allow them to ripen over a similar period.

At the correct stage for harvesting, very few varieties will have their full skin colour; some may have a flush or tinge of colour, others may still be green. The full colour will come later. Most storage pears attain perfection over a period, but once attained it lasts for only a short time – though only the connoisseur would detect a deterioration of quality early on.

Keep storing pears in a fairly dry atmosphere at 4–7°C (40–45°F) and lay them out on shelves or trays. Storage cabinets with pull-out slatted trays are ideal. If you are storing the pears in a shed keep it free from strong smells; oil, fertilizer, paint, binder twine and creosote tend to destroy the flavour and aroma of pears. When the stalk ends yield to very slight pressure, bring the pears into a temperature of about 15°C (60°F). They will then complete their ripening process quite soon.

Choosing for cross-pollination
Provide for cross-pollination by choosing a succession of pears. Choose varieties whose flowering periods overlap sufficiently, but avoid grouping certain varieties that will not cross-pollinate, even though their blossoms do coincide. Almost the only pear that is fully self-fertile is Fertility Improved, but it is not one of outstanding quality. The variety Conference produces some fruits from its own pollen in some seasons, but many of them are seedless and misshapen.

The queen of pears is probably Doyenné du Comice which is in season in early winter (November). Of the many available varieties, any of the others listed under Recommended Varieties would be suitable to go with it. If you only want two trees (the minimum for cross-pollination) select them from Conference, William's Bon Chrétien and Buerré Superfin, or from Doyenné du Comice, Marie Louise and Winter Nelis. William's Bon Chrétien is a dual-purpose variety, being a splendid dessert pear *and* excellent for cooking.

If you only have space for one bush tree, buy the Family Tree which comprises three varieties on one rootstock. Varieties are selected by the nursery for quality, effective cross-pollination and seasonal succession. Naturally, the yield of each type is only one-third of the total, but can still average about 30kg (15 lb) from a well-grown tree. One excellent combination offered is William's Bon Chrétien, Doyenné du Comice and Conference.

133

Rhubarb

Four rhubarb plants should be enough for the average family and six for a large one. There are two methods of establishing a rhubarb bed: one is to buy the planting crowns and the other is to raise your own roots from seed. If time is not important, growing from seed is cheaper and not difficult, but planting crowns gives a quicker return.

Preparing the soil

Rhubarb prefers a sunny, open site. It will grow in most soils but does better in a soil that is rich and light. As it occupies the ground for a long time (a good bed should crop for at least ten years) it makes sense to give it a good start. Begin by taking out a trench 90cm (3 ft) wide and a spade's depth, and then break up the subsoil. Before returning the topsoil, fork in some well-rotted manure or compost – about a bucket load to each plant. This should be done several weeks in advance of planting so that the soil has time to settle.

Planting or sowing

You can buy crowns from market stalls or nurserymen during the planting season. Choose roots that have at least one good bud or crown. The best planting time is early winter (November) followed by early to mid spring (February or March).

Sow seed outdoors in mid to late spring (late March or April) in drills 2–3cm (1 in) deep and 38cm (15 in) apart. Thin the plants to stand 15cm (6 in) apart and then let them grow on. It may be possible, by the end of the summer, to see which are the best roots to retain when thinning, but a better selection can be made if the plants are left for another season. You can then pull stalks from the rejected plants before they are discarded; don't pull any from the chosen roots.

In early winter (November) lift the roots carefully and replant them firmly 90cm (3 ft) apart, so that the topmost bud is just about 5cm (2 in) below the level of the surrounding soil.

Pulling the stalks

No stalks should be pulled in the first year after planting. In early autumn (August) the stalks yellow and die down naturally, and the goodness in them is returned to the crowns. By pulling too soon you delay

Champagne Early has a fine flavour

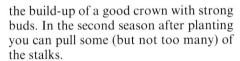

Above left: give a good mulch in autumn Above: cover crowns with removable box or bin to force. Above right: yellow leaves of forced rhubarb contrast with those of a normal crop (left)

the build-up of a good crown with strong buds. In the second season after planting you can pull some (but not too many) of the stalks.

Cut off any seed-heads that push their way up through the leaves (and put them on the compost heap) as the production of seed weakens the plants. Stop pulling rhubarb after mid summer (end of June). If you then want stalks for jam, take one or two from each plant. Always leave some stalks to feed the crowns for the following year.

When pulling rhubarb, slide a hand down the stem as far as possible and then detach the stalk with a quick, outward twist. One peculiarity of this plant, that should not be forgotten, is that while the stalks are edible the leaves should never be eaten as they contain oxalic acid and are poisonous.

Tending the plants
In autumn rake off the withered leaves and mulch the area with some good compost or manure. The goodness from this will be absorbed into the soil with beneficial results. Repeat this dressing annually to help keep the bed in the best possible condition.

When crowns produce only a succession of thin stalks it is a sign that the

roots need lifting and dividing. Fork them out, chop them up with a sharp spade and select only the strongest, outlying crowns for replanting. Only divide one or two roots at a time to make sure there is no break in the supply of stalks.

Forcing rhubarb
Rhubarb 'forcing' means persuading it to produce stalks before its normal season. There are two ways of doing this. For the first method you will need a greenhouse with some heating; a temperature of 10°C (50°F) is high enough. Dig up strong-growing crowns in late autumn and early winter (October and November) and leave them on the open ground so that the roots are exposed to the weather. In mid or late winter (December or January) take them into the greenhouse and plant them closely together in the soil border, or under the staging or in a deep box. If using boxes, put the crowns on a few centimetres of good soil and then cover them completely with more of the same soil.

There are two important points to remember with this type of forcing. The soil around the crowns must be kept moist, and they must be forced in the dark. Black polythene makes a useful screening material. If you are using boxes it is a simple matter to invert one box over another.

The disadvantage of this method is that, after forcing, the crowns are exhausted and are of no further use. Therefore you must either buy crowns specially for forcing, or take up valuable space in order to grow extra crowns for the purpose. But as rhubarb freezes well there is no longer

the same need to take this trouble in order to have rhubarb early in the year.

The second, and easier, way is to force the crowns *in situ* in the garden by covering selected roots with bottomless boxes, buckets or tubes. An old dustbin, with the bottom knocked out and the lid used as a cover, is ideal for this purpose. The point in having a removable cover is that it enables the crowns to be inspected without disturbing the box or bin. You can gain a little extra warmth by heaping strawy manure or decaying leaves around the bin. Alternatively, fill the bin loosely with hay or straw.

This practice, although giving later stalks than the greenhouse method, has the advantage that the crowns are not seriously harmed. Providing the same roots are not used for forcing each year, they soon recover. The simplest method of all (still giving stalks earlier than from unprotected roots) is to cover the roots in mid winter (December) with 30cm (12 in) of straw. You can leave the straw in place, after the rhubarb has emerged, where it will rot down to form humus.

Pests and diseases
The only calamity likely to affect rhubarb is crown rot. This bacterial disease causes rotting of the terminal bud, and may extend right back to the rootstock. Dig up and burn affected plants.

RECOMMENDED VARIETIES
Victoria Long, cherry-red stalks of excellent quality and flavour.
Champagne Early Fine-flavoured variety with long, bright scarlet stalks.
Glaskin's Perpetual Grows well from seed and produces a good yield over a long period.
Holstein Bloodred Vigorous grower and prolific cropper with juicy, dark red stalks.

Strawberries

The main requirement of strawberries is a well-drained, moisture-retentive soil enriched with organic matter. The modern varieties are largely free of pests and diseases and produce crops of finely-flavoured, brightly-coloured berries, varying in size from medium to very large.

Summer fruiters and perpetuals
There are two types of strawberries: the summer fruiters, that produce berries from mid to late summer (June to July), and the perpetuals that fruit in relays from mid summer to mid or late autumn (June to September or October) – if the plants are kept under cloches during the summer.

The summer fruiters will generally crop for three seasons, though the third season's yield will usually be light. The perpetuals are more or less finished after one season, except for the variety Gento that can give quite a good yield in its second year.

Although the total crop from perpetuals is heavy, the number of berries gathered at each picking is often small. One variety may give a total of 500g (1 lb) per plant, but from perhaps 15 or more pickings spread over eight or nine weeks. Other varieties, of which Gento is an example, can produce some huge berries. So if you want the weight to be made up in berry numbers as well as in size, you must buy an appropriate number of plants, say a dozen for a family of four, to give each person a worthwhile share of the pickings.

Soil requirements
Strawberries are essentially a rotation crop. The summer fruiters occupy their plot for two or three seasons, and new plants are put in elsewhere. The perpetuals remain for one season, or at the most two seasons, and again a fresh site is chosen for new plants. If you are growing plants in containers, use fresh soil for each new planting. Never plant into soil if the crop previously occupying it was infected with verticillium wilt – a fungus infection which affects strawberries. Potatoes and tomatoes are susceptible to this disease, and so are the weeds groundsel, thistles and plantains.

Rotate strawberries with crops needing and receiving good organic manuring – like peas and beans. These have nitrogen-fixing nodules on their roots, so cut off the

spent tops and leave the roots behind to supply nitrogen to the strawberries. Additional nitrogen-supplying fertilizers are not often required; an excess leads to leaf growth at the expense of berries, and this in turn hinders air circulation and sunlight penetration. These conditions invite grey mould (botrytis) that thrives in cool, damp conditions.

Strawberries like acidity, so do not add any lime to the strawberry bed. However, should you have limed the vegetable garden for a previous crop, this will not usually cause any trouble. One variety, Gento, does not appear to mind a limy soil, which makes it a good perpetual to choose for chalky districts.

On soils rich in humus you can achieve excellent results without using any fertilizers, but on less fertile land apply a general fertilizer (according to maker's instructions), that includes strawberries among plants for which it is formulated.

When to plant
Early autumn (August) is the best time to plant summer fruiters. You can then allow the plants to crop freely in the following summer. If you plant summer fruiters in the spring, remove all blossoms that appear, allowing the plants to build up strength for cropping the following year. Whether you plant in autumn or spring, remove the flowers appearing in early summer (May), but leave subsequent ones. Thereafter (with perpetuals that fruit again in the second year) leave all flowers intact.

How to plant
To prepare the soil, trench to about 15cm (6 in) to facilitate the placing of compost in the root zone. One barrowload per 8–10 sq m (10–12 sq yd) is a satisfactory dressing. A standard spacing is 45cm (18 in) between plants and 60–90cm (2–3 ft) between rows (depending on varieties). The summer fruiting variety Elista, however, can be planted with only 25cm (9 in) between plants. Plants must be set with their crowns level with the soil surface. If they are too high the new roots, that spring from the crown bases, will fail to contact the soil quickly enough and will perish; if too deep the crowns may rot, especially in wet summers.

Many nurseries sell pot-grown plants. These may arrive either in composition-

the soil). To make certain of rooting, however, peg the runners down with stones when the first leaves have appeared.

Allow no more than three runner plants (and preferably only two) to grow from each parent plant, using only the first to form on each runner. Never propagate from plants that are doing poorly; runner stock from poor parents will rarely succeed, and may well harbour disease.

Alternatively, keep two or so healthy plants just for runner production. Plant them away from the main strawberry bed and keep them 'de-blossomed'. If you choose this method, then remove and destroy runners from fruiting plants.

Some perpetuals do not make runners. Leave the runners on those that do, since the plantlets produce fruit in addition to that on the parents, thus increasing the total crop by up to about 25 per cent.

Mud and frost protection

When the first fruits have started to weigh down the stems, the plants can have a mat of straw laid round them to protect the berries from being splashed by mud. Another method is to lay strips of polythene sheeting, anchored by stones, along the rows. See that the soil is moist before laying down sheeting and that plants sit on a slight mound so that water does not collect around them. Black polythene sheeting is often recommended

because it suppresses weeds. However, clear sheeting has been shown to give bigger crops in recent experiments.

Tunnel and cloche cultivation

Polythene sheeting tunnels are the latest means of getting an early pick from the summer fruiters. This is useful if you want early strawberries for a special occasion; otherwise you may not find the extra attention they need worth the end results. There are various patterns of tunnel. The best is the type which has a bar running along the length of its ridge. The sides can then be rolled up and fixed to this bar at flowering time to allow pollinating insects free play. Without their help many flowers may fail to set or may produce small or malformed berries.

An advantage of tunnels is that they reduce the need for watering. Loss of water by evaporation through the leaves is greatly reduced – but, of course, the water must be there in the first place. This means giving the plants a thorough watering just before the tunnels are fitted, usually in early to mid spring (late February to mid March) for a first pick in early summer (the third week of May) in the south of England. After a wet winter, however, there will probably be enough moisture in the ground to make this initial watering unnecessary. Roll up the tunnels in any unseasonably hot weather. If you are using cloches or Dutch lights, take off

type pots that are planted directly into the soil, when they soon rot to provide free root growth, or else with their roots enclosed in a fibrous net (that also rots). In both instances the tops of the containers should be at soil level. Make sure, when buying plants, that they are certified as being from virus-free stock; most reputable nurseries now supply these.

Propagation by runners

Summer fruiters should have their runners removed in the first summer. These grow out from the parent plants and in due course form 'runner plants' that root on contact with the soil. In the second season you can leave them to grow on and use them to provide new plants for setting out in early autumn (August). They will then crop the following summer, thus giving you a continuation of summer harvests, and save the expense of buying new stock every third year.

Propagation is simple. Separate the plants from their parents by cutting the runners. Avoid cutting too close to the plantlet. Then lift them carefully and plant them out. Runners normally root readily in friable soil (or in a pot sunk in

Far left, above left and left: Tamella, Pantagruella and Baron Solemacher Below: for best flavour, pick and eat strawberries when they are 'dew fresh'.

alternate cloches at flowering time, and open Dutch lights fully. With all types of culture the coverings must be in position overnight for early berries. If frost is forecast it is wise to cover Dutch lights, cloches and tunnels with light sacking or something similar, removing this the following morning.

Protect plants in the open from frost in flowering time – early summer (May) – by covering them with newspaper or straw at night; remove it in the morning. Never put down a straw mulch under the plants until the frost has gone, the mulch can worsen frost damage to blossoms by insulating them from ground warmth.

Pests on strawberries
Strawberries fall prey to many pests, but most of them are easily controlled.

Slugs Mostly a problem on soils with a high content of organic matter. Put down metaldehyde pellets at fruiting time.

Red spider mite Mostly found on plants grown under cloches or polythene tunnels. It causes a mottling of the foliage, and plant growth is weakened. Spray with malathion before flowering, or make several applications of derris.

Aphides These pests cause a curling of the foliage, and sap the strength of the plant. More seriously they are carriers of virus disease. The variety Royal Sovereign is particularly susceptible to aphides. Spray well into the centre of the plant with derris, malathion or pyrethrum.

Squirrels and birds Both these animals are fond of strawberries. The best protection is netting.

Virus diseases
There are several types of virus diseases that attack strawberries. The superficial symptoms of these diseases are very similar – stunting of the plant and discoloration of the leaves.

Green petal, **arabis mosaic**, **yellow edge and crinkle** These are spread by eelworms in the soil and by aphides and leaf hoppers. To help control the spread of the diseases, spray with derris or malathion. Remove all weak and unhealthy plants and burn them. Buy certificated stock plants, and propagate only from healthy plants – and from these only for four or five years.

Fungus diseases
Leaf spot, red core, mildew and grey mould (botrytis) are fungus diseases which may attack strawberries.

Leaf spot Pick off and burn any leaves with greyish-red spots.

Red core This is only likely to occur in areas where drainage is poor. Gradually

all plants infected will appear stunted and die. If you cut into the roots, they will appear red in the centre. Spores of the fungus can live in the soil for twelve years or more. See that the ground is properly drained (by correct soil preparation) before planting. If plants become infected, burn them; strawberries should not be planted on the infected land again.

Mildew A dry-weather disease which shows as a white powdery mould. To control it, spray with dinocap, benomyl or wettable sulphur. Royal Sovereign is particularly prone to mildew. Although this variety is a fine summer fruiter it is much more prone to disease than the modern types, and therefore not recommended for beginners.

Grey mould (botrytis) This attacks mainly in wet summers. The fungus first appears in early summer (May), though it is invisible then, because only the spores are present. To defeat it at the outset, apply an appropriate fungicide. Several are available to gardeners, and are either protective formulations based on captan or thiram (don't spray during the three weeks before picking because of taint), or systemics based on benomyl. They are sold under brand names, complete with full instructions.

Tending the plants
The main jobs are weeding (best done with a hoe), removing or attending to the runners and watering in dry weather – especially important from first flower until just before harvesting. If you are using strips of polythene sheeting these will conserve root moisture and reduce watering, but they will prevent the

penetration of rain. So, as with tunnels, a thorough watering must be given before the strips are laid.

As soon as the final harvest has been gathered, the old leaves should be cut off plants that are to be left for a further year. Old foliage produces substances that inhibit the maximum development of flower-buds for the next season. The simplest way is to clip over with shears, taking great care not to cut the crowns or any young leaves surrounding them. The cut-off foliage is then gathered up and burnt. Prick over the surrounding ground lightly with a fork, and lay a light dressing of compost.

The exception to this treatment is Cambridge Favourite. With this variety, the removal of the leaves would result in a reduced crop the following year.

Straw protects berries from mud; as shown here with Cambridge Favourite variety

RECOMMENDED VARIETIES

SUMMER FRUITING	In season from mid to late summer (June to July)
Pantagruella	Early season; acid-sweet in flavour.
Cambridge Rival	Early to second early; medium to medium-large berries; shiny, darkish crimson at maturity; flesh pinkish, sweet and rich; moderate cropper.
Cambridge Vigour	Mid season; first berries medium-large, then smaller; scarlet at maturity; heavy yielder in maiden year.
Domanil	Mid to late; high proportion of large berries; heavy cropper.
Grandee	Mid season; produces some giant berries; heavy second-year cropper; a show bench variety.
Tamella	Mid to late; very heavy cropper; an outstanding strawberry for all purposes – highly recommended.
PERPETUALS	In season from mid summer to mid autumn (June to September)
Gento	The supreme variety to date; crops heavily on parent plants and runners; gives some very large, shining, scarlet berries.
Trelissa	Medium to large berries in abundance on parents and runners; can be trained against trellis work for decoration.
Baron Solemacher	A fine old favourite of the alpine type, producing masses of small berries of the best quality for making jam; does not make runners; a fine decorative plant for shady borders.

Raspberries and loganberries

Raspberries and loganberries thrive on most garden soils which retain summer moisture but do not become waterlogged in winter. The only basic soil type on which they will usually fail is the highly alkaline. If their roots are in chalk or limestone where the pH is above 7, iron deficiency will be a problem. The higher the alkalinity, the greater this problem will be. In theory you can overcome it by adding a proprietary iron compound, but this method can be expensive and might have to be adopted annually.

Some acidity, however, is safe; cane fruits will be happy in a soil with a pH of 6, which is slightly acid, or in one of 7, which is neutral, and they will tolerate acidity down to a pH of 5, but not below. You can always check acidity with a soil-testing kit, and apply lime as appropriate. The amount recommended by the manufacturers should be scattered evenly and forked in, preferably a few weeks before planting.

Preparing the ground
The best foundation is good quality compost dug deeply into the top 30cm (12 in) of soil at the rate of about a bucket – 9 litre (2 gallon) size – to a trench 60cm (2 ft) wide and 1·5m (5 ft) long, after removing perennial weeds and their roots.

Prepare the ground in late summer or early autumn (July or August), ready for planting either when plants become available from the nurseries – usually from late autumn (October) onwards – or in the spring. Do not skimp on the compost at this stage because the plants will rapidly produce masses of shallow roots, making it impossible to dig in compost later without damaging them.

This base dressing of compost can be supplemented by laying a mulch each spring along the raspberry rows in a continuous strip some 45cm (18 in) wide and 2–5cm (1–2 in) deep, and – if you have enough to spare – round the root area of loganberry plants as a circular mat about 45cm (18 in) in diameter. To be fully effective as a conserver of soil moisture and to suppress weeds, which are two of the prime functions of a mulch, the material must be generously applied. Some perennial weeds, like dock, may

still appear, but the roots are easily pulled out by hand.

Choosing the site
The main factor in choice of site is shelter from cold winds. At blossom time these can ruin the flowers, and at any period in the growing season they may cause leaf damage, sometimes to a severe degree. Every effort should be made to plant in a spot sheltered from northerly and easterly winds.

Westerly winds, on the other hand, cause little or no leaf scorch. However, if you have no choice but to plant in the path of any prevailing wind – and this is sometimes the case in country gardens – be sure the rows run along the wind rather than across it. Rows planted broadside could be badly blown about.

Spring frosts are seldom damaging because cane fruits come into flower when the frost hazard has passed.

How to plant raspberries
Plant your raspberries 45–60cm (18–24 in) apart, the latter distance being advisable for varieties making many canes (main stems), leaving a gap of 1·75–2m (6–6½ ft) between the rows. The roots should be covered to a depth of 7–8cm (3 in).

The simplest way is to take out a wedge of soil to the required depth and about a spade's width, and then, with someone

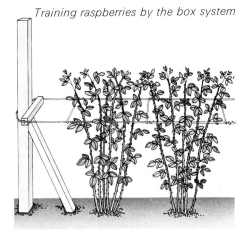
Training raspberries by the box system

holding the cane in position, replace the soil. Firm planting is essential; press home the soil (by treading it down) and then finish off the surface lightly. After planting, cut back the canes to 25–30cm (9–12 in) above soil level, so that the plants do not fruit the following summer, but spend the first year building strong roots and canes.

The best method of training raspberries is the box system. With a post at each end of the row, firmly staple two parallel wires at about 60cm (24 in) above ground level to each one and fit with cross wires twisted around them to separate the canes of each stool (the root or stump from which the stems grow) from those of its neighbour. If necessary the wiring can be repeated at about 1·25m (4 ft) above the ground to accommodate the tall-growing varieties. To hold the parallel wires at the right distance apart, nail or screw 15cm (6 in) distance pieces (battens) to the end posts, and to intermediate posts where the rows are long. The battens, which should be about 4cm (1½ in) in

Malling Promise, a strong and upright variety producing heavy crops of firm fruit, provided the stock from which the excellent Malling Exploit was derived

diameter, can be grooved to take the wires, or the wires can be stapled to un-grooved surfaces. You don't have to tie in the canes, and the cross wires are easily adjustable to accommodate new ones. In this way every stool with its canes is enclosed within its own 'box', which greatly facilitates the pruning out of old canes, and allows a good air flow between the canes. This is an important point: adequate air movement to dry the canes, leaves and berries quickly after rain is a necessary factor in the preven-tion of fungus diseases.

End posts need not be particularly heavy, since they take little strain, serving mainly to hold the wires taut: 5–6cm (2 in) in diameter and 2m (6 ft) long is usually adequate. Sink them 45cm (18 in) and strengthen them with wood strainers. The bottom 60cm (24 in) should be thoroughly treated with a standard proprietary preservative. Creosote in this case is not suitable because it gives surface protection only and can be harmful to plants.

Pruning the canes

Routine pruning (for all except autumn fruiting varieties) consists of removing all fruited canes after harvest, and all weak new ones, leaving about 6–8 of the best per stool. Tip back (cut the tops off) new canes in early spring (February) at 1·5m (5 ft) or so (or just below the point where they have bent over) to encourage fruiting. Autumn-fruiting raspberries are left unpruned until early spring (February) when old canes are cut back to just above ground level.

Pests and virus diseases

Although there may be occasional out-breaks of pests and diseases, routine detailed spraying will not be necessary. The virus diseases are, in principle, the only really severe threat, but the Malling raspberries recommended here are tolerant of virus infection in varying degrees. This means that if they do become infected they will not suffer to any marked extent, and often no leaf symptoms will appear.

The Glen Clova variety is, however, showing itself to be intolerant, and susceptible to cross-infection, so it would be unwise to plant it with a tolerant variety. For example, if Malling Jewel and Glen Clova were neighbours, the former might become infected (without showing any symptoms of the disease) and pass the infection to Glen Clova, which could then suffer. Planted on its own, however, Glen Clova has so far shown virtually no virus infection.

Virus diseases are transmitted by cer-tain greenfly species. The most common form of virus is probably mosaic. If the virus-transmitting greenfly feed on an infected plant and then (within 24 hours) feed on an uninfected one, they will transmit mosaic to the latter. It is almost impossible to keep down greenfly com-pletely, but if you are growing a virus-intolerant raspberry it pays to apply an annual winter wash of tar oil against the over-wintering greenfly eggs.

The nastiest pest is the grub of the raspberry beetle. A spray with a derris pesticide after full bloom and again 10 days later is the answer.

Deficiency diseases

The chief nutritional element which may be lacking from time to time is potash; deficiency in this will show as greyish or brownish leaf margins which become dead and brittle. To correct this, apply 15–25g per sq m ($\frac{1}{2}$–$\frac{3}{4}$ oz per sq yd) of sulphate of potash in the autumn.

LOGANBERRIES

Loganberries are usually planted about 3·75m (12 ft) apart and are cut back as for raspberries. The main training systems are the open fan, the 'modified open fan' and the 'rope' or 'arch' method. The two latter systems make use of practically all cane growth whereas half of this may have to be sacrificed with the open fan – resulting in much crop loss. But the open fan method is more convenient where space is limited, as the plants can be put in much nearer together only 2·5–3m (8–10 ft) apart.

Open fan Fix wires at about 60cm (2 ft), 1m (3½ ft), 1·5m (5 ft) and 2m (6 ft) from ground level to stout end and middle posts 2·5m (8 ft) long, which have been sunk 60cm (2 ft) into the ground. Arrange the fruiting canes fan-wise on the first wires, with a gap in the centre. Lead the new canes up through this gap and tie temporarily to the top wire. After harvesting cut the fruited canes right out at the base and tie the new ones in to replace them.

Modified open fan Fix wires at 60cm (2 ft), 90cm (3 ft), 1·25m (4 ft), 1·5m (5 ft) and 2m (6 ft) from ground level. Train the fruiting canes to more or less their full length, left and right of centre along the first four wires, while the top wire again takes the new ones.

Rope or arch Train all fruiting canes in one direction, and all new ones in the opposite direction. When more than one stool is planted, arrange the training so that the fruiting canes of one stool always meet the fruiting canes of its neighbour.

Separation of fruiting from non-fruiting wood makes picking and pruning much easier and reduces the risk of cane spot fungus, the spores of which are washed from old to new canes. (All methods of training provide for this separation.) Other pests and virus diseases are covered opposite.

Modern loganberry plants can produce a dozen or more canes each season, all of which you can tie in practically full length with the rope and modified open fan systems, thereby ensuring the maximum crop – which may be 4·5–5kg (10–12 lb) per plant when the plants are fully established. In all cases you need to sink stout posts 2·5m (8 ft) long, to a depth of 60cm (2 ft).

Above right: ripe loganberries
Opposite: main systems of loganberry training. Open fan, for use in limited space (far left, above), modified open fan (above left) and rope or arch (left)

RECOMMENDED VARIETIES

Skilful selection from among the modern varieties of raspberries and loganberries means that the gardener can enjoy the benefits of an extended picking season.

RASPBERRIES

The modern range of raspberries in Britain is composed chiefly of those raised at the East Malling Research station in Kent. In order of ripening the following are the best of those available.

Malling Exploit Early season variety fruiting in late summer (July). Canes abundant and vigorous; fruit large, bright red, firm and well-flavoured. Crops heavily and picks easily. Generally acknowledged to be superior to the earlier-raised Malling Promise from which it was derived.

Malling Jewel Early to mid season variety fruiting in late summer to early autumn (July–August). Cane growth strong but not abundant; fruit fairly large, medium to dark red, good flavour; picks easily and berries do not crumble. A reliable variety cropping well and regularly.

Malling Enterprise Mid to late season variety fruiting in early to late autumn (August–October). Canes strong but not usually abundant; fruit very large, medium red, firm, with excellent flavour; picks easily and does not crumble. Crops well, and tolerates heavier soil than other varieties provided drainage is adequate.

There are several more East Malling varieties, such as **Orion, Admiral** and **Delight,** on trial or being tested. Some are extremely heavy croppers producing fine quality berries, and will no doubt be released for general culture in due course. Two more outstanding varieties now available are **Glen Clova** from Scotland and **Zeva** from Switzerland. The former is an exceptionally heavy producer of top quality berries which are first-rate for eating and processing. The canes give a heavy mid season (early autumn) crop and a small mid autumn pick. Zeva starts to fruit in late summer and continues until mid to late autumn, though the summer crop is not abundant, and autumn is the period of heaviest cropping. The berries can be huge, sometimes 2–3cm (1 in or more) long, and the flavour is very fine. A distinct advantage of Zeva is that it needs no supporting system. It makes bush-like growth and can be grown as a single bush (where space is too limited for raspberry rows) even in a large tub or container. Finally, the autumn fruiting variety **September** is a splendid choice for those who want mid to late autumn raspberries, and the old favourite **Lloyd George** is still a winner if the improved New Zealand strain is bought. This latter is stocked by most leading fruit nurseries.

LOGANBERRIES

The best loganberry is the **Thornless**; it arose as a mutant or bud 'sport' of the thorned type which means it is identical to the original loganberry in all respects – except for having no thorns. Any natural plant variation is called a 'sport'.

Blackberries and hybrids

BLACKBERRIES

This fruit belongs to the genus *Rubus* and was originally named *Rubus frucoticosus*. Botanists later recognized much variation in wild blackberries and they divided them into more than 150 species.

Everyone who has picked the wild fruits will know that some are large, juicy and well flavoured, while others are small, woody and poorly flavoured. Seasonal conditions play a part, but the main reason for the difference in quality is the difference in species. Added to this is the fact that seedlings arise, of which some may be superior or inferior to the species from which they sprang.

Cultivated varieties

The best of the wild types have been selected for cultivation or used in breeding programmes for raising improved forms, and the list has now been reduced in the last thirty years from sixteen or so to about half a dozen. The most widely-known is probably Himalaya Giant, that was introduced to this country at the end of the last century by a Hamburg nurseryman, Theodor Reimers, who gave it his own name in Germany. It was known as Himalaya in Great Britain because it was thought that it arose from seed collected from the Himalayas but it is now known to be a species, probably a form of *R. procerus*, which grows throughout much of western Europe.

Himalaya is very vigorous, producing canes up to 3m (10 ft) long, which are heavily thorned. The jet-black berries are large (hence the 'Giant' part of the name), juicy and impressive looking, but can be disappointing in some seasons, with little discernible 'bramble' flavour, though this does come out well when the berries are used with apples to make jam. The variety is a prodigious cropper, sometimes giving 14kg (30 lb) per plant, and it rarely fails. It is in season from mid to late autumn (mid August to October). Its main drawback is the difficulty of handling the canes.

The earliest variety, starting to crop at the end of the summer and continuing for about a month (late July to late August) is Bedford Giant. This is said to be a seedling of the Veitchberry, which is a raspberry-blackberry hybrid. Bedford Giant is another vigorous, prickly grower producing abundant crops of large berries. The flavour is sweet and superior to

that of the Himalaya. Bedford Giant is rather susceptible to the bacterial infection crown gall; galls, that can be quite large, appear on the canes – sometimes at the crown and sometimes farther up. These are unsightly but, as far as research work has established, they do not unduly affect growth and cropping.

A fine variety for early to mid autumn (August to September) is John Innes, raised at the John Innes Horticultural Institution in England. This is juicy, sweetly-flavoured and crops heavily from canes up to 2·6m (8 ft) long.

Thornless varieties

However good the thorned varieties are there is little doubt that the thornless ones are preferable for the garden. Oregon Thornless, one of the most popular varieties, tends to be a lighter cropper than the thorned varieties, but it can yield well in a good year. It is a wild plant, native to Oregon, and was taken up there for domestic culture around the first quarter of the century, but it was introduced into Britain only recently. Growth is moderate, with canes reaching some 1·8m (6 ft). The berries are fairly large, sweet and with a good 'bramble' flavour. The parsley-leaved foliage is attractive, lending the plant a decorative aspect, and making it an ideal subject for a dividing screen between the flower and vegetable gardens. It crops from mid to late autumn (September to October).

Another excellent thornless type from the United States is Smoothstem, – resulting from a cross between Merton Thornless and the American variety Eldorado. It is in crop from the end of early autumn until late autumn (late August to October), producing very heavy yields of large berries.

HYBRIDS

The list of blackberry hybrids has shrunk considerably over the last four decades, perhaps because there was not a great deal to choose between most of them. The three main types now offered are those with deep red berries, represented primarily by the loganberry (described on page 141), those with purplish-black berries of which the chief example is the boysenberry, and the raspberry-blackberry hybrid – the Veitchberry.

Boysenberry This originated in California, and the first type seen in Britain was thorned. This type is still available but is likely to become superseded by the thornless variety now on sale. The berries are large, have a fine flavour, and ripen from late summer to early autumn (July to August). A yield of approximately 3·5–4·5kg (8–10 lb) is given per plant. The canes are up to 2–4m (8 ft) long. The berries make delicious jam. A useful feature of boysenberries is that they are good drought-resisters and will thrive on soils that might normally be too light for maximum production of blackberries.

Veitchberry This is a cross between the raspberry, November Abundance, and a large-fruited blackberry. It fills the gap between the summer-fruiting raspberries and the blackberries. The berries are

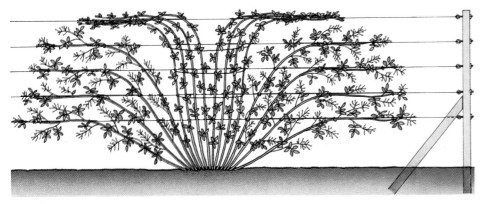

once-fruited canes can be left for a further season if desired, since these varieties will make a second year's flush of fruiting laterals from the previous season's canes, thus boosting the crop. In these cases, cut back (in winter) all laterals to basal buds on any canes to be left; new ones will grow out and fruit in the next summer. Often, however, there are enough. new canes, especially with Himalaya, to fill the allotted space without worrying about retaining any of the fruited ones, and in any case it is a mistake to retain wood for two seasons if this means congestion.

Pests and diseases
Blackberries and their hybrids are fairly sturdy plants but are prone to one or two ailments.

Blackberry mite A condition that frequently mystifies gardeners, particularly when the season is ideal for ripening, is failure of the berries to ripen fully. Many of the drupels (the small globules of which the berries are composed, and that contain the seeds) remain red. Himalaya is probably the most widely affected. This trouble is caused by the blackberry mite, sometimes called red berry mite, a microscopic species that feeds on the berries, preventing the drupels from ripening, and often causing distortion. Complete control is difficult to achieve but the mites can be substantially reduced by burning canes carrying infested berries immediately after harvest, and following this up next season with a spray of lime sulphur in early summer (mid May) at 500ml to 10 litres (1 pt to $2\frac{1}{2}$ gal) water; or a solution of wettable sulphur in water at 50g to 10 litres (2 oz per $2\frac{1}{2}$ gal) water just before flowering. Lime sulphur may cause some leaf scorch, but this is not usually enough to do serious damage. Wettable sulphur is not the same as sulphur dust; the latter is not formulated for use as a spray.

Virus diseases (such as stunt) affect blackberries and hybrid berries. They are spread by leaf hoppers and aphides. Burn affected plants, and only propagate from healthy specimens.

Far left: early-fruiting Bedford Giant
Centre left: popular Oregon Thornless
Left: thornless boysenberry, good for jam
Above: plants can be trained by modified
open fan method (as used for loganberries)

borne on vigorous canes and are finely-flavoured. This hybrid was raised at the famous English nursery of James Veitch.

Planting blackberries and hybrids
In practice any reasonably good soil will suit blackberries and their hybrids. They will always benefit from organic treatment, with compost being dug in before planting, at the usual rate for soft fruit of one barrowload per 10sq m (12 sq yd) or so, and thereafter used as a spring mulch over the root area. Plants given a good start and then well tended, will crop for ten to fifteen years, often longer; a planting distance of 2·5m (8 ft) apart is about right for John Innes, Oregon and Smoothstem; the others will need about 3–3·6m (10–12 ft).

Training the plants
Support the plants with posts and wires; ideally you should have four wires spaced at 90cm, 1·2m, 1·5m and 1·8m (3 ft, 4 ft, 5 ft and 6 ft) from ground level. The end posts should be 2·5m (8 ft) long, buried to 60cm (2 ft). Treat the bottom 75cm ($2\frac{1}{2}$ ft) with a standard preservative. Provide additional support by using inside strainer posts or outside wire struts, firmly anchored. Struts do, of course, take up extra room and can be effective trip wires for people not watching

their step, or for children in a hurry.

The same training systems are used as for loganberries (page 141). Thus you can train the canes on the open fan principle, with fruiting ones spread out fanwise left and right of centre along the first three wires, with a gap in the centre up which the current season's canes are led to a temporary position on the top wire. Alternatively, the fruiting canes can be led off along the wires in one direction, and the current season's ones in the opposite direction (the rope or arch method). These are arranged each year to ensure that where there are two or more plants, the fruiting canes of one plant meet the fruiting canes of its neighbour, while non-fruiting (i.e. current season's) meet similar ones.

Autumn and winter pruning
Prune all fruited wood as soon as possible after harvest. If you are using the open fan system, release the new season's canes from the top wire and tie them fanwise ready for fruiting the following year. With the rope or arch method the new canes are already in position. Remove the fruited ones; the space they occupy will, in due course, be taken over by the current growths of the following year.

With John Innes and Himalaya some

RECOMMENDED VARIETIES

BLACKBERRIES

Himalaya Giant	fruiting in early to late autumn (mid August to October)
Bedford Giant	fruiting in late summer to mid autumn (late July to late August)
John Innes	fruiting in early to mid autumn (August to September)
Oregon Thornless	fruiting in mid to late autumn (September to October)
Smoothstem	fruiting in mid to late autumn (late August to October)

HYBRIDS

Boysenberry	fruiting in late summer to early autumn (July)
Veitchberry	fruiting in late summer (July)

Gooseberries

For an early crop of gooseberries, try a variety such as Keepsake, whose berries make rapid growth from the time the fruits set to maturity. The main crop comes in mid season and is heavy, with medium-sized, pale green, slightly hairy berries.

Another good variety for an early pick, followed by a mid season main crop, is Careless. When fully ripe the berries are large, milky-white and practically hairless, with a transparent or semi-transparent skin. But avoid this variety if your soil is on the poor side, because it will not make much headway and the berries will be small. Improve the soil first and plant Careless later, when conditions are better. Good soil is necessary for all gooseberries but Keepsake is a more vigorous grower than Careless, and is a better choice if your soil is below par.

A fine mid season, deep red berry with a rich flavour is Lancashire Lad, which makes delicious jam. You can also pick it while still green, for cooking. The queen of the yellow-green varieties is the large-fruited Leveller, which also ripens in mid season and is ideal for showing. But, like all the highest-quality fruit, it does need the best conditions. On light soils that drain too freely it will be stunted, often with the greyish, brittle leaf margins that denote potash deficiency. And you will get the same results on heavy soils with impeded drainage.

If your soil is heavy but nevertheless well drained, a good choice would be the mid season, dark red Whinham's Industry. This is one of the best flavoured of all. The sweetest-flavoured mid to late season green variety is probably Lancer, which has translucent, thin-skinned, pale green berries tinged with yellow.

There are several other varieties available, but those listed here give first-rate fruits for dessert, cooking and jam making.

Preparation and cultivation

Gooseberries need a fertile, well-prepared soil, but not one that is too rich or overcharged with nitrogen; excessive richness will help to encourage American gooseberry mildew. Whatever your soil type, dig in thoroughly plenty of well-rotted compost before planting. A free root run and adequate drainage combined with a summer moisture reserve are the essentials for a good crop. The only fertilizer likely to be needed on any sort of routine basis, provided you maintain a good organic content, is sulphate of potash. The standard dressing is 25g per sq m ($\frac{3}{4}$ oz per sq yd) in early spring (February). However, if the leaves are a healthy green and show no signs of marginal scorch, not even this is necessary. But it must be applied if signs of potash deficiency appear.

Gooseberries detest the hoe. They make a massive, absorbing root system in the top few centimetres of soil, and like these roots to be left in peace. Annual mulching in spring (March–April) just after the fruits set will suppress weeds, maintain a moisture reserve and eliminate hoeing. If you cannot manage this every year, then as far as possible get the weeds out by hand in the root area of the bushes, and restrict the hoe to a narrow strip along the centre of the alleyways.

In any event there will not be many weeds from the mulched area, even if you treat it on a two-year basis, provided the compost is properly made and free of weed seeds. Remember that although hoeing cleans the soil initially, it stirs up the weed seeds that otherwise might have died, remained dormant, or had their new growth smothered by a mulch.

Gooseberries can be grown as cordons 30cm (12 in) apart, or as bushes 1·2–1·5m (4–5 ft) apart. Bushes must be grown on a short stem, while cordons should be free of suckers from below soil level, so plant both types no deeper than the soil mark on the newly-purchased plant. Spread the roots out to their fullest extent, cover them with friable soil, then tread in lightly. Add more soil and tread in firmly. Finish off with an untrodden surface. You do not want depressions round the stems collecting pools of winter rain.

Training cordons

Cordons are usually grown vertically, though you can train them obliquely if you prefer. Using light end posts, 1·2m (4 ft) long and sunk to a depth of 30cm (12 in) or 45cm (18 in) to be on the safe side, strain three wires between them at 30cm (12 in) intervals. Then fix bamboo canes about 1 m (3 ft) long to the wires, allowing one cane for each plant.

Left: top-quality large-fruited Leveller
Top right: prune a cordon in winter by cutting back sideshoots to three buds.
Top, far right: on a bush, cut back sideshoots to five leaves in summer

Cordons make neat path edgings, but remember in this case to allow the stems about 30–38cm (12–15 in) of soil width on each side so that the roots can forage well, and mulch this strip each spring. One of the objects of the system is to get quality berries, and an organic root covering is a definite aid to this.

Tip back the newly-planted cordons by some 15cm (6 in) and repeat in subsequent winters if necessary. Some varieties will reach the top wire with little tipping. At the same time, cut back sideshoots to three buds. Thereafter cut back all sideshoots to the fifth leaf from the base in mid to late summer (late June or early July) and to three buds each winter. The result will be fine berries growing from induced fruiting spurs along the cordons.

Pruning bushes

You can prune bushes in exactly the same way. In this case each branch is really a cordon, the only difference being that it grows naturally from the bush and is not trained. Tip back each branch of a newly-planted bush by half, and repeat the operation in subsequent winters as it becomes necessary.

Some varieties droop considerably. If this habit becomes too pronounced, prune back in winter to an upward bud just below the bend. Remove any weak or congesting shoots to maintain an airy atmosphere in the bushes.

Light pruning method

The method described above is the conventional one that has been used for many years, but light pruning (which was advocated by William Forsyth, gardener to King George III) can give just as good results and brings the bushes into crop earlier. In trials with Careless and Leveller, planted in mid spring (March) of one year and pruned lightly, they produced some 2kg (4 lb) of fruit per bush the following year.

With light pruning, the branches are not built up over successive winters and there is no sideshoot cutting. All the growths are left, except for poor or congesting shoots. Berries soon form on the uncut ones, usually in singles or perhaps doubles, from individual buds rather than in spur clusters. Each growth is cropped for a year or two, and is then removed in favour of a new one. Not all fruiting growths are removed in any one year; a pattern evolves in which there are always some shoots still in fruit and some maiden ones ready to fruit in their second summer. The only danger is overcrowding, so to prevent this, work on a basis of

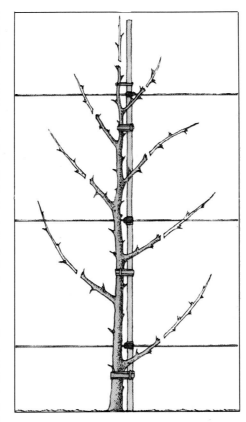

allowing at least one full hand's span between all adjacent growths. Be very strict over this.

Pests and diseases

There is one serious disease liable to attack your gooseberries and at least three fairly common pests.

American gooseberry mildew This shows first as thick, white, powdery patches on leaves and fruit while in the final phase there is a brownish, felty covering on the berries. It is essential to stop this fungus early, as soon as you see the first white patches on the young leaves and shoots. Apply a systemic fungicide at once and repeat at 10–14 day intervals if necessary.

Sawfly caterpillar These green caterpillars with black spots are very common pests on young bushes. They can strip a bush of every leaf. There are three generations annually, so if the first is not controlled there will be trouble at intervals throughout the season. The first batch of eggs is laid in late spring and early summer (April and May) on the undersides of leaves in the centre of the bush near ground level. They hatch about 2–3 weeks later. Look for the tiny, newly-hatched caterpillars and give them a few squirts of derris while they are still bunched in the centre of the bush. At this stage they are a sitting target and easily killed.

Magpie moth caterpillar These pests also eat the leaves, and are frequently confused with sawfly caterpillars. The magpie

moth caterpillars are 'loopers', drawing themselves into a loop each time they move forward, and have black and white markings with a yellow stripe along each side. They start feeding before flowering time, but often go undetected at this stage. A derris spray immediately before flowering will kill them, but if you miss this out, then apply derris after the fruits have set as soon as the caterpillars are seen.

Aphides These are the other main pests, curling the leaves and distorting young shoots. One species, the lettuce aphid, flies from gooseberries to lettuces, so there is a double reason for controlling it. The second sort flies to certain types of willow herb. Both overwinter on gooseberries in the egg stage, and can be eradicated with a tar oil spray. The alternative is a spray of malathion or a systemic insecticide just before, or immediately after, the flowering period.

RECOMMENDED VARIETIES

EARLY AND MID SEASON	
Keepsake	pale green
Careless	milky-white
MID SEASON	
Lancashire Lad	deep red
Leveller	yellow-green
Whinham's Industry	dark red
MID AND LATE SEASON	
Lancer	pale green

Blackcurrants

Blackcurrants thrive in organically rich soil. They can hardly have too much good quality, well-rotted compost. Dig it in before planting, at the rate of one full barrowload per 8–10 sq m (10–12 sq yd), and use it as a mulch every spring just after fruit set. If there is enough compost, cover the pathways as well as the plant rows. Use a depth of 8cm (3 in) if it can be spared. This will not only cut out hoeing, thereby leaving the near-surface root mass undisturbed, but it will ensure the greatest possible degree of summer moisture retention, and encourage each bush to make a really large root system. Abundant roots mean abundant top growth; the fruits are borne on shoots

Below left: plant bush in 10cm (4 in) deep hole and cut back shoots; below: plant cut-off shoots 15cm (6 in) apart

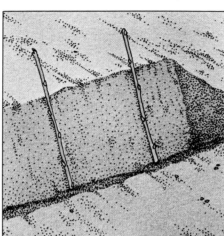

made the previous year, so the more two-year shoots, the bigger the crop.

Compost alone often will not boost growth and crops to the maximum. It may have to be supplemented with a proprietary fertilizer high in nitrogen in early or mid spring (February or March) at 25–35g per sq m ($\frac{3}{4}$–1 oz per sq yd).

Planting the bushes

It is imperative to get the plot really clean before planting. If such weeds as couch grass, bindweed and creeping buttercup are left, it will be almost impossible to eradicate them later from around the bushes without disturbing the roots.

Planting holes must be wide enough to take the roots comfortably and, more important, deep enough to ensure that the crotch of the bush is about 10cm (4 in) below soil level. New shoots are needed not only above ground but also below. The latter are 'stool' shoots, and can provide a significant portion of the crop.

Plant the bushes a minimum of 1·5m (5 ft) apart. Cut back newly-planted bushes to buds just above soil level. Do not crop them in their first summer as they must be given every chance to build up strongly. They will then crop well in the second summer and onward.

Raising from shoots

Use some of the cut-off shoots to raise more bushes. Trim them to 20–23cm (8–9 in), removing tip portions. Plant them 15cm (6 in) deep and 15cm (6 in) apart, with all buds intact, into a well-prepared nursery strip. The maiden bushes will be ready for planting out during the following winter.

Caring for growing bushes

Blackcurrant bushes have no permanent framework, but they send out many shoots from old wood. The aim in pruning is to have good supplies of maiden shoots each year for cropping the following year. Fruited shoots can be cut out when the fruit is picked, and this is often sufficient pruning. The other time to prune is in winter, leaving maiden branches, but cutting out fruited shoots. The two are easily distinguished; cropped shoots are darker than maiden ones, and carry the dried remains of the fruit strings.

Many fruited shoots will have maiden ones growing from them, and maiden tip extensions. Where a fruited shoot is supporting a maiden one, cut off the upper fruited part at the junction with the new shoot, and leave the latter intact. The

Below left: juicy fruits ripening and picked ready to eat (above)

basal portion of the old piece will then become a temporary support.

Where fruited shoots have no maiden side growths but do have good maiden extensions, leave them in. Such extensions can produce useful fruiting trusses. But where the extensions are very short and puny, cut out the shoots at the base. Cut out entirely any fruited shoots bare of maiden side growths and tip extensions.

Below: cut out fruited shoots at harvest time and, if necessary, in the winter

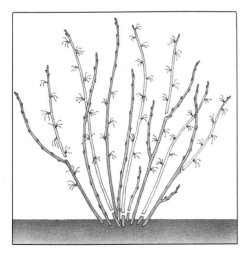

There may be weak maiden shoots deep within the centre of the bush. Their poor growth is due to lack of sunlight. Remove them as they are useless for cropping.

Protection from the wind
One of the commonest causes of crop failure is 'running off', when the flowers either shrivel or set fruit that falls soon after. This is the result of imperfect pollination due to strong, cold winds at blossom time. The winds not only damage the flowers but discourage pollinating insects, without whose help pollination is rarely satisfactory. If the garden is windswept, plant the bushes in the lee of any existing shelter from the east round to the north-west. The best shelter is an evergreen hedge. A temporary screen of sacking stitched to strong hazel rods is not as effective as the windbreak hedge, because it shelters only the bushes and not the surrounding area. If the area remains windblown, it will not attract pollinating insects.

Pests and diseases
The main pests infesting blackcurrants are aphides and gall mites ('big bud' mites).

Aphides These insects can do great damage to the leaves by sucking the sap and distorting them. The familiar sooty mould forms after an attack of aphides, often on the berries. The most practical control is a winter tar oil spray, thoroughly applied to kill the eggs. Alternatively, spray with derris, malathion, or a systemic in the spring as soon as aphides are seen on the undersurface of the leaves.

Gall mites These live and breed inside the buds, causing them to swell to several times the normal winter size. The buds are killed by the mites, which then infect new buds in the spring. The mites also transmit a virus disease called reversion, which does not kill but renders the bushes incapable of fruiting. Never use cuttings from infested bushes for propagation.

A limited measure of control may be achieved by picking off and burning swollen buds. The standard control is a spray of lime sulphur according to the maker's recommendation at the grape stage: that is, when the unopened flower buds hang like bunches of tiny grapes.

Some buds infested with gall mites may become detached from the plant and carried by the wind to nearby bushes, causing 'big buds' to appear on previously clean bushes. The mites may also be transported by various flying insects (particularly aphides) to which they cling. It is therefore a sound policy to spray with lime sulphur every year as an insurance against infection from any blackcurrant bushes in the vicinity.

The only variety of blackcurrant in present cultivation that has some degree of immunity to gall mites is Seabrook's Black. It is not completely immune, but may go for several years without an infestation.

Redcurrants and whitecurrants

Redcurrants eaten straight from the bush are among the most refreshing of soft fruit and are a delicious addition to fruit salads. They also make fine jelly and mix well with other fruit (especially raspberries) in jams, juices and desserts.

Whitecurrants are sweeter and are usually eaten as fresh dessert fruit.

Although redcurrants and whitecurrants will grow on a wide range of soils, they prefer a medium loam that is well drained but able to hold summer moisture, and is slightly acid or neutral (though they will normally be capable of standing some degree of alkalinity).

They do, however, react adversely to waterlogged roots and lack of potash. These often go together for, although potash is not necessarily absent in such soils, waterlogged roots cannot use it. Dry roots cannot make use of potash either, so if the soil is too light it will need good supplies of well-rotted organic matter to build up a moisture-conserving medium, and if it is too heavy it will need the same treatment to open up the soil and improve its drainage.

Bushes, cordons and espaliers

Both redcurrants and whitecurrants can be grown in bush form or as cordons and espaliers, and you can plant them in partial shade or in full sun. Redcurrant cordons can be trained against a north-facing wall if necessary, where they will do quite well, though their ripening period will be somewhat delayed. If possible choose a fairly sheltered spot for planting, otherwise there is a likelihood of wind damage.

The planting distances are 1·5m (5 ft) apart for bushes, 38cm (15 in) for cordons and 1·2–1·5m (4–5 ft) for espaliers.

You may want no more than one heavy-cropping bush. The variety called Earliest of Fourlands, for example, can produce about 5kg (11 lb) of redcurrants per bush in its fourth summer from planting, though average yields of all varieties could be some way below those of bumper years.

Bushes have a short stem from which the branches grow out to give an open centre bush. Plant to the soil mark at the base of the stem.

Each bush should have about eight cropping branches. Since the pruning of cordons and espaliers is the same as for

Above: Jonkheer van Tets — one of the best varieties for garden culture, it produces fine crops early in the season

Below: Red Lake is an American variety
Far right: White Versailles has sweet berries in very long bunches

bushes, a single cordon can be expected to produce one eighth of a bush crop, and a three-tier espalier (which would have six horizontal branches) would give about three-quarters of a bush crop.

Summer and winter pruning

Newly-bought bushes will not usually have eight branches, but they may have four, and these can easily be doubled by pruning.

After planting, cut back each branch by about half to an outward-pointing bud. During the next year extensions will grow, and generally each branch will send out a strong shoot from just below the extension, thus doubling the original number of branches. Tip these secondary shoots back by about half in the following winter and tip the leading extensions back by about one-third. Repeat as necessary in future winters, cutting all extensions back by one-third until the branches have reached the desired length. Some varieties grow strongly and quickly; with these, two (or at most three) winter cuttings are often enough.

Fruit is borne in clusters from short spurs along the branches; these are induced by summer and winter pruning. Summer pruning is done when the side shoots are mature along their basal portion, a stage that normally coincides with an increase in colour of the berries, about mid to late summer (late June). Cut the shoots back to within about 10cm (4 in), of the fourth or fifth leaf from the base. The branches are not cut. In winter cut the sideshoots again, to one or two buds from the base, leaving them as short spurs 13–20mm ($\frac{1}{2}-\frac{3}{4}$ in) long.

From time to time remove older branches to make way for new ones, maintaining a total of about eight branches.

The sideshoots of cordons and espaliers are treated in the same way, and the cordon rods and espalier branches are tipped as necessary in winter to stimulate extensions.

Feeding the plants

Red and whitecurrants do not need a great deal of feeding, but remember that heavy crops take their toll of soil foods. So keep the plants steadily supplied with moderate dressings of a combined organic fertilizer – applied annually or biennially as you think fit. Generally the lowest rate given in the maker's instructions will suffice; if they recommend, say, 70–100g per sq m (2–3 oz per sq yd), then use 70g (2 oz). Look out, however, for early stages of marginal leaf scorch, denoting potash deficiency. If this ap-

pears do not step up the routine dressing of combined fertilizer, but apply a separate dressing of sulphate of potash in autumn at about 17g per sq m ($\frac{1}{2}$ oz per sq yd). Do not use muriate of potash on currant bushes. Mulching, either in autumn or directly after fruit set, will help to conserve soil moisture.

Pest control

Aphides are the only serious pests. These can cause severe leaf damage. Distorted foliage with red blisters is a common sight on unsprayed bushes. Use a winter wash of tar oil to destroy the eggs. Alternatively you can spray the young aphides in spring with insecticides (such as derris or one of the systemics), but you must apply them

as soon as the pests appear. As hatching occurs over a period, it may be necessary to apply two sprays (especially of derris). With tar oil, however, only one application is needed.

Choosing varieties

Some varieties have a lax habit; the form of the bush is loose and droopy, and shoots can easily be broken by the wind. Avoid varieties that grow in this way and also those that make 'blind' buds – ones that fail to grow. The recommended varieties given here are all strong, heavy-cropping bushes with no blind buds and little or no tendency to loose, open growth. All of them may be expected to yield good-sized, high-quality currants.

RECOMMENDED VARIETIES

REDCURRANTS

Jonkheer van Tets Very early season variety ripening in mid summer (mid to late June); vigorous, upright growth; good cropper producing large fruit.

Earliest of Fourlands Early season variety ripening in mid to late summer (late June to early July); large bushes of erect habit producing firm, bright red fruit.

Laxton's No 1 Early season variety ripening in mid to late summer (late June to early July); produces heavy crops of good-sized fruit.

Red Lake Mid to late season variety ripening in late summer (mid July); an American variety producing long trusses of large, fine-flavoured fruit.

Wilson's Long Bunch Late season variety ripening in late summer (late July); produces large crops of medium-sized, light red fruit on very long branches.

WHITECURRANTS

White Versailles Mid season variety ripening in late summer (early July); strong-growing, fertile bushes producing large, pale yellow, richly-flavoured currants.

WAYS AND MEANS
Basic Tools

Forks and spades have either a D- or T-shape handle. Many gardeners claim that a D handle allows for better gripping. Try them out in the shop before you buy.

Forks are usually four-pronged and are useful for winter digging, especially on heavy soils.

Spades vary in blade width, from 16–19cm (6–8 in), and blade length, from 26–29cm (10–12 in). You'll find smaller sizes easier to use on heavier soils because less weight is lifted with each spade-load. Lighter, smaller forks and spades are made for women.

A **Dutch hoe** takes the backache out of weeding, and saves time.

When making seed drills you will find a **draw hoe** invaluable. A hand version, known as an **onion hoe**, has a narrower blade and is ideal for cultivating small patches, raised beds, and plants in pots and tubs.

No gardener can do without a **hand fork** and **trowel**. The forks have long and short blades of varying widths; the long, thin ones are excellent for prizing out long-rooted perennial weeds.

You will need a **rake** for breaking down clods to a workable tilth. They range between 30–40cm (12–16 in) wide; when buying ensure that the metal rake is well fixed to the handle.

Wooden ones are wider and are recommended only for very large gardens.

Stainless steel tools cost about twice as much as others, but they are a worthwhile investment. They last much longer, are quick to clean and don't rust. They also slip easily into soil. The handles are made of polypropylene or wood, the former being much lighter.

Pruning can be done with a **pruning knife** or **secateurs**. Well-versed gardeners recommend a sharp knife for most jobs, but many people prefer to use secateurs for trees, shrubs and roses.

The knives must be made of well-hardened steel; cheap ones or pen knives will tear at plant stems and invite infection.

There are two types of secateurs: parrot-billed (scissors action), and anvil (the single blade cuts against a metal block). They should be well-made with sharp blades; blunt ones will only crush plant tissue and frustrate the pruner.

You will need a **reel** and **line** and a **measuring rod** or **tape** in the vegetable garden and for marking out borders.

Wooden or **plastic labels** are best for marking seed-sowings.

Use **gardening gloves** for heavy work and pruning roses.

Your tool shed will not be complete without a **watering can**. Get a 7–9 litre (1½–2 gallon) size with a rose. It is advisable to have a second can for weedkillers.

A **hose** saves time when watering plants. Invest in a frost-proof one. A **hose reel** will also cut watering time and save wear and tear on the hose.

A **bucket** will serve to carry odds and ends until you acquire a **wheelbarrow**. When you choose a wheelbarrow don't forget to consider its weight when filled and its size in relation to your garden paths.

For hedges, lawns and mixed borders you will require a good pair of **shears**. These and other lawn equipment are described on the facing page.

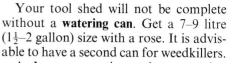

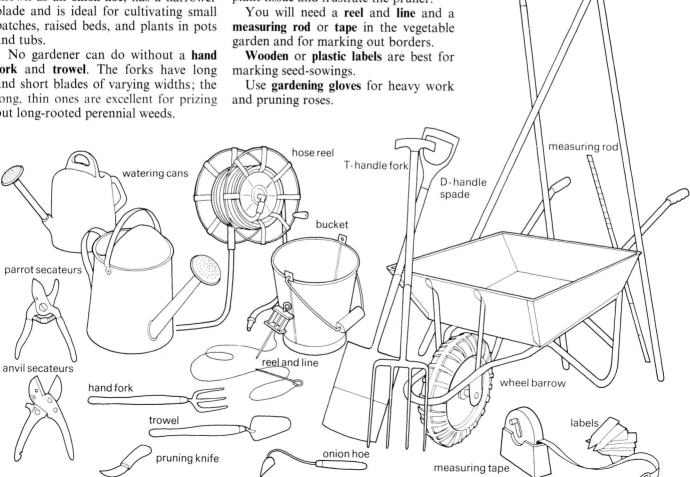

draw hoe

rake

Dutch hoe

measuring rod

hose reel

T-handle fork

D-handle spade

watering cans

bucket

parrot secateurs

anvil secateurs

hand fork

trowel

pruning knife

reel and line

onion hoe

wheel barrow

labels

measuring tape

Lawn equipment

All but the smallest lawns need to be cut with a mower, but before you decide which type to buy compare the various models and list your requirements (this also applies when buying other lawn care equipment). Certain mowers work better on short grass and edges, others on long grass, and all grass boxes are not equally efficient. Choose a lightweight model with adjustable handles if you have steps to negotiate or storage problems.

Hand lawn-mowers
Although it can be tiring to hand mow a large lawn, it is certainly very economical to use a hand machine for small and medium-sized ones. They are also considered to give a better finish than power-operated machines.

Nowadays, due to skilful engineering, cylinder hand mowers are very easy to push and operate. They come in two types: roller and sidewheel and each has its advantages.

Roller types have a small roller in front of the cylinder and a large one behind. The two rollers help to give lawns the striped effect for which many people aim. They also make it easy to cut edges and narrow strips of grass as they simply overhang where necessary. However, these roller types do not operate well if the grass is more than 5cm (2 in) long.

Power lawn-mowers
Power lawn-mowers are precision instruments and often have to stand up to years of rough usage, so you should always buy the best you can afford.

Mains-powered electric mowers are cheap to run and noiseless; but mains-operated types are not suited to large lawns or rough ground. Petrol-driven mowers give more power but can be difficult to start, and require a regular maintenance programme. Apart from the choice between electric and petrol power, the mower may cut by the cylinder or rotary method; the former type cut with a scissor-like action, the latter by beheading the upstanding grass. Cylinder types are good for fine lawns, but not so efficient for grass longer than 5 to 8cm (2 to 3 in) high. The rotary type deal better with long grass and are easier to handle though they do not give a striped lawn effect.

Sidewheel mowers have only the small roller in front of the cutting cylinder and are better for cutting long grass, but they require a balancing act to cut lawn edges, and on soft ground the two side wheels can leave track marks.

Roller mowers cost about twice as much as the sidewheel types and always have the grass box attachment in front. Grass boxes may be fitted to the front or rear of sidewheel models, according to the make. They are usually more efficient when the box is fitted in front of the cutting cylinder.

With cylinder mowers the grass is cut between the cylinder blade and a fixed blade. The effective cutting width, known as the cylinder length, is usually 25 or 30cm (10 or 12 in), although one sidewheel model is available with a 40cm (16 in) cylinder.

The cutting height adjustment and ease of altering it varies according to the model, so compare these facilities before buying. Both power and hand-driven cylinder mowers are available, but rotary ones are always petrol-driven or electrically operated.

Shears for cutting
The first item for your list is a good pair of shears. There are long-handled and short-handled, edging and cutting shears. Blade sizes vary from 15–25cm (6–10 in); handles can be wooden, metal or plastic, and some models are available with rubber buffers to absorb jarring and reduce fatigue when cutting.

The traditional short-handled shears are invaluable for cutting long or short grass. To avoid having to bend, you can get the same blades attached to long handles. There are two basic models in this range, one for edging and the other for general cutting. You can also buy spring-loaded hand shears which allow for one-handed operation; one type comes with an orbital handle so that it can be adjusted to cut at any angle between horizontal and vertical.

The lawn edge trimmer, a modification of edging shears, has spring-loaded blades and you push it along to cut overhanging grass. It has a broad, non-slip rubber roller that guarantees easy guiding and balancing, even on undulating ground.

Brushing and raking
All lawns require brushing and raking to keep them looking well-groomed and pleasant to sit on. A besom, or birch broom, is ideal for sweeping off leaves, but a good stiff broom is required for getting rid of wormcasts.

Steel, spring-tined lawn rakes are essential for removing debris and for scarifying the lawn surface. You can get fixed, or adjustable, tined models, the latter being preferable as they can be used for any job from moss-collecting to leaf-raking.

There is also a lawn comb – a cross between a lawn rake and a garden rake, but it has no particular advantage over other rakes. Wooden lawn rakes are prone to breaking and so are not recommended. The traditional garden rake is best for spreading top dressing on lawns.

Rolling the lawn
It is worth borrowing or hiring a roller each spring to put a new face on your lawn. Winter frosts often lift the turf and rolling will consolidate the surface. It need only be done in spring. It is important to sweep off all wormcasts and debris beforehand and to roll only when the surface is dry and the soil below is damp. Don't roll when the grass is thin or wet and never use a roller weighing over 2 cwt. Bumps should be levelled out properly because rolling will not squash them down.

Tools for aerating
For this you need only use a garden fork. Push it in 7–10cm (3–4 in) deep, at 7–10cm intervals. Easier to use is a fork-like tool fitted with hollow, or solid, tines (sometimes called mechanical spikes), and it gives better results. Wedge-shaped blades can also be attached and are good for compacted areas as they prune the roots and so encourage stronger root growth. For larger areas use an aerator with spiked wheels and interchangeable tines.

Feeding and weeding
Fertilizer-spreaders ensure an even distribution of lawn feeds and lawn sands. Fertilizers and 'feed and weed' mixes come in several forms and should be applied with the spreader in strict accordance with the manufacturers' instructions.

A certain number of weeds eventually die as a result of constant mowing but a few stubborn types will remain and must be dealt with by other methods. Apply spot weedkillers from a small bottle with a squeezy-type top, or dig out stubborn weeds with a hand fork, or a long, narrow trowel.

Tidying up the edges
Finally, to ensure that your lawn never encroaches on the flower borders you should edge-up with a good half-moon edging iron at least twice a year.

The greenhouse

The acquisition of a greenhouse opens up an exciting new area of gardening, where you don't have to worry about extremes of weather or damage from cold, wind or excessive rain. You can regulate the amount of water your plants receive and, because fertilizers are not washed away by rain, you can feed them correctly.

Temperature and ventilation can be adjusted and, by applying shading, even the light may be altered to suit plant preferences. Pests and diseases are easier to combat and the plants are protected from damage by birds and small animals.

Which type?
Most greenhouse styles offer the choice of a glass-to-ground or a base-wall design. The glass-to-ground type allows very efficient use of space for growing. When staging is fitted, there is enough light beneath for the accommodation of a varied selection of plants. The all-glass house is also ideal for tall subjects like tomatoes and chrysanthemums. By arranging your space carefully you can grow many different kinds of plants together. For example, you can grow tomatoes along the south side, followed by chrysanthemums – putting the pots on the floor. Your staging can then run along the north side, providing a surface on which to grow a variety of pot plants, with some space below for plants that like a certain amount of shade (as do many house plants). On the end wall you can train climbers bearing either beautiful flowers, or edible crops like cucumbers.

But for some purposes a greenhouse with a base wall of brick, concrete or timber boards (usually called a 'plant house') is preferable. Plants liking deep shade can be grown below the staging. This design is more economical to heat artificially and therefore is preferable when the greenhouse does not get much sun. It is also a good choice where high temperatures have to be maintained for propagation or for tropical plants (many of which do not demand much light). Greenhouses with a base wall at one side and glass-to-ground at the other are also available. These should be oriented east-to-west, if possible, with the base wall on the north side.

Planning ahead
Before buying your greenhouse, make sure that you are not infringing any rules or regulations by erecting it in your garden. If you are a tenant you should seek your landlord's permission; should you move, you can take the greenhouse with you. If you are a freeholder and wish to have a permanent structure (like a lean-to against the house wall) you will almost certainly require planning permission from your local council.

You must also do some advance thinking about the foundations of the greenhouse. You can lay old railway sleepers or concrete footings, or build a low, cemented brick wall on which the greenhouse can be free-standing or screwed into position. Do have a path of concrete, brick or paving stones down the centre of the house, for dry feet and clean working.

The best positions
Freestanding, rectangular greenhouses get most benefit from the sun if you orientate them east-to-west, with the long sides facing north and south. The 'high south wall' greenhouse *must*, in fact, lie this way to catch as much winter light and sun as possible. Staging, if used, should run along the north side.

With a lean-to, you may have no choice in the siting, but what you grow in it will depend on which way it faces. An east- or west-facing lean-to is usually fairly versatile since it gets some sun and some shade. If north-facing it will be very shady and is best devoted to pot plants (such as cinerareas, cyclamen, primulas and calceolarias) and house plants for permanent decoration. A south-facing lean-to can become very hot in summer and, unless you want to install shading, you should choose sun-loving plants like cacti and succulents.

Types of material
You should consider the cost of subsequent maintenance as against initial outlay when choosing your materials.
Glass or plastic? Glass has the unique property of capturing and retaining solar warmth. It also holds artificial warmth better. Polythene has a limited life and for long-term use a rigid plastic (like Novolux) is the wisest choice. Plastic surfaces are easily scratched by wind-blown dust and grit, causing dirt to become ingrained and a loss of trans-

parency over a period of years. Plastic also becomes brittle with weathering and may disintegrate.

However, plastic is advisable if the site is likely to be the target for children's games or hooligans out to break glass, or where quick erection or portability is desirable, or where temporary weather protection is all that's necessary. Moulded fibreglass greenhouses are also available, but tend to be expensive and the fittings have to be free-standing.

Aluminium frames Aluminium alloy (often white-coated) is now tending to replace timber for the frame as it has many advantages. It is lightweight yet very strong, and prefabricated structures are easily bolted together. Sophisticated glazing, using plastic cushioning strips and clips instead of messy putty, means that the greenhouse can easily be taken apart for moving. There is no fear of rot, warp or trouble from wood-boring insects, or need for maintenance, like painting or treating timber.

Timber frames These may look better in a period-style garden. Select one of the more weather-resistant timbers such as cedar, teak or oak, but remember that all timber needs painting or treating with a wood restorer or preservative from time to time.

A 'vertical-sided 'barn' or 'span' model (far left) with timbered base walls on three sides. The 'Dutch light' house (left) is always a glass-to-ground structure; it has sloping glass walls which are designed to trap the sun's rays.
Ornamental houses (right) come in many shapes and sizes.
A 'lean-to' can be set against a garden wall or a house wall.

Providing shade
If your greenhouse receives plenty of sun you will need shading in the summer.

Slatted blinds, run on rails over the exterior of the roof, are efficient but costly. They also have to be made to fit. Interior blinds are far less efficient in reducing temperature, since the sun's heat-producing rays have already entered the greenhouse, though they do help to prevent direct scorch.

The simplest and cheapest effective method of shading here is with an electrostatic shading paint that is not washed off by rain but can easily be removed by wiping with a dry duster. You apply and remove it like a blind.

All year round ventilation
Ventilators are usually fitted in the roof and sometimes in the sides as well, reducing excess heat in summer and controlling humidity at all times. Thermostatically-controlled units that open and shut the ventilators automatically according to the temperature inside the greenhouse are very useful.

Types of heating
It makes sense to heat your greenhouse, if only to keep out frost, since this greatly widens its usefulness. Your heating need not be costly if you don't waste it.

Oil heaters Both oil and paraffin are easy to store and portable heaters are particularly valuable as supplementary heating in periods of extreme cold or during power cuts. Use paraffin heaters that are specially designed for greenhouses; the blue-flame design is best.

Electricity is trouble-free and gives accurate temperature control, but it can be expensive if used wastefully. Fan heating

is very effective providing the fan and heat output are controlled together (preferably with a separate, rod-type thermostat); avoid a heater with a continuously-running fan. Ventilation becomes almost unnecessary with this system, and if you line your greenhouse with polythene to form a kind of double glazing you can cut fuel consumption by up to half.

Convector heaters and electrically-heated pipes are also efficient when used together with an accurate thermostat. If you decide on electricity you will need to run a cable from the house: be sure to have this done by a qualified electrician.

Natural gas There are special greenhouse heaters using natural gas, with good thermostatic control. They can also be adapted to work from bottle gas, though this makes them more expensive to run.

Natural gas, oil and paraffin, when burned, all produce carbon dioxide and water vapour. The carbon dioxide is beneficial to plants, but the water vapour can be a nuisance in winter when you will do better to keep the greenhouse dry. You will need some ventilation to keep down humidity and supply air for the fuel to burn, but this cold air does mean that some of the heat is lost.

Other types of heating Solid fuel (with the heat distributed by hot water pipes) and oil-fired boilers are still relatively cheap methods of heating. Hot water pipes, linked to a boiler, maintain high temperatures but are costly to install.

Heated propagators You will need some form of heated propagator so that you can germinate seeds without heating the whole greenhouse to a high temperature. Electrically-heated models are simple and cheap to run.

Automatic watering
There is a wide choice of equipment here. The water can be fed to the plants by overhead sprays, trickle-feed pipelines, by capillary sand benches or capillary matting. In the case of capillary watering, the sand or matting under the pots is kept constantly moist by whatever automatic system is installed.

One automatic watering system uses a photo-electric cell (connected to a special electric circuit) that registers the amount of sunlight prevailing, and controls the water flow accordingly. Once you have installed such a system you can leave the greenhouse unattended for weeks.

Artificial lighting
A paraffin lamp will give you enough light in the evenings for most jobs, but if the greenhouse has an electricity supply you can install either a lamp-holder and lamp bulb or a fluorescent tube.

Frames and cloches

A frame – or two – costs little to buy, or to make yourself quite easily, and it can be fitted into most gardens. Nearly everything you grow in a greenhouse can also be grown in frames, allowing for the restrictions in height and size.

Even if you have a greenhouse, frames can take over much of the work to leave more space for decorative plants and those demanding full greenhouse height.

First you must decide whether to buy a ready-made frame or make one yourself from a frame kit of glass-to-ground design with timber or metal sections. An all-glass frame is suitable unless you want extra warmth for propagation, or for growing cucumbers or melons.

Lids, known as 'lights', can be bought separately and you can place these over your own timber or brick-built sides, or even set one over a pit dug in the ground, adding to it as required. The lights can be easily stored away in the summer, when not in use.

Modern frames are often fitted with sliding glass sides, to give access or for added ventilation, and lights that slide aside as well as lift up so that they can be removed conveniently and completely for easy working.

Choice of material

Aluminium alloy framework has many advantages: it is long-lasting, requires no maintenance and, being lightweight, is ideal for moving about. If you prefer timber, choose wood that is noted for its weather resistance, because frame sides are likely to come into contact with damp soil for long periods. Avoid soft woods treated with creosote as the vapour continues to be harmful to plants for some time. Green Cuprinol is suitable, but before using any other preservative check the maker's literature to be sure that it is safe for plants.

Plastic, instead of glass, for garden frames is light, easily portable and obviously advisable where small children are using the garden. From a gardener's

A large glass-to-ground frame, with aluminium-alloy framework, being used to house trays of seedlings and plants waiting to be transplanted

point of view, however, glass has many advantages (see previous comments on choosing a greenhouse). You must use glass if the frame is to be heated, and would be advised to do so in windy areas as plastic can blow away.

Siting the frame

If you use a frame as an adjunct to your greenhouse (and it has vertical sides), you can push the frame close up to one side. This helps to reduce possible warmth loss from both the greenhouse and the frame.

If using a frame for greenhouse and pot plants, put it in a shady place – against the north side of your greenhouse is ideal. But most vegetable crops, and those alpines which you may be housing in frames when not in flower, prefer

to be in a bright, open position.

With many frames it is often convenient to set them back-to-back, or alongside each other in rows. To obtain more height, stand your frame on a base of bricks or concrete blocks, or place it over a pit (providing you make sure that water does not collect in it).

Electric soil-warming cables

Frames do not have to be 'cold'; you can heat a large one with a small paraffin lamp provided you take great care to see that there is always ventilation. But installing electric soil-warming cables is by far the best method. Lay them in loops across the floor of the frame, making sure that they do not touch each other. Place a little sand on top and keep it moist: this will hold the cables in place and conduct the warmth more uniformly. Use only about 2–3cm (1 in) of sand, then a thermostat can be installed above the sand level to control the frame's temperature.

If you need extra warmth (as for pot plants) run cables round the frame sides as well. With glass-sided frames, fasten the cables to wooden battens with cleats and thrust the battens very firmly into the ground.

If you are growing plants to be rooted into a deep layer of compost (such as

salad crops, cucumbers and melons) site the warming cables near the bottom of the compost. In this case a thermostat of the rod type should be thrust into the compost. Temperature can also be controlled manually or by a time switch. The considerable bulk of compost will hold warmth over the periods when the electricity is off.

Wattage depends on the size and purpose of your frame; decide after you have consulted the suppliers of such equipment.

You can use small heated frames inside the greenhouse for high-temperature propagation, or for housing a small collection of low-growing tropical plants. An aluminium framework, glass sides and top, and 2–3cm (1 in) or so of sand over the cable, are recommended. The wattage required is usually about 20W per 1000 sq cm (20W per sq ft) of frame floor, and a thermostat is essential.

Frame cultivation

If possible, avoid using soil. Instead, line a trough or pit with polythene sheeting, slitted here and there for drainage, and fill it with a proprietary potting compost. You can grow excellent, high-quality salad and other crops with little risk from pests or diseases.

Where you are moving pots or other

Above left: timber-sided frame, with glass lights, shelters bedding plants prior to planting out. Above: rows of barn cloches protect lettuce that are almost ready for cropping

containers in and out, firm the floor and cover it with polythene, over which is spread coarse sand or shingle. If you keep this damp, it will moisten the air in the frame; the polythene will help to keep out soil pests.

Grow house plants, and pot plants like cineraria, calceolaria, primula and cyclamen, in frames until the decorative stage when they are ready to transfer to the house, conservatory or greenhouse. Use frames to raise bedding plants and for many forms of propagation from cutting and seed. You will also find them especially useful for crops like lettuce, radish, beet and carrots that you want in the kitchen even before winter is over.

Keep plants like dormant fuchsias, chrysanthemums and pelargoniums (that are used for summer garden or greenhouse decoration) in frames during the winter when they often look far from attractive. Store dormant tubers and bulbs there to leave the greenhouse less cluttered. Some crops, like strawberries and violets, lend themselves particularly to frame culture.

Keep glass frames (and cloches) as clean as possible to admit maximum light and discourage plant pests and diseases. Remove any mud splashes by careful use of a hose, if necessary.

CLOCHES

Early cloches were of glass and often held together by clumsy wires that were difficult to manipulate. Modern designs are simpler and often make use of plastics, which are very suitable for this purpose as cloches are frequently used only for weather protection, high temperatures being rarely necessary.

Select your type

There are tent, barn and T-shaped cloches, and a flat-topped 'utility' one. These are usually held together by special metal or plastic clips. Some cloches can be opened for ventilation or for watering, others have perforated tops to allow the rain to enter. Plastic ones with a cellular structure give greater warmth retention.

You can make simple and effective tunnels, ideal for protecting rows of vegetables, by sandwiching lengths of polythene between wire arches at intervals along the row, or by aligning ordinary cloches end-to-end. Anchor your plastic ones carefully in windy areas as they can easily blow away; use stones, bricks, wooden or metal pegs, or some special cloche fitments.

Cloches are most useful from autumn to late spring for providing protection from excessive wet and cold. Set them in place to dry and warm the soil before you dig and fertilize it, in preparation for sowing or planting.

Cloche cultivation

Use individual cloches for protecting isolated tender plants (such as fuchsia) in beds and borders, and protect groups of hardy and half-hardy annuals until they become established. You can also root cuttings directly into the ground of a nursery bed if you use cloches to cover them.

Many flowers grown for cutting benefit from cloche protection, especially low-growing bulbs in pots or bowls. Other favourite cloche flower crops are anemones, hellebore (Christmas rose), lily of the valley, violet and polyanthus. You can harden off bedding plants under cloches if frame space is not available. Also use them to protect sweet peas in the early stages.

In the vegetable garden, cloches give you year-round cropping. If you plan carefully you can move them from one

Top: tunnel cloches of polythene sheeting are versatile. They can be cut to any length, depending on whether you want to cover one plant or a whole row. Above: corrugated plastic cloches are used here to cover strawberry plants; being lightweight these cloches need to be anchored against the wind with wire hoops. End pieces can be added to give the plants greater protection

crop to another as needed, thus putting a limited number to maximum use.

Working with cloches

You do not need to remove cloches for watering; the water that drains off them will seep into the soil provided that it has been well prepared. It should be porous and moisture-retaining, but well-drained. Work in plenty of humus-forming material, like peat or rotted

garden compost. To avoid the wind rushing through your cloche tunnels, block the ends. This also applies to individual cloches used as miniature greenhouses to cover single, or small groups of, plants. When the weather permits ventilation, move the cloches along to leave a small gap between each one and remove the ends of tunnels.

Leave plenty of room between rows for comfortable access and keep the soil along the sides of the cloche rows well hoed to allow water retention. Soluble fertilizers can also be applied along the outside edges of the cloches.

Store glass cloches, and plastic tent and barn types, on their ends and stacked inside each other. For this purpose put down some clean boards (or lay a section of concrete) in a corner of the vegetable plot, and cover it with roofing felt for glass cloches.

Seed sowing and pricking out

Many different plants are raised from seed sown in containers in a greenhouse: summer bedding plants, flowering pot plants, and vegetables like tomatoes, lettuce, celery, cucumbers and marrows. But the techniques of sowing and subsequent care are similar.

Late winter and spring is the main period for most sowings; more precise timing is usually given on the seed packets. The procedure does, however, need prior preparation. A heated greenhouse, or a propagator, is necessary for germination (that is, starting seeds into life).

Seed trays and pots
Seed trays, approximately 5–6cm (2–2½ in) deep, are available in either wood or plastic. Plastic ones last for many years,

if well looked after, and are easy to clean. Hygienic conditions are important if you are to raise healthy seedlings, so be careful to clean the seed trays thoroughly before use.

For very small quantities of seed use plastic pots 9 or 13cm (3½ or 5 in) in diameter. These are also recommended for very large individual seeds, such as marrows and cucumbers. Again it is extremely important to wash all pots carefully before use.

Types of compost
Garden soil is not a very suitable medium in which to grow seedlings as it is full of weed seeds and harmful organisms, and it may not provide the correct conditions required by the seed for successful germination. Instead, buy one of the ready-

mixed seed-sowing composts, the most popular being John Innes Seed Compost, consisting of loam, peat, sand, superphosphate and ground chalk.

Alternatively there are many brands of seed compost which consist only of peat with added fertilizers; these are known as 'soilless' composts because they do not contain loam. When using soilless compost you have to be especially careful with watering, for if it dries out it can be difficult to moisten again; over-watering may saturate it and cause the seeds to rot.

Building in drainage
Be sure that surplus water is able to drain from all containers. When using John Innes composts it is essential to

Pricking out seedlings with a dibber

Place a layer of crocks in the bottom of flower pots to provide drainage

place a layer of crocks (broken clay flower pots or stones) at least 13mm ($\frac{1}{2}$ in) deep over the bottom of the pot. Cover the crocks with a little roughage, such as rough peat. If you use seed trays, crocks are not needed, just cover the drainage slits with some roughage.

Soilless compost can be used without any crocking – unless it is going in clay flower pots, in which case you must cover the large hole at the bottom with crocks.

Once you have arranged the drainage material add the compost to about 13mm ($\frac{1}{2}$ in) below the top of the tray or pot, to allow room for watering. Firm it gently all over with your fingertips, paying particular attention to the sides, ends and corners of seed trays. Make sure that the surface is level by pressing gently with a flat piece of wood that just fits into the tray or pot. Soilless compost should not be pressed hard but merely shaken down by tapping the container on a hard surface or lightly firming with the wood.

Very tiny seeds (like lobelia and begonia) should be sown on a fine surface. So before pressing down, sieve a layer of compost over the surface using a very small-mesh sieve. Alternatively you can sprinkle a thin layer of silver sand over the compost before sowing. Do not use builder's sand as this contains materials toxic to plants.

Water the compost lightly, using a fine rose on the watering can, before you sow.

Sowing the seeds

Seeds must be sown thinly and evenly otherwise the seedlings will be overcrowded and you will find it difficult to separate them during pricking out (transplanting). They will also have thin, weak stems and be prone to diseases like 'damping off'.

Small seed is usually sown broadcast

(scattered) over the surface of the compost. Take a small quantity of seed in the palm of one hand – just sufficient to sow a tray or pot. Hold your hand about 30cm (12 in) above the container and move it to and fro over the surface, at the same time tapping it with the other hand to release the seeds slowly. If you move your hand first backwards and forwards and then side to side this will help to spread the seeds evenly. You may find it easier to hold the seeds in a piece of paper, instead of in your hand.

It is difficult to sow very small seeds evenly, some being as fine as dust, but if you mix them with soft, dry, silver sand (using 1 part seeds to 1 part sand) this helps to bulk them up and makes them easier to handle.

Large seeds, which are easily handled, can be 'space-sown' – that is placed individually, and at regular intervals, on the surface of the compost. Tomato seed, for instance, can be treated in this way.

Very large seeds, such as cucumbers, peas and various beans, are best sown at two per 9cm ($3\frac{1}{2}$ in) pot. If you use

1 *Cover drainage materials with compost, firming it gently with the fingertips*

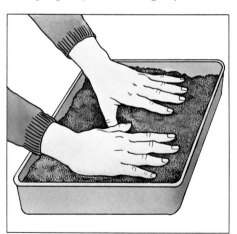

3 *Scatter a little seed into tray by tapping it gently from your open hand*

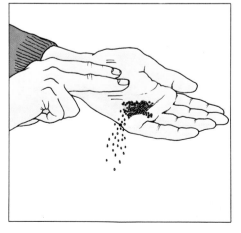

peat pots, they can later be planted, complete with young plant, into the final pot or open ground. When they have germinated, remove the weaker seedling, leaving the stronger one to grow on.

Pelleted seeds

This term describes seeds that are individually covered with a layer of clay which is often mixed with some plant foods. They are easily handled and can be space-sown in boxes or pots. The compost around pelleted seeds must remain moist as it is moisture which breaks down the coating and allows the seeds to germinate.

After sowing

Seeds should be covered with a layer of compost equal to the diameter of the seed. It is best to sieve compost over them, using a fine-mesh sieve. However, do not cover very small or dust-like seeds with compost as they will probably fail to germinate.

If you use John Innes or another loam-

2 *Level the surface of the compost by pressing with a flat piece of wood*

4 *With large seeds, sow two in a small pot and remove the weaker seedling*

1 Sieve compost over seeds; 2 Stand tray in water till surface looks moist. 3 Use a dibber to lift seedlings and transfer them to a new tray, where they will have room to grow on

containing compost the seeds should then be watered, either using a very fine rose on the watering can or by standing the containers in a tray of water until the surface becomes moist. (This latter method is not advisable for loam-less composts as they tend to float; moisten them well before sowing the seed.) Allow the containers to drain before placing them in the greenhouse.

A good, or even better, alternative to plain water is a solution of Cheshunt Compound, made up according to the directions on the tin. This is a fungicide which prevents diseases such as damping off attacking seedlings.

Aids to germination

Place the pots or trays either on a bench in a warm greenhouse or in an electrically-heated propagator. Most seeds need a temperature of 15°–18°C (60–65°F) for good germination. The containers can be covered with a sheet of glass that, in turn, is covered with brown paper to prevent the sun's warmth drying out the compost. Turn the glass over each day to prevent excess condensation building up on the inside. Water the compost whenever its surface starts to become dry. As soon as germination commences remove the covering of glass and paper, for the seedlings then require as much light as possible if they are to grow into strong, healthy plants.

Pricking out

Once the seedlings are large enough to handle easily prick them out into trays or boxes to give them enough room to grow. Generally, standard-size plastic or wooden seed trays are used that are 6cm (2½ in) deep; there is no need to put drainage material in the base. The trays are filled with compost in the way described for seed-sowing, again leaving space for watering. A suitable compost would be John Innes Potting Compost No. 1 which can be bought ready-mixed. It consists of loam, peat, coarse sand, John Innes base fertilizer and ground chalk. Alternatively, use one of the soil-less potting composts that contains peat, or peat and sand, plus fertilizers. Make sure the compost is moist before you start pricking out.

You will need a dibber for this job – either a pencil or a piece of wood of similar shape. With this lift a few seedlings at a time from the box or pot, taking care not to damage the roots. Handle the seedlings by the seed leaves – the first pair of leaves formed. Never hold them by the stems which are easily damaged at this stage.

Spacing out

The number of seedlings per standard-size box will vary slightly according to their vigour. Generally 40 per box is a good spacing (5 rows of 8). For less vigorous plants you could increase this to 54 per box (6 rows of 9).

Mark out the position of the seedlings with the dibber before commencing, ensuring equal spacing each way. Next make a hole, with the dibber, which should be deep enough to allow the roots to drop straight down. Place the seedling in the hole so that the seed leaves are at soil level, and then firm it in by pressing the soil gently against it with the dibber.

If only a few seeds have been sown in pots each seedling could be pricked out into an individual 7cm (3 in) pot. But if you have single seedlings, such as marrows, already started in 9cm (3½ in) pots, these will not need to be moved.

After pricking out, water in the seedlings (with a fine rose on the watering can) preferably using Cheshunt Compound. Then place them on the greenhouse bench or on a shelf near to the glass, as maximum light is essential. Continue to water whenever the soil surface appears dry.

Windowsill propagation

If you do not have a greenhouse, heated frame, or propagator, you can still raise seedlings in the house. Ideally the germination conditions should be as similar as possible to those which are recommended for greenhouse cultivation. Windowsills are the best places for raising seeds, and if they are wide ones you can use standard-size seed trays.

However it is usually possible to fit a few pots onto the narrowest of windowsills. For best results use trays or pots that are fitted with propagator tops. The temperature on the sill must not drop below the average room temperature and south- or west-facing sills are obviously best.

Make sure the seedlings are never deprived of daylight or allowed to get cold at night. Never draw the curtains across between the plants and the warm room air on cold nights, if necessary bring them into the room. Finally, to maintain strong and even growth, turn all pots and trays around every day.

Use a pot with a propagator top when starting off seedlings on a windowsill

Potting off and potting on

Nowadays plastic pots are generally used in preference to clay, but whichever type you have ensure that they are clean and dry before using them.

POTTING OFF

As soon as cuttings have developed a good root system they should be carefully lifted from their trays and put into individual pots about 7·5–9cm (3–3½ in) in diameter. When seedlings are large enough to handle easily they can be treated in the same way (as an alternative to pricking out into trays).

For this first potting, use a fairly weak compost, such as J.I. No 1, or an equivalent soilless type consisting of loam, peat, coarse sand, John Innes base fertilizer and ground chalk.

Allowing for drainage

Drainage material is not necessary in plastic pots as the holes are devised so that the compost does not leak. Furthermore, there is a trend towards using less drainage material in the bottom of small clay pots. When there are some drainage holes provided, place a few crocks (pieces of broken clay pots or stones) over the drainage holes and cover with a thin layer of roughage such as coarse peat or partially-rotted leaf mould. If you are using soilless compost, crocks or drainage materials are not normally necessary. Place a layer of compost over the drainage material and firm lightly with your fingers.

Transferring the plants

Hold the rooted cuttings or seedlings in the centre of the pot, with the roots well spread out, and trickle compost all around until it is slightly higher than the rim of the pot. Give the pot a sharp tap on the bench to settle the compost well down and lightly firm all round with your fingers. Make sure the compost is pushed right down to the bottom.

Some soilless composts, however, require little or no firming, so check the manufacturer's instructions first.

Remember to leave about 13mm (½ in) between the surface of the soil and the rim of the pot to allow room for watering.

After potting off, water the plants thoroughly, using a fine rose on the watering can, to settle them in further. Then they can be returned to the greenhouse bench.

POTTING ON

Plants need potting on to prevent them becoming 'pot-bound' (when the roots are packed very tightly in the pot). If this happens the plants will suffer from lack of food, growth will be poor and they will dry out very rapidly and require frequent watering.

However, it is worthwhile noting that some plants, such as pelargoniums, are more floriferous (bear more flowers) when slightly pot-bound.

Plants should be moved to the next size of pot, for instance from a 9cm (3½ in) to a 13cm (5 in), from a 13cm (5 in) to a 15cm (6 in) and so on. The reason for moving only to the next size pot is that plants dislike a large volume

Before placing a pot-bound plant in its new pot, carefully remove old drainage crocks from the base of the rootball

of soil around their roots because they cannot absorb water from all of it and, therefore, it is liable to remain wet. This can result in root rot and the possible death of the plant. Small moves allow plants to put out new roots quickly.

Composts and drainage

Richer composts (those containing more plant foods) are generally used for potting on. If you prefer the John Innes type, then use No 2, which contains twice as much fertilizer and chalk as No 1. Some plants (for example chrysanthemums,

tomatoes and strawberries for fruiting under glass) like an even richer compost, such as J.I. No 3 – particularly when they are moved into their final size of pot).

Drainage material, as described under potting off, is generally advisable when using soil composts in pots that are 13cm (5 in) or larger. A layer of crocks about 2–3cm (1 in) deep should be sufficient, plus roughage.

Repotting the plant

Remove the plant from its pot by turning it upside-down and tapping the rim of the pot on the edge of a bench. The rootball should then slide out intact. On no account disturb this ball of roots and soil, but remove old crocks, if any, from the base. Scrape off any moss or weeds on the surface with an old wooden plant label or similar object.

Place enough soil in the new pot so that, when the plant is placed on it, the top of the rootball is about 13mm (½ in) from the top of the pot. This will allow for a light covering of compost with room for subsequent watering. Firm the compost lightly with your fingers and then stand the plant in the centre of the

new pot. Trickle fresh compost all round the rootball until you reach the top of the pot. Give the pot a sharp tap on the bench to get the compost well down and firm it all round.

If you are using soilless composts, follow the maker's instructions for firming. You will probably need to add more compost to reach the desired height. Finally, water in the plants, using a fine rose on the watering can.

Potting on is best done when plants are growing actively in spring and summer – or in the autumn, although growth will then be slowing down. Plants potted in spring and summer will quickly root into the new compost because of the warmer weather.

Plant propagation: Cuttings

A cutting is a part of a plant—a piece of stem, leaf or root—which is induced to form roots of its own and thus develop into a young plant that is identical with its parent.

Many plants can be propagated from cuttings but the type of cutting to prepare depends on the plant. A wide range from hardy shrubs to greenhouse plants can be increased from softwood cuttings. These are prepared from very soft young shoots early in the year, generally in the period from late spring to mid summer (April to June), although some may be taken even earlier than this.

Cuttings, whether softwood or any other type, must be prepared with a very sharp knife or razor blade to ensure clean cuts. Ragged cuts resulting from using a blunt knife may take too long to heal, and could eventually result in the cutting rotting instead of making roots.

Softwood cuttings

Hardy shrubs that can be propagated from softwoods include weigela, deutzia, philadelphus, buddleia, caryopteris, hypericum and many other deciduous kinds. The cuttings of these can be about 8cm (3 in) in length, and should be cut cleanly just below a leaf joint, or node. Such a cutting is generally known as a 'nodal' cutting.

The lower leaves should be carefully cut off as close to the stem as possible. The bases of the cuttings can then be dipped into a proprietary hormone rooting powder or liquid to encourage rapid root formation.

Softwood cuttings are liable to lose water very quickly and wilt, so they must be inserted in the rooting medium as quickly as possible. The usual compost for rooting is a mixture of equal parts of moist sphagnum peat and coarse horticultural sand.

A small number of cuttings can be rooted in pots of a convenient size, but larger quantities should be inserted in seed trays. The container should be filled with compost to within 13mm ($\frac{1}{2}$ in) of the rim and firmed moderately well with the fingers. Cuttings are placed in holes made with a dibber – a piece of wood shaped rather like a blunt pencil. In fact, a pencil makes a good dibber. The base of each cutting should be in close contact with the bottom of the hole. Firm in with the fingers and when the container is full water generously with a fine rose on the watering can.

Softwood cuttings of hardy herbaceous perennial plants such as delphinium, lupin, phlox, chrysanthemum, gaillardia and scabious, and of half-hardy perennials like dahlia and glasshouse chrysanthemum, are prepared and inserted in the same way. Remove young shoots when 8cm (3 in) long, from as close to the crown of the plant as possible.

Other plants that can be raised from softwood cuttings are tender greenhouse plants such as begonia, coleus, fuchsia, impatiens and tradescantia. Cuttings of fuchsia can be prepared by cutting the base between two nodes or joints—these are known as 'internodal' cuttings.

Growing conditions

All softwood cuttings need plenty of warmth in which to root, and a humid or moist atmosphere. The simplest method of providing these conditions is to enclose a pot of cuttings in a polythene bag, which should be tied at the top, or place a jam jar over the cuttings, and stand it on a windowsill in a warm room, preferably above a radiator. A more sophisticated approach is to invest in an electrically heated propagating case, which is generally placed on a greenhouse bench. This should be set to give a temperature of 52°C (70°F).

The covers should be removed for an hour or two, several times a week, to

Softwood cuttings: **1** *cut shoot from plant with sharp knife or razor;* **2** *trim cutting cleanly to just below base of leaf joint;* **3** *cut off lower leaves as close to the stem as possible;* **4** *dip base of cutting in proprietary hormone rooting powder;*

5 *using dibber, insert cutting in compost, made of moist sphagnum peat and coarse horticultural sand;* **6** *firm round cutting;* **7** *water well in, using fine spray on watering can;* **8** *place in propagator or mist unit or,* **9** *put pot in polythene bag*

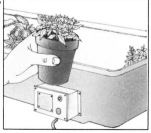

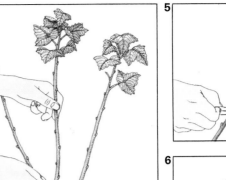
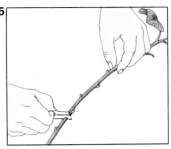
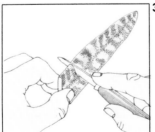
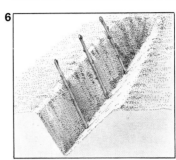

Semi-ripe cuttings:
1 *remove lower stems;*
2 *rub off lower leaves;*
3 *insert cuttings in compost*
Hardwood cuttings:
4 *cut ripe or woody shoot;*
5 *trim to four or five buds;*
6 *put cuttings in prepared,*
V-shaped trench, replace soil
and firm well in

allow the containers to dry off, because a great amount of condensation forms in these enclosed conditions.

The most adventurous way of rooting cuttings is to install a mist-propagation unit in your greenhouse. This provides heat at the base of the cuttings and sprays the leaves intermittently with water, which prevents the cuttings from wilting and dying. Reasonably simple and cheap units are available to amateur gardeners.

Some softwoods can be rooted simply by standing them in jars of water on a warm windowsill indoors. Plants which respond to this treatment include coleus, fuchsia, impatiens, tradescantia and zebrina – all popular house plants.

Semi-ripe cuttings

Many plants can be prepared from semi-ripe (or semi-mature) cuttings. These are prepared from shoots which are ripening or hardening at the base but are still soft at the tip. The time to take these is late summer to late autumn (July to October).

Evergreen and deciduous shrubs, heathers, conifers and half-hardy perennials like pelargonium (geranium), heliotrope and gazania, can be increased from semi-ripe cuttings.

Cuttings generally vary in length from some 10–15cm (4–6 in), but those of heathers should be only 5cm (2 in) long. These can simply be pulled off the plant, whereas cuttings of other subjects must be nodal and prepared with a knife.

Growing conditions

Preparation and insertion are the same as for softwoods, but less heat is needed for rooting. A cold frame makes an ideal rooting environment, but of course if you have a propagating case or mist unit then root them in these.

Hardwood cuttings

Hardwood cuttings, which are inserted in early and mid winter (November to December), need no heat at all to root. Common examples of shrubs and soft fruits raised from these are privet, willow, shrubby dogwood, Chinese honeysuckle, blackcurrant, redcurrant and gooseberry.

Choose current year's shoots which are completely ripe or woody and cut them into 23–30cm (9–12 in) lengths with sharp secateurs. Cut just above a bud at the top and just below at the base. With redcurrants and gooseberries remove all the buds except the top three or four. Dip the base of the cutting in a hormone rooting powder or liquid.

The cuttings are inserted to two-thirds of their length in a V-shaped trench made with a spade in a sheltered well-drained spot outdoors. Firm them in well. They will be well rooted by the following autumn (September).

Leaf cuttings

Some house, and greenhouse, plants are propagated from leaf cuttings in spring. With peperomia, saintpaulia, streptocarpus and gloxinia use a whole leaf with the leaf-stalk attached. The complete leaf-stalk is inserted in a peat and sand compost so that you leave only the leaf-blade exposed.

In the case of a plant like *Sansevieria trifasciata* (Mother-in-law's tongue),

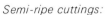

Leaf section cuttings: **1** *cut whole leaf from plant;* **2** *cut leaf into 5cm (2 in) sections;* **3** *press section (top end facing upwards) into peat and sand compost*

Whole leaf cuttings: **4** *cut leaf from plant;* **5** *insert whole leaf-stalk into peat and sand compost, leaving leaf-blade exposed;* **6** *firm compost round cutting*

163

one of the long leaves should be cut into 5cm (2 in) sections. Each section is pressed into peat and sand compost to about half its length. Make sure you insert each section the right way up.

Rex begonia can be propagated by removing an entire leaf, cutting through the main veins in several places on the underside and laying the leaf, top side uppermost, on the surface of a tray of compost. Hold the leaf down with small stones. Young plants will form where you have made the cuts.

Like softwood cuttings, leaf cuttings need plenty of warmth and humidity to enable them to root.

Leaf-bud cuttings
A leaf-bud cutting is a portion of stem about 2·5cm (1 in) long, with an entire leaf attached at the top, and a bud in the axil (the point where the leaf joins the stem). Rubber plant, camellia, clematis, passion flower and ivy can be propagated by this method, which should be carried out in late spring (April). Insert cuttings so that the leaf only is above the compost and root in warm, humid conditions.

Eye cuttings
Grape vines and their close relations (parthenocissus and ampelopsis) are propagated from eye cuttings in mid winter (December). You will probably need a propagating case for this method as a base temperature of 52°C (70°F) is required for rooting. Use well-ripened or hardened current year's wood. Cut it into 4cm (1½ in) sections, each with a dormant 'eye' or bud in the centre. Remove a thin slice of wood on the opposite side to the

1–3 leaf cutting using whole leaf laid on compost, with main veins cut; 4–6 root cuttings, using thick and thin roots

Top: pull pink shoots to obtain pipings
Above: for leaf bud cuttings use a portion of stem bearing a leaf and a leaf bud

bud. These cuttings are pressed horizontally into pots of peat and sand compost, with the buds uppermost, and just sufficiently deep to ensure that they remain stable. Water in and place in the rooting environment.

Pipings
Pinks are raised from a special type of cutting known as a piping. In late summer or early autumn (July or August) pull out the tops of young shoots: they should snap out cleanly just above a leaf joint or node. Each one should be left with three or four pairs of leaves, after the lower leaves have been carefully pulled off. Using a dibber, insert the pipings around the edge of a small pot containing peat and sand compost. Water well in and then place in a cold frame to root.

Root cuttings
Finally, root cuttings can be used to propagate shrubs like rhus, sambucus, aralia, campsis, celastrus, chaenomeles and rubus; trees such as ailanthus, catalpa, paulownia, robinia and elm; hardy herbaceous perennials like anchusa, echinops, eryngium, gaillardia, Oriental poppy, border phlox, *Primula denticulata*, *Romneya coulteri*, symphytum or verbascum; and the alpines *Morisia monantha* and *Pulsatilla vulgaris*.

The time to take root cuttings is when the plants are dormant, a good period being mid winter (December). Use young roots of no more than pencil thickness; the roots of some plants, such as phlox, primula, morisia and pulsatilla, will be thinner than this.

The roots can be obtained by scraping the soil away from large plants, removing a few roots, returning the soil and firming. Small plants can be lifted, a few roots removed and then replanted.

The roots should be cut into 5cm (2 in) sections with a knife or secateurs. Thick roots are inserted vertically, and to ensure that you keep them the right way up the tops of the cuttings should have a flat cut and the bases a slanting cut. The top of a root cutting is always that part which was nearer to the stem of the plant.

The cuttings can be rooted in pots or boxes of peat and sand compost. Thick cuttings should be pressed vertically into the medium so that the tops are just below soil level. Thin cuttings cannot be pushed in vertically, so are laid horizontally on the surface of the compost and covered with a further 13mm (½ in) layer. Place in a cold frame or greenhouse to root. The top growth will be produced first so do not be in too much of a hurry to lift the cuttings for planting out.

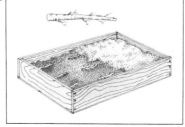

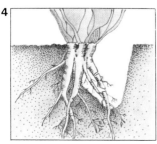

Plant propagation: Division and layering

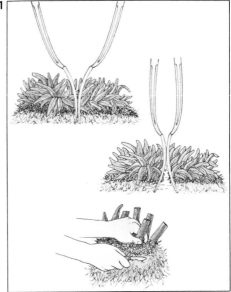

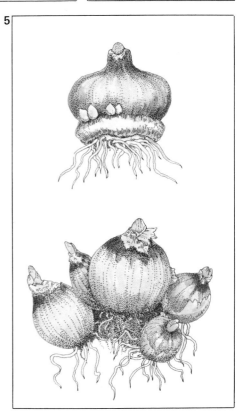

The simplest method of plant propagation is division, or the splitting of plants into a number of small portions. It is the principal method of increasing herbaceous border plants and other hardy perennials; most of these need lifting and dividing every three to four years to ensure that they remain vigorous and continue to flower well. Many other kinds of plant can also be increased by division.

Perennials and alpines

The best time to carry out this operation is in mid spring (March–mid April), just as the plants are awakening from their winter rest; plants in flower should be left until they finish flowering. Lift the clumps carefully with a fork and shake off as much soil as possible. Large tough clumps can be divided by inserting two digging forks back to back through the centre and pulling the handles apart. The two portions can then be split by the same method. Discard the centre of each clump and replant only the young outer portions. Each division should consist of a number of growth buds and a good portion of roots.

Top left: preparing divided perennial plants for replanting; 1 dividing clump of perennials with forks and trimming damaged roots; 2–4 cutting, trimming and replanting young rhizomes; 5 corm producing cormlets, and below, bulblets forming round parent bulb

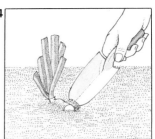

Those perennials that flower early in the year, such as doronicum, pyrethrum, epimedium, symphytum, pulmonaria and primula (including primroses and polyanthus), should be divided immediately after flowering. Some perennials are best not divided at all, as they resent being moved: these include romneya, paeony, helleborus, alstroemeria, echinops, eryngium, *Papaver orientalis*, (Oriental poppy) and Japanese anemone. Plants that grow from a single stem, cannot, of course, be divided.

Many alpine plants form mats or carpets of growth and these too can be lifted and pulled apart to provide a number of smaller plants. Thyme, raolia, sedum, gentian, saxifrage and campanula can all be split in early spring.

Dividing rhizomes and tubers

Some plants, of which the iris is the best-known example, form 'rhizomes', which are simply swollen stems situated at or just below soil level. There are many kinds of iris, such as the bearded iris, which is a superb border plant, and the dwarf kinds admirably suited to a rock garden.

When you divide iris—which should be immediately after flowering—each division should consist of a short portion of rhizome with some roots and a fan of leaves attached.

Many people keep dahlias from one year to another. Before planting them out in the spring, the dormant clumps can be split into smaller portions. Dahlias are best cut with a knife; make sure that each division consists of a portion of old stem with dormant growth buds at the base, and at best one tuber attached.

Bulbs and corms

Bulbs, such as daffodil, tulip and hyacinth, and corms, for example gladiolus and crocus, form offspring around their bases, and these are known as bulblets and cormlets respectively. If the parent bulbs and corms are dug up after the foliage has died down, these youngsters can be removed and stored dry until the correct planting time, which is autumn (September or October) for most, and mid to late spring (March–April) for gladiolus. Plant them fairly shallowly. Some bulbs and corms may take two or three years to flower, so be patient.

Simple layering: **1** *twist stem sharply to break surface tissue or* **2** *make cut in underside of stem;* **3** *bend stem at wound and peg to soil with wire pin;* **4** *cover pegged section with soil;* **5** *tie end of stem to bamboo cane:* **6** *when roots have formed, sever new plant from parent stem*

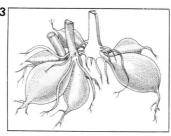

House plants

Some house plants can be split up in spring when they start to become too large, such as ferns, aspidistra, chlorophytum, and other clump-formers. Remove each plant from its pot, shake the soil away and pull apart. Repot each portion, using fresh compost.

Offsets

An even easier method than lifting and dividing is simply to remove offsets from plants complete with a few roots attached. Offsets are small plants found growing around the parent. Carefully tease them away with a hand fork to ensure you do not damage the roots or disturb the main plant.

Sempervivum (houseleek), androsace, some saxifrages, sansevieria and many cacti and succulents form offsets.

Suckers

There are many shrubs that produce 'suckers'—shoots which arise from below ground, usually from the roots. This is one of the ways in which plants increase naturally. With some, such as raspberries, masses of shoots are produced all round the parent plants.

In the winter or in early spring (November–March), when the plants are dormant, suckers can be carefully dug up with some roots attached and planted elsewhere. Shrubs which are often pro-

1 *Removing offsets from sempervivum;* **2** *lifting rooted suckers from raspberry plants;* **3** *dividing dahlia tubers*

pagated by this method include *Rhus typhina*, symphoricarpus, cornus (dogwood) and aralia. It is also the way to increase raspberries.

Layering

Layering is also an easy method of propagating plants. Simple layering consists of pegging down a branch or shoot into the soil, where it will form roots. It can then be detached from the parent plant and planted elsewhere. You may notice, when out in the country, that some plants, such as beech and bramble, layer themselves quite naturally without the help of man.

Almost any tree or shrub can be propagated by simple layering, provided a shoot can be brought into contact with the soil. The best time for this operation is in the spring or early summer when plants are actively growing. Choose young shoots or stems for layering as these will root quicker than older growth. The ground in which the stems are to be layered should be well prepared beforehand. Fork it over and break it down to a fine tilth. Mix plenty of moist peat and coarse sand with the soil to a depth of 15–25cm (6–9 in). Now all is ready.

About 30cm (12 in) or so from the tip of the shoot or stem it should be wounded in some way, so as to encourage quicker rooting. The easiest way to wound the stem is to grip it with both hands and give it a sharp half-twist to break some of the tissue. Another method is to cut diagonally halfway through the stem with a sharp knife, making a cut 4–5cm ($1\frac{1}{2}$–2 in) in length. This will result in a 'tongue' in the stem, which should be kept open with a small stone or piece of wood.

Using a piece of galvanized wire bent to the shape of a hairpin, peg the prepared shoot down where it was wounded into a 7–8cm (3 in) deep depression in the soil. Cover with soil and firm with your fingers. Tie the end of the stem protruding through the soil upright to a short bamboo cane. Keep layers well watered whenever the soil starts to become dry.

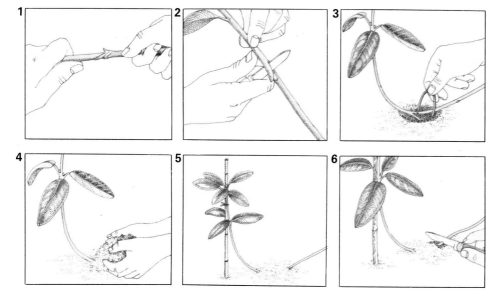

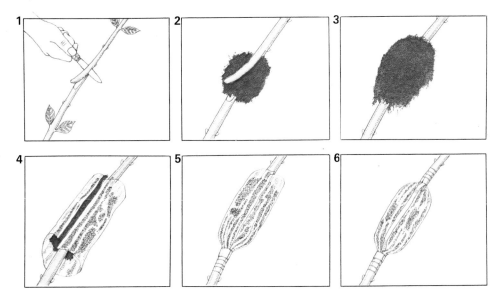

Air layering: **1** *make diagonal cut, half way through stem;* **2** *treat with hormone rooting powder and wedge open with moss;* **3** *bandage cut with moss;* **4** *wrap with polythene sheeting;* **5** *seal lower end below cut;* **6** *seal upper end and join*

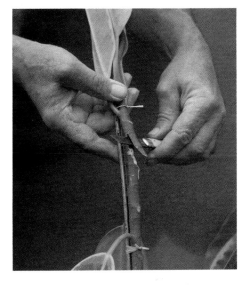

Above: air layering of ficus elastica *rubber plant, showing correct angle of cut*

vines. Wound the long stems and peg them down at intervals along the ground, so that you get a number of new plants from one stem. All should have rooted within a year.

Tip layering

Blackberries, loganberries and other hybrid berries are propagated by tip layering. In late summer or early autumn July or August simply bury the extreme tip of a young stem 7–8cm (3 in) deep in the soil. It should be well rooted by the following early winter (November), when it can be planted out.

Air layering

This is a useful method where stems cannot be pulled down to the ground. Again it is suitable for any tree or shrub, spring or early summer (March–May) being a good time to do it.

Use a young stem and cut diagonally halfway through it, making the cut about 5cm (2 in) in length. Make this wound about 30cm (12 in) from the tip and keep the cut open by packing it with moist sphagnum moss. You can first treat the cut with a hormone rooting powder or liquid to speed root production.

The prepared part of the stem should then be 'bandaged' with moist sphagnum moss, held in place by wrapping with a piece of clear polythene sheeting. Each end of this polythene 'sleeve' must be tightly sealed with self-adhesive water-proof tape. The overlapping edge of the polythene must also be sealed with tape.

You will know when roots have formed as they will be seen through the poly-thene. At this stage sever the rooted layer and plant it out.

House plants such as ficus (rubber plant) croton, philodendron, dracaena and cordyline can also be air-layered. It is done in the way described for outdoor plants, making the cut near the top of the plant. If the plant is kept in a warm place, rooting will be a matter of weeks. If the stem of the parent plant is cut hard back after removing the layer, it should produce new growth from the base.

Finally, strawberries are also propagated by layering. In the summer they produce 'runners', or stems which grow along the ground, and at intervals along these new plants are formed. To encourage these to root quickly, peg the first plantlet (the one nearest the parent) on each runner into a pot of potting compost sunk in the soil. Remove any plantlets beyond the first one. They will quickly root, and in early autumn (August or early September) should be severed from the main plant and planted elsewhere.

Some plants, such as the common shrubs forsythia, syringa (lilac), weigela, hebe (veronica), privet and philadelphus (mock orange), will form a good root system in a year. Others may take longer to root well, particularly magnolia, hamamelis (witch hazel), rhododendron, azalea and camellia. When the layers have rooted lift them carefully with a fork and sever from the parent close to the new root area. Set out as soon as possible.

Serpentine layering

This is a minor modification of simple layering, and is done with plants possessing long stems, particularly climbers like clematis, jasmine, lonicera (honeysuckle), wisteria, passiflora (passion flower) and

1 *Serpentine layering;* **2** *pegging down strawberry runners;* **3** *tip layering*

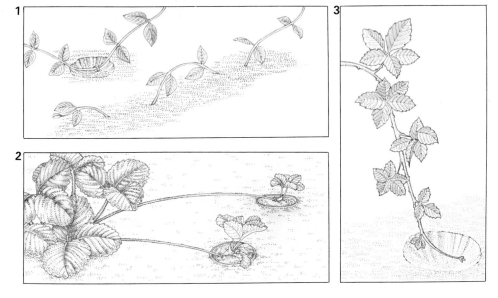

Weeds and weed control

There are two basic types of weeds – perennial and annual: the former are far harder to eliminate.

PERENNIAL WEEDS

Most perennial weeds are quick-growing and tenacious, often re-growing from roots or rootstocks. They are, therefore, very difficult to get rid of. Herbaceous types, such as couch grass, bindweed (convolvulus and calystegia species) and ground elder are often notoriously deep-rooted. They store food in their fleshy roots, rhizomes, stolons, tubers or bulbs. It is easy to remove the visible vegetation but difficult to eradicate the roots. With woody plants, such as brambles and ivy, it is harder to get rid of the growth above ground, but comparatively easy to eradicate the roots, which must be burnt.

Manual weeding

Good hand-weeding is still one of the best ways to rid yourself of perennial weeds. Some well-timed work with a trowel will save you much time and trouble later on – providing you don't leave any of the roots in the soil.

If working near decorative or vegetable plants where you don't want to use chemical weedkillers, then manual weeding becomes a necessity. You may need to use a fork, trowel, knife or even a mattock (like a pickaxe). Be careful that you don't just carve them up; this merely helps to propagate them and makes more work in the future. Dig up the weeds, complete with roots, and then burn them or put them in the garbage bin.

When cultivating fresh ground it is essential to remove all the roots and underground storage systems; although hard work, it pays to lift them out by hand. Don't use a rotary cultivator on couch grass or dock-infested land as it will only chop up the weeds and encourage regrowth. Hoeing can have the same effect on a smaller scale unless you take care to remove the root, not just chop off leaves.

Weedkillers

Weedkillers are categorized according to their mode of action, so that you can buy whichever is most suited to your needs.

Total In an area devoid of decorative or culinary plants you can use a 'total' weedkiller, such as aminotriazole, to 'sweep the board'. A total weedkiller will kill all plants with which it comes into contact. You must take great care not to let it drift onto other plants or onto your neighbour's property. There have been many skirmishes over the garden wall as a result of misapplied weedkillers. After using it, remove and burn the debris and plant nothing in the ground for two to three months. If treatment with a total weedkiller is followed by a dose of a residual weedkiller (such as simazine) you will have a weed-free site for several months.

Another total weedkiller is sodium chlorate. It has to be used with great care as it spreads in the soil and can kill plants some distance away from the spot it was applied. Another danger is that, mixed with many other substances, it may be spontaneously inflammable, and it is therefore dangerous to store. It has a residual effect for up to a year.

Total and residual weedkillers are best for clearing paths and driveways.

Above right: the seed clock of the dandelion (Taraxacum officinale), ready to spread a new generation over the garden. Right: daisy (Bellis perrenis)

Residual or pre-emergent These will not kill established weeds but they help to prevent the germination of most weeds for up to three months. There are various degrees of persistence.

Simazine has a long persistence, but it can be harmful to some shrubs (such as deutzia). Propachlor lasts for shorter periods but is less toxic and so is useful for herbaceous borders and shrubberies.

This type remains in a narrow band of the topsoil, so that any weed seeds germinating in this zone take up the chemical and die. It is possible to apply residual weedkiller where bulbs are planted, because their roots are located below the weedkiller band, and they grow quickly through it without suffering any damage. Plants such as runner beans, sweet peas, daffodils and hyacinths will all grow through the weedkiller layer after it has become inactive.

Selective Some weedkillers are termed 'selective' as they kill dicotyledons (broad-leaved plants), but will not damage many monocotyledons – such as grasses. Selective ones like 2,4-D, MCPA, 2,4,5-T or fenoprop (hormone types) kill by causing the plant to overgrow its food reserves so that it literally grows itself to death. Use this kind with great care as the slightest drift will damage crops; tomatoes are especially sensitive to them.

Non-selective The well-known paraquat and diquat weedkillers will only kill perennial weeds while they are still at seedling stage. After a few weeks they become immune and these preparations merely burn off their foliage and allow the roots to re-grow. They are de-activated immediately they meet the soil and are therefore safe to use provided they do not drift. But they must be kept away from children and animals: under no circumstances store them in old lemonade or other misleading bottles.

Methods of application

Always read the maker's instructions on the package and follow them closely; they have been based on years of research. Our recommendations give the chemical name, so when buying proprietary brands check the package label and see that it contains the correct constituents for your purpose. Keep a separate watering can for use with chemical weedkillers, and use a rose fitting or dribble-bar attachment for controlled application.

Specific treatments

Some perennial weeds are particularly stubborn and require special treatment.

Oxalis Remove these plants, which defy all chemical killers, with a sharp knife. Be sure to get up all roots and little bulbs.

Couch grass and perennial oat-grass These persistent grasses, with rhizomes, put up a fight against eradication. The only effective control is dalapon. If they are found in flower or vegetable beds 'spot' apply several doses of dalapon and then dig out the remains.

'Spot treatment' involves applying the weedkiller to the weeds only. It is done most easily by using a bottle with a pourer top or a squeezy-type container.

Docks Repeated action with dichlobenil (not easily obtainable), or spot treatment with 2,4-D, MCPA, fenoprop or mecoprop will keep the plants down. They are difficult to control because the roots, if broken on being dug out, will grow again.

Perennial nettle, bindweed, ground elder and blackberry These tend to grow near hedges or in shrubberies, and once established are likely to remain permanent residents. Apply 2,4,5-T or brushwood killer (usually a mixture of 2,4-D and 2,4,5-T) but avoid spraying onto other plants.

A good way to minimize drift is to make up a solution of this weedkiller in a container and dip the tips of the weeds in it. This will then be taken up through the plant by the sap stream – and kill it. You may need to make several applications over a few days for them to be effective. This method also works on many wild, shrubby plants such as dog rose and ivy (*Hedera helix*).

Thistles These are particularly obstinate weeds that may need pulling out by hand.

Above: bindweed (Convolvulus arvensis)

Above: couch grass (Agropyron repens)
Below: dock (Rumex obtusifolius)

Below: annual nettle (Urtica urens)
Bottom: creeping thistle (Cirsium arvense)

PERENNIAL WEEDS Guide to treatment

PLACE	TYPICAL WEEDS	TREATMENT	OTHER ADVICE
NEW LAND & WASTE LAND	Bindweed; blackberry; couch grass; docks; ivy; ground elder; nettles; oat-grass; thistles	Apply total weedkiller, e.g. aminotriazole; clear away debris and dig carefully, removing all roots, tubers and bulbous roots. Throw away or burn these.	Take care not to let the spray drift on to your own plants or over to other gardens.
LAWNS	Creeping buttercup; daisy; dandelion; plantain; speedwell	Mowing and raking; apply 2,4-D and mecoprop mixtures (ioxynil is needed for speedwell). Lever out old grass and weeds with a sharp trowel or knife.	Do not use 2,4-D or mecoprop on new lawns until the grass is at least six months old; use ioxynil for weeds on young lawns.
	Moss	Lawn sand or mercuric chloride.	Take care not to let children or animals near either of these dangerous poisons.
SHRUBBERIES & MIXED BORDERS	Bindweed; couch grass; docks; ground elder; thistles	Dig out all roots; apply a residual weedkiller to prevent fresh germination; dichlobenil kills many perennial weeds.	Check all instructions to make sure that your borders do not contain plants that are sensitive to some of the residual weedkillers.
ROSE BEDS	Couch grass; many germinating perennials	Treat couch grass with dalapon and remove by hand; simazine will prevent germination and dichlobenil completely kills many of these perennial weeds.	Take care not to let weedkiller get on to roses, especially if in leaf; apply simazine in early spring to last through most of the plant-growing season.
HERBACEOUS & FLOWER BORDERS	Many germinating and established weeds	Propachlor is a good residual weedkiller to check further germination, provided all established weeds are removed by hand or fork first.	Ensure that weather is warm and soil moist before applying propachlor.
FRUIT	Established and germinating perennials (especially couch grass and creeping buttercup in strawberries)	Use diquat or paraquat between rows to kill new weeds; dalapon for couch grass; dichlobenil for established weeds; simazine residual weedkiller around trees, bush and cane fruit.	Dig out weeds from strawberry plants as they are very sensitive to weedkillers, especially when in full leaf.
VEGETABLES	All weeds	Don't let weeds get too large before treatment. Hoe frequently to remove germinating weeds; use propachlor for some crops, but check instructions first to ensure safety of growing plants.	Hoeing is best done on warm days as weeds die from exposure and will not re-root in soil tilth; pull out any large weeds after a shower of rain.
PATHS & DRIVES	All weeds	Apply a total weedkiller, such as aminotriazole, sodium chlorate or simazine.	Avoid contact with cultivated plants in the vicinity.

Above: sow-thistle (Sonchus asper)
Below: chickweed (Stellaria media)

Wait till the ground is slightly moist, and be sure to wear gloves. Repeated doses of 2,4,5-T will help to weaken them.

Lawn weeds

The rosette-forming types (such as daisy, dandelion and plantain) are the most successful on lawns as they tend to escape the lawn-mower blades. To spot-apply weedkillers to lawn weeds use a small dropper bottle.

Dandelion, daisy, creeping buttercup, ribwort and plantain Proprietary lawn weedkillers containing MCPA and 2,4-D with mecoprop or fenoprop usually bring quick death, but must be applied in strict accordance with the makers' instructions.

Speedwell Mecoprop/ioxynil mixture is required to check this weed.

Yarrow Use repeated doses of mecoprop. Feeding the lawn with sulphate of ammonia should hasten the expiry date.

Couch grass and perennial oat-grass Two very difficult grasses to remove from lawns. Close and frequent mowing will go a long way towards finishing them off; otherwise you must dig them out with a knife. Effective weedkillers cannot be used as they would kill the lawn as well.

ANNUAL WEEDS

Annual weeds, by definition, mature, flower, seed and die within one year. 'Seed' is the operative word here, because this is the method by which they reproduce and infest the garden. It is also the key to their control; if you can remove the

seed before it reaches the soil you can stop the next generation of weeds before it starts.

Many species of annual weeds grow quickly and succeed in completing several generations each year. The seeds seem to be able to germinate at any time of the year, even the middle of winter. So never assume that weeds are 'out of season'; although they may grow more slowly in winter they are always lurking.

Some of the most common annual weeds that you are likely to encounter are: chickweed, speedwell, groundsel, knot-grass, shepherd's purse, annual nettle, charlock, sow-thistle, scarlet pimpernel, goose-grass and wild radish.

Weeding by hoeing

One of the most common, and time-honoured, ways of controlling annual weeds is by hoeing. The secret of successful hoeing is to choose a day that is dry, sunny and, preferably, has a steady breeze. All these factors help to dry out the weed seedlings on the soil surface and prevent them re-rooting.

Persicaria (Polygonum lapathifolium)

Don't just decapitate the weeds when you hoe; make sure the roots are removed.

In a way, you make extra work for yourself by hoeing because you constantly bring more weed seeds to the surface where they germinate. Seeds can remain viable in the ground for years, waiting until they come near to the surface before starting to grow. Some seeds are very sensitive to the amount of daylight available and can only spring into life when they are in the topmost layer of soil. Regular hoeing, however, will keep weed seedlings under control.

Controlling with weedkillers

Most annual weeds are more easily controlled by weedkillers than their perennial counterparts. A whole range of annuals succumb to applications of dichlobenil or propachlor. Both these weedkillers are residual, but last only a few months. Diquat and paraquat are

Red deadnettle (Lamium purpureum) also known as bad man's posies

very useful for killing germinating weed seedlings. You can spot apply these anywhere provided you take care not to let them drift onto other plants.

Unlike many perennials, annual weeds germinate within the narrow soil-surface band to which the weedkillers have been applied; therefore they die almost as soon as they start growing. So, on the whole, these weedkillers tend to be more effective against annuals. Always remember where these chemicals have been put down and make sure that no horticultural activities 'break the band' as this will allow the weeds to come through unscathed.

Special treatments

There are a few stubborn annual weeds that do not succumb easily to dichlobenil and propachlor. These usually need an application of another type (or mixture) of weedkiller.

Rayless mayweed (pineapple weed) Treat with mecoprop or mecoprop with ioxynil.

Common persicaria Several doses of propachlor or dichlobenil may be required before you eventually get rid of it.

Red deadnettle Repeated applications of mecoprop will be needed.

Annual lawn weeds

As well as the tough perennial lawn weeds, you are also likely to encounter some troublesome annual ones. One good preventive measure is to use a grass-collecting box on the lawn-mower. This will stop many weeds falling back on the lawn and propagating themselves.

Chickweed Best controlled with mecoprop which is often applied with 2,4-D as a general lawn weedkiller.

Lesser yellow trefoil Several applications of mecoprop may be needed; or use fenoprop.

Lesser common trefoil This weed often flourishes where grass is short of nitrogen. Feed the lawn with sulphate of ammonia in spring to lessen the chance of this weed getting established.

Pests: Prevention and control

The word 'pest' conjures up, for many people, a vision of hordes of greenfly on roses or blackfly on broad beans. The vision is quite justified because both are pests and both tend to infest on an epidemic scale. Agriculturists and horticulturists view any organism that interferes with crops as a pest – whether it be a virus or a predatory animal.

This section leaves aside the viruses (and fungi and bacteria) and the animals like rabbits and moles and concentrates on insects and insect-like pests, including also slugs and snails (molluscs) and eelworms (nematodes).

Insects are the largest group of creatures on earth. In evolutionary terms they are highly successful, and have proved to be man's fiercest competitors. Historically, insects have caused more deaths to mankind than all wars put together.

Insects will attack most plants, whether they live in the garden, the house or the greenhouse. Like all illnesses and disorders, prevention is better than cure and the best way to reduce your losses is to ensure that your plants are healthy when planted and then well cared for. Many physiological disorders of plants (caused, for instance, by too little water or too much nitrogen fertilizer) pave the way for attack by pests. So as soon as you notice any signs of distress or damage—act promptly.

Knowing what to look for

The pest itself may be almost invisible. Eelworms, for instance, are difficult to see under a microscope. But their size bears no relation to the damage they can do. Even visible pests may not always be sitting in full view. You may have to dig underground and study the roots to determine the cause of the trouble, or wait for night to catch such insidious creatures as slugs.

Pests which attack leaves and flowers are the most easily identified because the damage occurs rapidly and is usually quite recognizable. Two main groups of pests attack leaves: those which have biting mouthparts (for example beetles) and those with sucking mouthparts (such as greenfly). They may hide inside or outside the leaves or, like the notorious leaf-miner, burrow between the middle layers of leaf tissue.

Larger pests (like caterpillars) are usually more noticeable but they may attack and run (or fly) away, in which case you should spray, or lay bait, against the next visit.

Fortunately there are many methods of control at your fingertips, providing you diagnose the enemy correctly and act as swiftly as you can.

Understanding the enemy

Knowing something about the life cycles and habits of pests can help you in anticipating and preventing trouble. For instance a major factor in determining how active they are is temperature; the warmer it becomes the busier they get. And up to 35°C (95°F) they breed faster too. Cold winters greatly decrease the numbers tending to spend the entire season in the garden.

Day length also plays a part in controlling the breeding seasons and migration patterns of many insects. This is why they always become scarce in autumn, even before cold weather arrives. Clear away and burn garden refuse every autumn because it provides ideal shelter for overwintering pests. Many overwinter as eggs which can also be destroyed by the use of insecticides.

Use of insecticides

Most pesticides are sold under trade names, partly because the chemical names and formulae are cumbersome and difficult to remember. You can, however, be sure of getting the right product by reading the contents on the label and checking with the chemical, or proper, name given here. Full chemical names are

Left: aphides attack indoor and outdoor plants. Below left: cabbage-root fly larvae is a danger in the vegetable garden. Bottom left: onion fly, enemy of the onion bulb family. Below: cabbage white butterfly, whose caterpillars cause such damage. Below centre: cabbage white caterpillar eating brassica leaves. Bottom: the ubiquitous slug, menace of all gardens. Bottom right: potted palm showing red spider mite damage

often abbreviated, for instance benzene hexachloride is known as BHC. (It is also sometimes called gamma-BHC.)

Always use protective clothing. Rubber gloves are important and be sure always to wash hands and face thoroughly after using insecticides. Never allow children or animals to be with you when sprays are being applied, and don't let them eat anything that has just been sprayed. Also wash out all spraying equipment after use—but not in the kitchen sink.

In some cases you may be able to use physical methods of combat such as picking caterpillars off plants and burning them. These are always preferable to spraying, because all sprays have some adverse effect on the plant. This is why you must adhere strictly to the manufacturer's recommended rate of application.

How insecticides work

Insecticides kill in two main ways; first as a stomach poison, when the pest either eats it with the leaf or sucks it up with the plant sap. Alternatively, if the pest is sprayed directly, the chemical will poison through the 'skin' or suffocate the pest. The method you choose depends on several factors, such as climate, type of insect and type of plant involved.

Non-systemic ('knock-down') insecticides Many early insecticides killed either by blocking the breathing processes or by poisoning when absorbed through other exterior surfaces. But they did not persist for long and had to be used frequently in order to be effective. However, some are still very useful for certain purposes.

Pyrethrum and derris, for example, are both very effective general insecticides. They are derived from plants and do not persist for long. This means they are safe to use on vegetables—even up to the day before harvesting. Derris, however, is harmful to fish so do not use it near stocked pools.

But DDT, used by gardeners for so many years, has now been withdrawn from the gardening market as other, newer insecticides have proved to be safer and equally (if not more) efficient. Trichlorphon is one good modern substitue for DDT.

Systemic insecticides The systemics are absorbed by the plant and dispersed throughout its entire system; any biting or sucking insect will ingest them while feeding and be killed. These pest-killers remain in the plant for several days (sometimes even weeks) and they act against a wide variety of pests.

But too often spraying can result in the development of pests that are resistant to them. So spray on sighting the enemy rather than 'just in case'.

Dimethoate and formothion are systemic insecticides that control most aphides, red spider mite, scale insect, mealy bug, caterpillars and leaf hoppers. Systemic insecticides are also one of the most successful ways of killing many of the root-feeding insects, such as lettuce root aphid.

PESTS Guide to treatment

PLACE	COMMON PESTS	PLANT AREA	TREATMENT	OTHER ADVICE
GREENHOUSE PLANTS	Aphides Whitefly	Leaves Stems Flowers	Treat as for house plants or fumigate greenhouse with nicotine, dichlorvos or BHC.	Make sure all vents are closed while fumigating. Do not enter until fumes have dispersed.
	Scale insect	Leaves	Wipe off, but if badly infested spray with malathion, nicotine or systemic insecticides.	Scrape insects off where possible.
	Red spider mite	Leaves	Spray malathion, derris or pyrethrum.	Pick off and burn badly-infected leaves.
	Mealy bug	Leaves Stems	Spray with systemic or non-systemic insecticides.	Scrape insects off where possible.
	Leaf hopper	Leaves	Spray with BHC, malathion or nicotine, often available in aerosol or smoke form.	
	Leaf miner	Leaves	Spray with BHC or malathion.	Pick and burn infected leaves.
	Vine weevil	Roots	Remove and destroy grubs found when repotting plants. Drench soil of infected plants with BHC solution.	Incorporate naphthalene or paradichlorbenzene among the crocks when known susceptible plants are repotted.

Leaf hopper

PLACE	COMMON PESTS	PLANT AREA	TREATMENT	OTHER ADVICE
HOUSE PLANTS	Aphides Whitefly	Leaves Stems Flowers	Non-systemic sprays: e.g. derris, pyrethrum, are often sufficient. For bad attacks use systemics, e.g. dimethoate.	Check all newly-acquired potted plants and eradicate any pests to prevent them spreading among your existing plants.
	Mealy bug	Leaves Stems	Spray with systemic or non-systemic insecticides, or dab with methylated spirit.	Scrape insects off where possible.
	Scale insect	Leaves	Wipe with a soft cloth dipped in soapy water or methylated spirits, or treat as for aphides and whitefly.	Place your house plants in the greenhouse when you fumigate and do both jobs at once.
	Leaf hopper	Leaves	Spray with BHC, malathion or nicotine (often available in aerosol form).	
	Leaf miner	Leaves	Spray with BHC or malathion.	Pick and burn infected leaves.
	Vine weevil	Roots	See GREENHOUSE PLANTS	

Aphid

PLACE	COMMON PESTS	PLANT AREA	TREATMENT	OTHER ADVICE
FLOWER GARDEN	Aphides Whitefly	Leaves Stems Flowers	Spray with systemic insecticide such as dimethoate or formothion.	Malathion is also effective.
	Scale insect	Leaves Stems	Spray with malathion or systemic insecticide.	Scrape off insects where possible.
	Earwigs	Flowers	Reduce populations by spraying with BHC or trichlorphon prior to flowering.	Place inverted, straw-filled flower pot traps on 1m (3 ft) canes near plants; burn resulting earwig nests.
	Capsid bug	Leaves Stems Flowers	Spray with BHC or malathion as soon as damage appears.	Prompt action is essential.

Earwig

PLACE	COMMON PESTS	PLANT AREA	TREATMENT	OTHER ADVICE
VEGETABLE GARDEN	Caterpillars	Leaves	Spray or dust with BHC, malathion or derris.	Pick caterpillars off where possible.
	Cutworm	Roots Stems	Work BHC dust or bromophos into the soil when planting.	Prevention is better than cure.
	Slugs Snails	Leaves Stems	Spray or apply pellets of metaldehyde or methiocarb.	These pests usually attack at night.
	Pea/bean weevil Grubs Thrips	Leaves Pods Peas	Apply BHC dust or fenitrion.	Apply when first flowers open and again 2 weeks later.
	Flea beetle	Leaves	Apply BHC dust when sowing seeds and at seedling stage.	Keep seedlings covered with dust until true leaves appear.
	Aphides	Leaves Shoots	Spray with systemic insecticides or malathion.	Watch for a reinfestation.
	Whitefly	Leaves	Spray with pyrethrum, dimethoate or BHC.	Malathion is also effective.
	Cabbage-root fly Carrot fly	Roots	Dust or spray BHC.	Keep seedlings covered with dust until true leaves appear.

Thrips

PLACE	COMMON PESTS	PLANT AREA	TREATMENT	OTHER ADVICE
FRUIT GARDEN	Caterpillars	Leaves	Spray or dust with BHC, malathion or derris.	Pick caterpillars off where possible.
	Aphides	Leaves Shoots	Spray with a systemic insecticide.	Watch for a reinfestation.
	Woolly aphides	Stems	Spray malathion or a systemic insecticide.	Systemic insecticides can be used, but at least 21 days before harvesting.
	Maggots	Fruits	Spray fenitrothion, BHC or derris.	Spray twice, in mid and late summer, as prevention.
	Gooseberry sawfly	Leaves	Spray thoroughly with derris or malathion.	Attacks usually occur in early summer.
	Capsid bug	Leaves Fruits	Spray with BHC or malathion as soon as damage is noted.	Prompt action is essential.
	Red spider mite	Leaves	Spray malathion, derris or pyrethrum, or a systemic.	Spray systemics 21 days before picking.

Codling moth maggot

PLACE	COMMON PESTS	PLANT AREA	TREATMENT	OTHER ADVICE
FLOWER GARDEN CONTINUED	Caterpillars	Flowers	Spray with BHC or trichlorphon.	Pick caterpillars off by hand.
	Leaf miner	Leaves	Spray with BHC or malathion or use systemic insecticide.	Pick off and burn badly-infected leaves.
	Frog hopper (Cuckoo spit)	Leaves Stems	Spray with malathion, BHC, derris or pyrethrum.	Can be washed off with spray of soapy water.
	Slugs Snails	Leaves Stems	Spray or apply pellets of metaldehyde or pyrethrum.	These pests are most active at night.
	Thrips	Flowers	Spray pyrethrum.	Prompt action is important.
	Red spider mite	Leaves	Spray malathion, derris or pyrethrum.	Pick off and burn badly-infected leaves.

Scale insect

Fungus diseases: Prevention and control

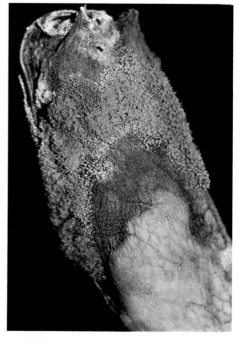

Fungi, bacteria and viruses are the three main causes of plant disease, and of these the most important to the gardener are the fungi. Unlike insects, they can only live in and with the plant they infect, and they are common in all plants, large or small – from the tiniest seedling affected by 'damping-off' to the tall and sturdy elm tree laid low by Dutch elm disease.

Although it is quite often a simple matter to recognise that a plant is diseased – discoloration, distortion of growth, even a general air of listlessness, are all easily observed symptoms – it is usually much harder to diagnose exactly what is wrong with it. It is important, therefore, to learn to recognize the different kinds of fungal infection, so that the right remedies can be applied where possible and without delay.

Propagation of fungi

Most fungi propagate by spores (which are very similar in kind, although not in appearance, to the seeds of plants), and these can be carried from plant to plant by the wind, rain, soil or plant debris, animals and birds, and other means. Each fungus will produce many spores, and this is one of the reasons why they spread so quickly and potentially dangerously through a bed of plants, a greenhouse, or a whole garden.

Other fungi, and particularly those that attack roots, spread by means of mycelium (a fibrous growth that has much the same function as the roots or stems of plants).

The majority of fungi spread and do most damage in moist, warm conditions. To reduce the likelihood of fungal infection of roots, therefore, it is important to keep the soil well drained; and in the greenhouse adequate ventilation is essential. However, some fungi (of which the powdery mildews are an outstanding example) show a distinct preference for drier conditions.

Fungus infection of seedlings

'Damping off', or seedling blight, is common when seeds are raised under unhygienic conditions. The disease is often due to a complex infection by different species of fungi, some of which are closely related. Pythium species and phytophthora species (sometimes known as watermoulds) thrive under wet conditions, and their spores are present in all soils. This is why it is essential to germinate all seed in sterilized (and therefore fungus-free) soil or compost, and to use clean pots and trays.

On sterilized soil damping-off will rapidly emerge through a batch of newly-emerged seedlings, and it is worthwhile to water with Cheshunt compound before and after germination. If the disease does take hold, watering with Cheshunt compound, captan, thiram or zineb may check it.

Plants that are growing well are less liable to attack, but even sturdy seedlings will still succumb if they are not well-cared for: over-watering and lack of ventilation are the principal cause of infection at this stage. Seedlings that have been too well nourished with excessive nitrogen may show similar symptoms.

Fungal attack of roots

The majority of species of fungus attack the leaves and other aerial parts of the plant, but there are some that spread through the soil.

Bootlace fungus The mycelium grows to look exactly like a black bootlace, but wherever it encounters dead wood it is

Above right: grey mould (botrytis) attacks many plants, especially in wet weather
Right: damping off (seedling blight) is a fungus infection
Below: bootlace fungus grows from the roots beneath the tree bark

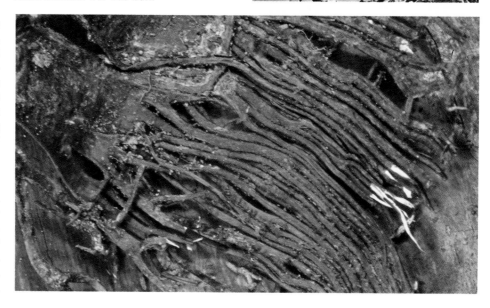

likely to throw up a toadstool, which releases spores into the air. The 'bootlace' grows from the roots beneath the bark of the tree, where it also forms yellowish-white sheets of fungus that have given it the alternative name 'honey fungus'. A tree that is badly affected must be dug up and burnt; and the soil must be sterilized with a mixture of 1 part of formaldehyde to 6 parts of water, applied at a rate of 27 lit per sq m (5 gal per sq yd). Where infection is not too serious, a creosote-like chemical, Armillatox, may be sufficient to control the disease and allow the tree or bush to recover.

Club root Very common and attacks all members of the brassica or cabbage family (and this includes wallflowers). The plants look weak and yellow and the roots are swollen. Liming the soil helps to prevent the disease; so does a crop-rotation system. Calomel dust applied at planting time reduces the likelihood of attack, and dipping the roots in benomyl just before planting has also proved effective.

Crown gall Produces symptoms similar to clubroot, but attacks many different kinds of plant. It is favoured by wet soils: provide adequate drainage, and avoid injury to the roots. Dipping plants in a copper fungicide such as Bordeaux mixture at planting time provides protection.

Brown core Attacks polyanthus and primula roots, and the plants then become weak and sickly. Burn all affected plants and grow no others of the family on that ground for several years.

Above left: conifer gall, a white blight, may affect any conifer tree. Left: club root attacks the brassica family
Below left: roses are susceptible to powdery mildew
Below: downy mildew likes the damp

Violet root rot Affects several plant groups and is easily recognized by the characteristic strands of purple mycelium on the plant roots. Destroy all infected plants and introduce resistant crops. Violet root rot only rarely occurs in land that is in 'good heart' and so attention to drainage and soil fertility is the best means of prevention.

Black root rot Most likely to strike where plants are grown in the same place every year; it also affects pot plants. Drench the soil with captan solution.

Fungal attack of shoots and leaves

Many different fungi attack shoots and leaves, and the following are the most common examples.

Grey mould (botrytis) Prevalent in wet weather, it attacks numerous plants. Remove the infected plants to control spread of the disease, but for really effective control use benomyl, captan, thiram or zineb.

Powdery mildew Found on almost all plants, and there is often a specific species for a particular plant. This is a fungus which favours drier weather for attacks. Plants most commonly infected are roses, gooseberries, apples and Michaelmas daisies. The mildew forms a white powder on the leaves, shoots and flowers. Greenhouse plants also suffer. Cut out infected shoots on trees and shrubs the following autumn, otherwise re-infection can occur. Spray with benomyl, dinocap or thiophanate-methyl. On plants which are not sulphur-shy, sulphur or lime-sulphur sprays may be used. Many varieties of apple are sulphur-shy, for example, so it is important to make sure before using the spray. Generally the container for the mixture lists the plants and varieties for which it is unsuitable.

Downy mildew By contrast with the powdery types, downy mildew thrives in damp, cool conditions. Grey or whitish furry growths appear on leaves and spread very rapidly. Zineb is the best chemical to use.

Potato blight Related to downy mildew, and the treatment is similar. Remove and burn any plants that become very diseased.

White blister Similar to downy mildew, but the spores are liberated from blisters or pustules. The only course is to burn the affected plants, but individual diseased leaves may be removed and burnt if the infection is caught in time.

Silver leaf Affects plums, peaches, cherries and ornamental prunus, turning the leaves silvery. Cut out diseased material and treat all wounds with a protective bituminous paint.

FUNGUS DISEASES OF PLANTS
Non-systemic (knock-down) fungicides

INFECTIONS CONTROLLED	PLANTS COMMONLY INFECTED	CHEMICAL NAME	FORM AVAILABLE
Galls	Azaleas	Bordeaux mixture	Powder
Wilts	Clematis and paeonies		
Peach leaf curl	Many ornamental plants and fruits	Lime-sulphur	Powder or concentrated suspension
Blight	Tomatoes and potatoes		
Cane spot/spur blight	Raspberries	'Liquid copper'	Concentrated solution
Powdery mildews	Many fruit and ornamental varieties	Sulphur	Powder
Scab	Apples and pears (**Caution**: do not use lime-sulphur or sulphur sprays on sulphur-shy varieties)	Several special formulations of the above are available	

INFECTIONS CONTROLLED	PLANTS COMMONLY INFECTED	CHEMICAL NAME	FORM AVAILABLE
Onion white rot	Onions	Calomel	Powder
Club root	Brassicas and wallflowers		
Moss and turf diseases	Grass/lawns	Other mercury-based mixtures	Mixed with lawn sand

INFECTIONS CONTROLLED	PLANTS COMMONLY INFECTED	CHEMICAL NAME	FORM AVAILABLE
Black spot	Roses	Cheshunt compound	Powder for solution
Leaf spots	Many garden plants	Captan	Wettable powder or dust
Scab	Apples and pears (**Caution**: do not use on fruit to be bottled or used for deep freezing)	Dinocap	Wettable powder, dust, liquid or smoke
Soil-borne infections	Many seeds and seedlings		
Grey mould/downy mildew/potato blight	Many plants	Thiram	Concentrated solution
		Zineb	Wettable powder
Rusts	Many ornamental plants and fruits in the garden	Mancozeb	Wettable powder
Spur blight	Raspberries	Several formulations and mixtures of the above are available	

Systemic fungicides

INFECTIONS CONTROLLED	PLANTS COMMONLY INFECTED	CHEMICAL NAME	FORM AVAILABLE
Grey mould	Many fruits and vegetables, growing and in storage		
Leaf spots	Many ornamental plants, soft fruit and celery	Benomyl	Wettable powders
Scab	Apples and pears	Thiophanate-methyl	Wettable powders
Powdery mildews	Roses, other ornamentals and fruit		
Black spot	Roses		

Fusarium wilt Often the cause of plants looking sickly, with yellowing leaves which appear to wilt, even in wet weather. This fungus blocks the 'plumbing' system of the plant. The spores lie in the soil for considerable periods; it can be sterilized with formaldehyde, but growing on fresh soil is often the only solution.

Apple scab Common throughout the growing season, attacking ornamental malus species such as crab-apple, pears and culinary apples. It infects leaves, stems and fruits, producing olive-green blotches on the leaves, and brown or black scabs on the fruit. Spray with lime-sulphur when flower buds emerge, but do not use on sulphur-shy varieties (see instructions on the spray container). Benomyl, captan or thiram may be sprayed from bud-burst until late summer (July). Rake up all dead leaves and burn them in the winter to prevent further spread.

Rusts Attack many plants, but hollyhocks are particularly prone. All rusts appear as orange, yellow or brown powdery masses. You can obtain resistant varieties which prevent spores germinating on the leaves. Mancozeb, zineb or maneb fungicides sprayed at fortnightly intervals should cure most rust infections.

Below: apple canker spreads along the bark, killing young shoots, and should be treated without delay
Bottom: the fruiting fungus of silver leaf appears on the bark of affected trees
Below right: rust — a mass of orange, yellow or brown pustules on the leaves
Below, far right: beware apple scab on leaves, stems or fruit in summer

Black spot Attacks roses and is probably one of the most common of fungal diseases. It starts as dark brown spots which grow up to 2cm (1 in) across. Infected leaves fall during mid summer. It also affects stems and will remain on the plant to re-infect the following season. Burn all diseased leaves and stems, and spray with benomyl, captan or zineb at the initial infection stage.

Cane spot and spur blight Affect raspberries and loganberries. Both form purple blotches; spur blight becomes mottled with black, and cane spot as it develops becomes white. Apply a copper fungicide such as Bordeaux mixture at bud-burst and, in the case of cane spot, again when the fruit has set. Thiophanate-methyl or benomyl may be used throughout the blossom period.

Stem cankers Attack many trees and shrubs. The first signs are poor, weak growth and soft patches of bark. These patches later erupt into unsightly reddish-pink pustules that spread along the bark, causing the shoots to die back. There is no chemical control for the disease, and the only solution is to cut off and burn all infected stems at once. Paint the wounds with a protective bituminous paint, such as Arbrex.

Diseases affecting tubers

These diseases can affect the other storage organ type plants as well as tubers.

Basal rot Often occurs on crocuses, narcissi and lilies. It spreads from the base as a brown rot, eventually rotting the whole bulb. It will attack at any time, even when bulbs are in storage. Cut out infected areas, dust with quintozene.

Smoulder and dry rot Attack bulbs, although smoulder is only usual on narcissus. Dry rot has a wider range and can be stopped by dipping healthy bulbs in solutions of benomyl or captan. Smoulder tends to occur in storage and a cool dry storage place helps to prevent it. If you see any signs during the growing season, spray zineb at fortnightly intervals. Other storage rots and some bulb or corm scabs should be treated in a similar manner to dry rot.

White rot and neck rot White rot is very common on spring onions and on main-crop types during the growing season. It persists in the soil and if your crop has been infected grow onions on a new site the following year. Calomel dust in the seed drills reduces the danger.

Parsnip canker Appears as brown patches and cracks on the shoulder of the parsnip, which can then be attacked by pests. The best remedy is to rotate crops or grow resistant varieties.

Fungicides

All fungicides are phytotoxic to some extent—that is, they affect the growth of the plants which they protect. It is essential that only recommended quantities and dilutions are used. Some fungicides based on lime and sulphur are particularly bad at scorching leaves if over-used. The systemic fungicides like benomyl and thiophanate-methyl are often more effective but cost more.

Removal of infected tissue will often stop the spread of a fungus and this is a point that cannot be over-emphasized. Strict garden hygiene is one of the main ways of preventing infection.

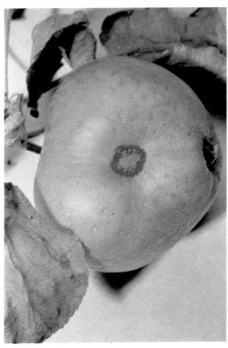

Watering the garden

Plants need water for many reasons. Seeds will not germinate without water and plants can only use the nutrients in the soil if they are in soluble form. Water gives the plant its shape and stiffness; without it the plant becomes limp. If the water loss becomes too great the stomata (holes) in the surface of the 'skin' close and the basic plant processes come to a halt. You must, therefore, ensure that plants always have enough water for all their needs.

During dry weather you must give your plants the water that nature has failed to provide. Too often, however, the mistake is made of watering irregularly and in insufficient quantity. It is essential to give enough water to penetrate the soil down to the layer where the plant roots are growing. If you only sprinkle the surface, the water will simply evaporate in the heat of the sun.

How much water?

Apply sufficient water to penetrate the soil to a depth of at least 15cm (6 in) – preferably more. This means applying at least 2–3cm (1 in) of water, depending on the soil type. The lighter and more sandy the soil, the deeper this amount of water will penetrate. If you are using a sprinkler, you can measure the amount of water being applied by placing a number of tin cans over the area being watered. When there is 2–3cm (1 in) of water on the bottom of the tins you will know it is time to turn off the sprinkler. Eventually you can estimate the time required to cover the area, and the rather tedious

business of setting out cans will be unnecessary. If you water with a hosepipe then you will have to dig down into the soil with a hand trowel to see how far the water has penetrated.

Start watering before the soil dries out to any great depth; a good guide is when the top 2–5cm (1–2 in) is becoming dry. In hot, summer weather you may have to water at least once a week.

It is usually best to apply water in the evening, as then none will be evaporated by the sun and it will penetrate the soil to a good depth.

Many people do not realize that wind is a major drying agent (especially in spring and early summer), so watering will be necessary after windy weather.

Sprinklers and hoses

Applying all this water will be very time-consuming if you have to rely on a hosepipe alone. It is therefore a good idea to attach a sprinkler of some kind to the end and let it distribute the water.

There are many types on the market to suit all pockets. The cheapest are those with no moving parts (mini-sprinklers), but which produce a fine circular spray from a static nozzle. Often the base of these is equipped with a spike which you push into the ground to hold the sprinkler firmly.

Rotating sprinklers are slightly more expensive. They have two adjustable nozzles on an arm which is spun round by water pressure, giving a circular pattern. These are probably the most popular for private gardens.

The more sophisticated oscillating sprinklers apply water in a square or rectangular pattern. A tubular bar with a row of nozzles (non-adjustable) moves backwards and forwards, watering a very large area. It is worked by water pressure. Some can be adjusted to water a small or large area.

Sprinkler hoses are perforated plastic hoses of various kinds which are connected to the main hosepipe and produce a gentle spray of water along their complete length. One of these can be laid along rows of crops, or between plants.

You will, of course, want a good reinforced plastic or PVC hosepipe; a 13mm ($\frac{1}{2}$ in) diameter hose is a suitable size for general use. A wide range of sprinklers and hoses is, of course, available to suit individual requirements.

Below: a perforated hose sprinkler, handy for long borders
Above right: use a fine rose for watering cuttings and seedlings

A rotary type sprinkler that waters in a regular circular pattern

Oscillating sprinkler that will deliver an even spray into a corner

Watering vegetables

Most vegetables benefit greatly from regular watering, especially crops like runner, French and broad beans, peas, marrows, lettuce, radish, cucumbers and tomatoes. Vegetables such as cabbages and other greenstuff, and root crops like potatoes and carrots, can get by without regular watering, although their yields will not be so heavy.

All newly-transplanted vegetables must be well watered in if the ground is

dry and then kept moist until established. You can water these individually with a watering can.

Germinating seeds

Seeds must be kept moist to encourage them to germinate. This is especially true of the modern pelleted seeds, which will fail to grow if they lack sufficient moisture.

Fruit trees and bushes

Fruit trees, provided they are well established, will not come to much harm if you do not water during dry spells, but the fruits may be smaller than normal. However, black, red and whitecurrants, raspberries, strawberries, gooseberries, blackberries, loganberries and other hybrid berries really do need watering in dry weather if they are to crop well.

Flowers in beds and containers

It may not be possible to water everything in the garden, especially in a very dry season when there may be restrictions on the use of sprinklers in the garden. If this is the case, the flower garden must take third place – after fruit and vegetables,

which you will be growing to supplement the family budget. However, flowers in containers (such as tubs, troughs, hanging baskets and window boxes) will soon die if not watered regularly. These dry out rapidly in hot weather and may well need watering twice a day – in the morning and again in the evening.

Watering the lawn

Lawns rapidly turn brown in dry weather, although they will green up again once the rains start. To keep a lawn green in the summer you will need to begin watering before it starts to turn brown and continue at weekly intervals, or more frequently, thereafter. Remember also not to cut a lawn too short in dry weather – so raise the mower blades.

Mulching the soil

There is a method of conserving moisture in the soil which will enable you to cut down on watering. It is known as 'mulching' and consists of placing a 5–8cm (2–3 in) layer of organic matter around and between plants – covering the root area. Use garden compost, well-rotted farmyard manure, leaf mould, spent hops, straw, grass mowings or sawdust.

Another method is to use black polythene sheeting. To anchor it to the ground, bury the edges in 'nicks' made with a spade in the soil; then place a few stones or bricks on top. You can buy rolls of special black mulching polythene.

All plants benefit from being mulched, for moisture is conserved and so they do not dry out so rapidly. If you have to limit mulching, however, then concentrate on your vegetables and fruits, rather than on your flowerbeds.

Left and below: mulching trees and shrubs with compost will conserve moisture

Feeding plants

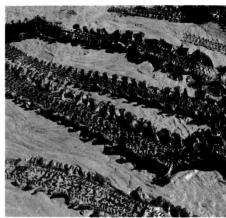

Plants, like people, need a regular supply of food if they are to survive and grow well. The main ways of feeding your plants are by applying fertilizers and bulky organic matter (like manure) to the soil. Manure supplies some nutrients, but its most important function is to improve the soil structure by adding organic material. This turns the soil into a healthy medium in which plants can thrive. Fertilizers provide some, or all, of the basic plant foods (nitrogen, phosphates, potash and trace elements) in concentrated form.

When digging, particularly in late autumn or early winter, it is wise to incorporate in each trench well-rotted farmyard manure, garden compost, seaweed or hop manure. These materials will supply bulky organic matter and a variable amount of plant food. None of them, however, supplies adequate nutrients for the plants to make optimum growth; therefore fertilizers will have to be added at planting time to ensure that the plants are sufficiently provided with the food they require.

The organic matter is digested by bacteria in the soil and turned into humus. This humus is like a sponge; it holds water and prevents rapid drying-out of light soils. It also helps to break up sticky clay soils by improving drainage. Organic material is, therefore, essential because it greatly improves the soil's structure.

MANURES

Never apply manure at the same time as lime (calcium). This is because the lime can liberate any available nitrogen in the form of ammonia, which may then be lost through evaporation. Also, never grow root crops on ground where fresh manure has been used, for your vegetables may well produce deformed roots.

Seaweed as manure

If your garden is near the coast, use seaweed as a manure. It is excellent for digging – wet or dried – into the soil in the autumn. Seaweed is one of the oldest manures known and contains many plant foods. It is now possible to obtain specially refined seaweed manures from gardening shops. Use these carefully, according to maker's instructions, as they are rather concentrated.

Manure for mulching

Rotted manure or garden compost makes a good mulch for established plants such as trees, shrubs, top and soft fruit, vegetables, roses, dahlias and chrysan-

Above left: Ascophyllum nodosum, 'egg' or knotted wrack, exposed on the rocks at low tide and ready for collection – it can be used wet or dry
Top: fronds of sea belt Laminaria saccharina, *left on the beach at low water*
Centre: shoddy, or animal hair, laid around the base of a shrub — it is useful as an organic form of plant food
Above: spreading top-dressing of dry fertilizer around the base of the shrub in summer months with a balance of nitrogen, phosphate and potash mixed to suit the particular plant
Right: adding rotted manure to a trench

themums. Place a layer of mulch, 5–8cm (2–3 in) thick, around the plants in spring. It will then provide some food and humus and help prevent evaporation of moisture from the surface soil.

FERTILIZERS

Bulky organic matter is not capable, by itself, of supplying all the foods the plants will require, so fertilizers must also be added to the soil.

As a general rule, dry fertilizers should be applied to moist soil, or else well watered in after application if the ground is dry. Always apply them evenly, and discard or break up any lumps; these can 'burn' roots. Apply all fertilizers carefully and according to maker's instructions. If you exceed the recommended rate of application you may seriously injure your plants.

Before sowing or planting, the usual procedure is to rake in a dry fertilizer which contains the major plants foods (nitrogen, phosphates and potash). There are many of these 'general-purpose' or compound fertilizers on the market. Probably the best known is National Growmore, which is available under numerous brand names. This is suitable for all vegetables, fruit and flowers. You can also apply it as a top dressing in spring or summer by lightly raking it into the soil surface around any of your established plants.

Special dry fertilizers for specific crops (such as roses and tomatoes) are available. These contain the correct balance of nitrogen, phosphates and potash suited to the particular plant.

Lawn fertilizers

There are several proprietary lawn fertilizers which make the lawn 'green up' quickly and grow well due to the high proportion of nitrogen they contain. Feed your lawn once or twice during spring and summer to ensure a lush, deep-green sward. Autumn lawn fertilizer, which is applied in mid autumn (September), contains more potash; this helps to 'ripen' the grass and make it more resistant to hard winter weather.

'Straight' fertilizers

You can also apply 'straight' fertilizers to plants, especially as a supplement to the ready-mixed, general-purpose kinds applied earlier in the growing season; but you must be aware of specific food requirements of individual plants before trying out these fertilizers. Be sure to handle them carefully and accurately.

Sulphate of ammonia and nitro-chalk supply nitrogen which encourages plants to make lush, leafy growth. They are quick-acting fertilizers and should be used very sparingly. They can be used on lawns and also on green vegetables such as cabbage, kale, broccoli and spinach. Apply them in spring and summer only.

Sulphate of potash and muriate of potash both supply the potash (potassium) essential for the production of fruit and flowers. It also helps to ripen the stems, which is necessary for the successful overwintering of all hardy plants. Potash can be applied in summer or early autumn. Wood ashes contain potassium

Above: applying chemical fertilizer by spoon in small measured quantities
Above right: sieving leaf mould into a wheelbarrow for use as compost
Right: fertilizer spreaders give even results
Far right: applying lime by hand

and, once they have weathered for 3–6 months, can be dug into the soil during autumn digging or raked into the surface.

Superphosphate of lime supplies phosphate (phosphorus). This is also essential for good root production and all-round growth. It is usually applied in spring and summer at the rate of 3g per litre ($\frac{1}{2}$ oz per gal) of water and applied to the soil around plants about once a week. Avoid getting it on the foliage.

Liquid fertilizers

Use liquid fertilizers in conjunction with powdered or granulated fertilizers – not as a substitute. They should be considered as supplementary feeds to boost the growth of plants. They are generally used in the summer when plants are in full growth. Being liquid, they are quickly absorbed by plants and rapidly stimulate growth.

Dilute liquid fertilizers according to maker's instructions, and apply them to moist soil. Use them as frequently as once a week and on all kinds of plants in the

house, greenhouse and garden. You can apply them most easily with a rosed watering can.

There are many brands of liquid fertilizer on the market, some of which are formulated for specific crops.

Foliar feeding

Foliar feeding is a fairly recent technique of applying liquid fertilizers to plants. The fertilizer is sprayed or watered onto the leaves where it is quickly absorbed by the plants and circulated in the sap stream. The nutrients are made im-

mediately available to plants. This makes them particularly useful to transplanted plants before their new roots have become established.

You can buy special foliar feeds from gardening shops. Alternatively you can apply any liquid fertilizer to the foliage and it will be quickly absorbed.

Sulphate of ammonia can be dissolved at the rate of 3g per litre ($\frac{1}{2}$ oz per gal) of water and applied to leaves to promote growth of foliage. Likewise sulphate of potash will encourage fruiting and ripening of growth.

LIME

Lime is another plant food and this is applied on its own, generally in the winter after autumn digging, in the form of dehydrated lime. It is mainly the vegetable plot that will require lime and an application every two or three years will be adequate.

Lime lowers the acidity of the soil, and as many plants (especially vegetables such as brassicas) do not thrive in an acid soil, liming enables you to grow a wider range of plants. But do not lime if you have a naturally alkaline or limy soil with a pH of 7 or above. Hydrated lime is the type generally used.

Making a compost heap

Waste not organic materials from the house or garden and want not for compost is a maxim worth following. Compost, when rotted down, will improve and maintain your soil by adding humus-forming matter, plant foods and beneficial bacteria.

Compost is not difficult or time-consuming to make. Certain types of plant and household waste can be used to make it. Suitable plant waste includes grass clippings, flower and vegetable stems that are not too tough, light hedge trimmings, wet peat, wet straw and annual weeds. Leaves can be used, but not in great quantities as they are more valuable for use as leaf mould. A separate bin can be kept in the kitchen for such household waste as tea leaves, vegetable trimmings, hair, egg shells and vacuum cleaner dust. Bonfire ashes, animal manure, and sawdust are also suitable.

Not suitable for the compost heap are coarse plant material such as cabbage stems and tree prunings, diseased plants, pernicious weeds like docks, dandelions, and bindweed roots, any dead plants on which weedkiller has been used, and cooked matter, such as meat or fish.

As a compost heap is not particularly sightly, it is best situated in the working part of the garden and screened from the house. It should be protected from hot sun or cold winds, but not be against a wall or hedge. An ideal site is beneath a tree. The shape of the heap can be

If you lack the space for a compost heap as described, a bin will also give you good results. Below are three main types

circular or rectangular, although most people find a rectangular one easier to cope with. The best size to aim for is about 1m (3 ft) wide, 1½–2m (5–6 ft) long, and 1–1½m (3–5 ft) high when completed.

It pays to construct the site of the heap correctly, rather than tipping the waste straight onto the ground. First dig a shallow pit – about 15cm (6 in) deep. Place the soil on one side as you will need it later. Then put down in the pit an 8cm (3 in) layer of broken bricks or stones mixed with coarse tree prunings, woody cabbage stems, straw and similar tough plant material. These will help essential drainage and allow plenty of air penetration.

When the base is prepared, begin to build up the compost heap. This should be done roughly as follows:

Layer 1: about 15cm (6 in) of organic material.
Layer 2: a sprinkling of a proprietary compost accelerator according to the manufacturer's instructions. This should supply the essential bacteria, nitrogen and chalk necessary to break down the raw matter into usable compost.
Layer 3: a 2–3cm (1 in) layer of soil, taken from the dug-out heap.
These three layers are repeated until the heap reaches the required height.

Follow these rules for successful composting:
1 Always be sure that each layer of organic material is well firmed down (but not too tightly compressed) by treading on it or beating it flat with a spade blade.
2 If using grass clippings in large quantities, mix them with other materials

or they will form a soggy mass in the heap.
3 Check from time to time to make sure that the heap is moist. If it has dried out, either sprinkle water over it or, preferably, hammer stakes into the heap to make holes and then pour water into the holes.
4 To finish off the heap, level the top and put a 2–5cm (1–2 in) thick layer of soil over the top and around the sides to act as a cover.

A properly made compost heap provides material to be used either for digging into the ground or for mulching. Mulch is a top dressing layer on the surface of the soil around the plants. The compost will be ready to be dug in after about 10–14 weeks in summer or 14–18 weeks in winter. When the compost is ready for use the heap will consist of a brownish black, crumbly, pleasant-smelling and easily handled material. If the heap doesn't seem to be rotting down well in the allotted time, something has gone wrong with the construction. If this happens, it is worth the trouble of digging a second shallow pit alongside and rebuilding the first heap into that, turning the top to bottom and sides to middle and following the sandwich layer principle again. In any case, as one heap is finished, a second one should be started so that there is always a supply of essential humus-forming material ready to add to the soil.

The method of compost-making described here is simple and cheap. If, however, you have a very small garden, it may be easier for you to buy a proprietary bin compost unit, which has its own instructions for use.

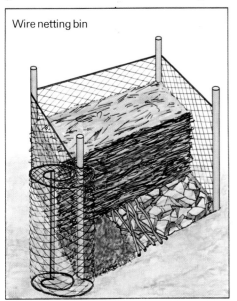

Wire netting bin

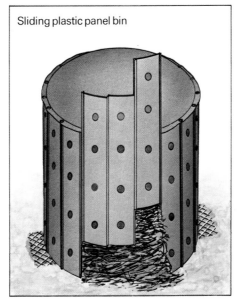

Sliding plastic panel bin

Slotted wood bin

Top dressing, mulching and hoeing

'Top dressing' is the term for any plant food or soil conditioner that is applied to the soil surface. 'Mulch' usually refers to top dressings that are composed of bulky organic materials – such as compost or manure. Mulches help to suppress weeds, so if you are not applying a mulch then hoeing will be necessary, and must be done correctly.

TOP DRESSING

A top dressing may be left scattered on the surface of the soil or raked into the topsoil. Lawn top dressings are often brushed into the topsoil with a stiff broom.

A good general-purpose fertilizer, such as Growmore, is very useful for all kinds of plants and is probably the top dressing most used by gardeners. Put down such a fertilizer (used according to maker's instructions) before applying a mulch. Top dressings of lime, applied during winter or early in spring, are of great value to the vegetable garden – especially where brassicas (cabbages, sprouts etc) are being grown.

When applying soluble chemical fertilizers, take great care to follow the maker's instructions exactly; too strong a solution can cause damage to plant roots. With many top dressings it is also important to keep them well clear of plant stems and leaves.

MULCHING

A mulch, whether it be a layer of organic matter or polythene sheeting, is usually placed over the soil in the root area of plants. Organic materials that can be used for mulching are well-rooted farmyard manure, garden compost, leaf mould, peat, spent hops, rotted grass clippings, straw, pulverized bark and rotted sawdust. Peat, straw and bark supply very little in the way of plant foods but are used for moisture conservation and weed suppression.

Reasons for mulching

One of the most important reasons for applying a mulch is to conserve moisture in the soil during dry weather, by helping to prevent its evaporation.

Mulching also prevents the growth of annual weeds, and some perennial weeds can be smothered with a polythene mulch. Furthermore, by placing an organic mulch between rows of vegetables and fruits you can avoid making the soil surface hard and compacted as you walk between the rows. An organic mulch may also supply plant foods – though not all materials will supply nutrients.

When to mulch

The best time of the year for putting down a mulch is in the spring and early summer (between March and the end of May). Apply it to moist, weed-free soil over a top dressing of fertilizer. An organic mulch should be spread around the plants, or between rows of crops, to a depth of 5–10cm (2–4 in). Obviously the greater the depth, the more effective it will be. Spread it evenly and ensure it covers the plants' root area.

What to mulch

In the fruit garden it is well worth mulching black, white and redcurrants, gooseberries, raspberries, blackberries, loganberries and rhubarb, as these fruits thrive on a good supply of matter and moisture. The ideal is an annual mulch of well-rotted manure or compost. With strawberries the usual practice is to give a mulch of straw, after danger of frost has passed, to prevent the fruits from coming into contact with the soil and getting mud-splashed or eaten by slugs.

Top fruits, such as apples, pears and plums, can be lightly mulched with manure or compost, about every two or three years. Too heavy a dressing of manure or compost to fruit trees may result in over-vigorous growth at the expense of fruiting. Instead, use material with a low food content, annually, to conserve moisture and help to prevent weed growth.

All vegetables, particularly peas, beans, cauliflowers, tomatoes, marrows, celery and lettuce, benefit from a

becoming trodden down as a result of the regular attention these plants need.

Remember that all newly-planted trees and shrubs should be mulched after watering to prevent the soil drying out rapidly; drying out can have a serious effect on the plants if they have not yet established fibrous feeding roots.

If you have to water mulched plants, apply it in good quantities, because an organic mulch can absorb a great deal of water. Unless you water heavily, it may never reach the roots of the plants.

Inorganic mulches

Rock gardens can have a layer of stone chippings or shingle placed over the entire soil surface to keep in moisture and prevent too much annual weed growth. The rock plants will grow much better under these conditions.

Black polythene sheeting is another useful inorganic mulch and it is possible to buy strips specially for mulching. Place it over the soil to prevent weed growth and evaporation of moisture. It can be used in all the areas described above, with the exception of rock gardens. Its only drawback is that it can look rather unsightly.

To hold the polythene in position, first make v-shaped nicks in the soil, with a spade, on either side of the strip to be mulched. Then tuck the edges of the sheet into the nicks and firm the soil with your feet. You can then make slits in the polythene and plant through them.

HOEING

If you do not mulch plants then you will have to hoe around them to keep weeds in check – unless you prefer to use chemical weedkillers. Regular hoeing is necessary to catch weeds in the seedling stage. It is much easier than hoeing out large weeds that may well root into the soil again if left on the surface. It is important to work the hoe shallowly so as not to damage any plant roots that may be growing near the soil surface.

The best time for hoeing is on a warm day when the soil surface is dry. The weeds will then quickly shrivel up and die. When you hoe try to achieve a nice, fine loose tilth on the surface. The layer of dry, loose soil will act as a mulch, conserving moisture in the undisturbed soil below.

In the vegetable or fruit garden, where footprints do not matter, you will probably find a draw hoe much quicker, working in a forward direction and walking over the hoed ground. But in the ornamental area use a Dutch hoe, moving backwards. The double-bladed push-pull type of hoe is popular and speedy.

moisture-conserving mulch, though one that supplies plant nutrients as well is obviously the best.

Mulch the flower garden to keep the soil moist and minimize weeding. Use manure around trees and shrubs, applying a light dressing every two or three years. An annual application of peat, leaf mould, bark or spent hops can be given in the 'in-between' years; again the idea is to avoid over-lush growth. All surface-rooting shrubs, such as rhododendrons,

azaleas and heathers, appreciate a mulch of peat or leaf mould each year to keep their roots cool. The same principles apply to herbaceous border plants.

Give roses an annual mulch as they require plenty of feeding. Apply a deep layer of well-rotted farmyard manure or garden compost.

Dahlias and sweet peas need moist soil and benefit greatly from a straw mulch if they are being grown in their special beds. This also prevents the soil surface from

Brussels sprouts like a fortnightly dose of fertilizer (left), while an onion hoe (below) helps keep them free of weeds

Above: black polythene sheeting may not look very elegant, but here it provides potatoes with a useful inorganic mulch

Index

Page numbers in italic refer to illustrations.

Kingfisher daisy 50
Knot grass 171
Kohl rabi 109
Korean chrysanthemum 38

Laburnum 13, *18*, 20-1
Laburnum anagyroides 21
Laburnum vossii 21
Laminaria saccharina 182
Lamium purpureum 171
Larkspur 45, 53
Lathyrus odoratus 44, 45
Laurustinus 31
Lavandula 13, 29
Lavandula spica 29
Lavatera 45
Lavender 13, *28*, 29, 57
Lawn 9, 10; to roll and mow 17, 151; to sow 16-17; to turf 14-15; to water 181
Lawn fertilizers 183
Lawn-mowers 151
Lawn weeds 171
layering 166-7
leaf-bud cuttings 164
leaf curl 125
leaf cuttings 163-4
leaf hopper 173, 174, *174*
leaf miner 174
leaf mould 125
leaf spot 138, 178
Leek 119-20
Lenten rose 35, 36
Lettuce 80-3, 181, 186
lettuce root aphid 173
Leucojum aestivum 40
Leucojum vernum 40
Lilac 13, 21, *21*
Lilium candidum 13
Lime 184
Limestone soil 12
Ling *9*
Linum grandiflorum 44
liquid fertilizers 184
Livingstone daisy *49*, 50
loamy soil 12
Lobelia 50, *50*
Loganberry 141, 142, 167, 181, 186
Lonas 48
Lonicera 13, 33, 167
Lonicera x americana 33
Lonicera japonica 33
Lonicera periclymenum 33
Lonicera purpusii 33
Lonicera sempervirens 33
Lonicera tellmanniana 33
Love-in-a-mist 45
Love-lies-bleeding 45
Lunaria 13, *53*
Lupin 34, 38, *38*, 45
Lychnis 45

Madonna lily 13
Madwort 45
maggots 175, *175*
Magnolia 167
magpie moth caterpillar 145
Mahonia 13, 29
Mahonia aquifolium 29, *29*
Mahonia bealei 29
Mahonia japonica 29
Malcolmia 13, 45
Mallow 45
Mangetout 110
manures 182-3
Maple 13, 18
Matthiola *55*
mealy bug 173, 174
Mesembryanthemum *49*, 50
Mentzelia lindleyi 45, *45*
Mexican orange blossom 13, 25
Mignonette 45
mildew 60, 112, 138
Mile-a-minute vine 33
Monarch of the Veldt 51
Morisia monantha 164
mosaic disease 82
moss 170
Mother-in-law's tongue 163
mulching 181, 182, 186-7
Mullein *54*, 55

Narcissus 40, *41*, 43, 179
Narcissus actaea 43
Narcissus pseudonarcissus 41
Nasturtium 13, 45
neck rot 179
Nemesia 45, 50, *51*
Nemophila 45
Nepeta 13, 39, 57
Nettle 169, *169*, 170, 171
New Zealand spinach 85

Nicotiana 45, 50
Nigella 45

Oat-grass 169, 170, 171
offsets 166
Olearia 13, 29-30
Olearia x haastii 29
Olearia x scilloniensis 30
Olearia stellulata 30
Onion 76-9
onion fly 79, 120, *182*
onion hoe 150, *187*
onion white rot 178
Oriental poppy 34, 38, *39*, 164, 165
Oxalis 169

Paeony, 165, 178
Pansy 52, *52*, 54
Papaver 13
Papaver nudicale 54
Papaver orientalis 38, *39*, 165
Papaver rhoeas 45
Parsnip 94
parsnip canker 179
Passion flower 164, 167
patio area 8, 10
Paulownia 164
Pea 110-12, 181, 186
Pea weevil 112, 175
peach leaf curl 178
Pear 130-3, 186
peaty soil 12
Pelargonium 163
pelleted seeds 158
Peperomia 163
Perennial broccoli 106, 107
Perilla 45
Periwinkle 13, 31, *33*
Perpetual spinach 85
Persicaria 171, 171
Peruvian squill 40
pests and pest control 172-5
Petits pois 110
Petunia 45, 50
Phacelia campanularia 45
Philadelphus 162, 167
Philodendron 167
Phlox 50, *50*, 164
Pickling onions 79
Pineapple weed 171
Pink 13, 37, 45, 164, *164*
pipings 164
Plantain 170, 171
Plantain lily 13, 37, *37*
Plum 186
Polyanthus 57, 165, 177
Polygonum 13, 33
Polygonum baldschuanicum 33
Polygonum lapathifolium 171
Pompon chrysanthemum 38, *38*
Poplar 18
Poppy 13. *See also* Californian, Iceland *and* Shirley poppy
Portulaca 50
Pot leek 120
Potato 72-5, 181, *187*
potato blight 73, 125, 177, 178
potato eelworm 73
potting off, potting on 160-1
powdery mildew 177, *177*, 178
power lawn-mowers 151
pricking out 159
Primrose 57, 165
Primula 165, 177
Primula denticulata 164
Prince of Wales feathers 49
Privet 163, 167
propagation: by cuttings 162-4; by division and layering 165-7
Pulmonaria 165
Pulsatilla vulgaris 164
Pyracantha 13, 30, *31*
Pyracantha atlantioides 30
Pyracantha coccinea 30
Pyracantha rogersiana 30
Pyrethrum 13, 38, *38*, 165

Quince 13, 25

Radish 86-7, 181
Raolia 165
Raspberry 139-40, 141, 166, *166*, 178, 181, 186
raspberry beetle 140
Rayless mayweed 171
Red cabbage 100-1
red core 138
Red deadnettle 171, *171*
red spider mite 125, 173, 174, 175, *183*
Redcurrant 148-9, 163, 181, 186
Reseda 45
rhizomes, to divide 166

Rhododendron 13, 30, 167, 187
Rhubarb 134-5, 186
Rhus 164
Rhus typhina 166
Ribwort 171
Ricinus 50
Robinia 164
rock garden 187
Romneya 165
Romneya coulteri 164
root cuttings 164
root funguses 176-7
Rosa 13
Rosa filipes 63
Rosa longicuspis 63
Rosa wichuraiana 60, 63
Rose 13, 177, 187
    climbers 33, 60-3, 66, 68, 69
    floribunda 58-9, 68, 69
    hybrid tea 56-8, 59, 67, 79
    miniature 57, 69
    pruning 67-9
    rambler 60, 63, 68, 69
    shrub 69
    siting and planting 64-6
Rubber plant 164, 167, *167*
Rubus 164
Ruby chard 90
Rumex obtusifolius 169
Runner bean 114-15, 169
Russian vine 13, 33
rust 178, 179, *179*

St John's wort 13, 29
Saintpaulia 163
Salad onion 79
Salpiglossis 50-1, *50*
Salvia 51
Salvia horminum 45
Sambucus 164
sandy soil 12
Sansevieria 166
Sansevieria trifasciata 163
Savoy cabbage 100
sawfly caterpillar 145
Saxifrage 165, 166
scab 178
Scabiosa caucasica 34, *36*
Scabious 34
scale insect 173, 174, *175*
Scarlet pimpernel 171
Scilla peruviana 40
Seakale beet 90
seaweed as manure 182, *182*
Sedum 165
seed sowing 157-9
seedling blight 176, *176*
semi-ripe cuttings 163
Sempervivum 13, 39, 166, *166*
Senecio cineraria 36
serpentine layering 167
Shepherd's purse 171
Shirley poppy 45, 53
shoddy *182*
Shrubby dogwood 163
shrubs 13, 22-32
Silene 45
Silver birch 13, 19
silver leaf 177, *179*
Skimmia 13, 31
Skimmia japonica 31
slugs 45, 117, 175, *183*
smoulder 179
snails 175
Snapdragon 48
Snowdrop *40*, 41
softwood cuttings 162
soil, types of 9, 12
soil-warming cables 155
Sonchus asper 171
Sow-thistle 171, *171*
sowing a lawn 16-17
spacing out 159
spades 150
Spanish broom *9*
Spartium *9*
Speedwell 170, 171
Spider flower 49
Spinach, spinach substitutes 84-5
Spinach beet 85, 90
Spindle bush 13, 28
Spindle tree 13, *20*, 21
Spring cabbage 98-9, 100
Spring onion 79
Spring or summer snowflake 40
Sprouting broccoli 106, 107
spur blight 178, 179
Star of the Veldt 50
Statice 51, *51*
Stellaria media 171
stem cankers 179
stepping stones 45

Stock 52, 54, *55*
Strawberry 136-8, 167, *167*, 181, 186
Streptocarpus 163
stunt 143
suckers 166
Sugar pea (mangetout) 110
Summer cabbage 100
Sunflower 45
Swede 109
Sweet buckeye 20
Sweet pea *44*, 45, 53, 169, 187
Sweet William 52, 54
Swiss chard 90
Sword lily 13
Symphoricarpus 166
Symphytum 164, 165
Syringa 13, 21, 167
Syringa vulgaris 21

Tagetes 13, 45, 51
Taraxacum officinale 168
Thistle 169, *169*, 170
Thorn tree 18
thrips (thunder flies) 112, 175, *175*
Thyme 13, 39, 165
Thymus serphyllum 39
tip layering 167
Tobacco plant 45, 50
Tomato 121-5, 181, 186
tomato blight 178
tools 150
top dressing 186
Tradescantia 162, 163
Tree of heaven 18
trees 13, 18-21; to plant 19
Trefoil 171
Tropaeolum 13, 45, *45*
trowel 150
Tulip *42*, 43, 166
Tulipa kaufmanniana 42, 43
turfing a lawn 14-15
Turnip 108-9
Turnip greens 108

Ursinia 51
Urtica urens 169

Veitchberry 142
Venidium 51
Verbascum 164
Verbascum bombyciferum 54, 55
Verbascum Broussa 55
Verbena 45, 51
Veronica 167
Vervain 51
Viburnum 13, 31
Viburnum betulifolium 30, 31
Viburnum burkwoodii 31
Viburnum davidii 30, 31
Viburnum fragrans 31
Viburnum opulus 31
Viburnum tinus 31
Viburnum tomentosum 30-1, 31
Vinca 13, 31-2
Vinca major 31, 32, *33*
Vinca minor 32
vine weevil 174
Violet root rot 177
Viper's bugloss *52*, 53
Virginian stock 13, 45

Wallflower 52, *52*, 53, 54, 177
Water-lily tulip *42*, 43
watermoulds 176
watering 180-1
weeds, weed control 9, 168-71
weedkillers 168-9, 171
Weeping willow 18
Weigela 162, 167
white blister 177
white rot 79, 120, 179
Whitecurrant 148-9, 181, 186
whitefly 174, 175
Wild radish 171
Willow 163
Wind flower 13, 38
windowsill propagation 159
Winged pea 110
Winter aconite 41
Winter cabbage 100
Winter radish 87
Wisteria 167
Witch hazel 13, *28*, *28*, 167
woolly aphides 175

Xeranthemum 48

Yarrow 171
yellow edge and crinkle 138

Zebrina 163
Zinnia 45, 51, *51*